ARBEN

David Arben's
Life of Miracles & Successes

An Authorized Biography
By Dr. John Jackson & Rebecca Jackson

Naches Press
Santa Cruz, California

Library of Congress Control Number: 2019917428

Printed in the United States of America

2 3 4 5 6 8 9 10

ISBN 978-1-7338755-1-6

www.davidarben.com

Dedicated to Abraham, Chaya, Israel, and Zysla

Contents

Foreword

I had the pleasure of making music with David Arben for many years in Philadelphia, where I was music director. I remember working with him as a soloist in a Mozart concerto. His wonderful interpretation still lives in my best memories of musicians — his clear sound, wonderful phrasing, moving musicality. I am proud to be his friend and admirer, and I am sure that his biography will be illuminating for musicians and for all who love music!

Riccardo Muti
Music Director
Chicago Symphony Orchestra
October 2016

Preface

"The writing of many books is endless, and excessive devotion to books is wearying to the body."

— Ecclesiastes 12:12

Did Solomon, a notably wise figure, have it right? Can book writing and reading weigh us down more than providing uplift? Maybe this depends on multiple factors. Obviously, today's electronic publications eclipse the literary output of any prior era. Still, wouldn't weighing a particular work's pros and cons hinge on the subject matter, its author, and a reader's life circumstances? So, why did we write *Arben: David Arben's Life of Miracles and Successes*? And more importantly, would reading it adequately reward an investment of your limited and consequently precious time?

Our subject is the person you would most like to meet, but just don't know it yet, because you probably have never heard of him. Who might find in David Arben a kind of lighthouse for the soul? Let's go over the profile. Ever felt desperate for that special someone to truly understand you? David went on hunger strike at age seven to convince his parents of a heartfelt desire to play violin. At any point did escape from life-threatening danger seem improbable? The young Arben exited Warsaw Ghetto through a tunnel under the wall. Feel sympathy for the plight of innocent orphans? Our protagonist, age thirteen, suffered agony after the murder of his whole family.

Have you or someone you know trod the surreal soil of a near death experience? Arben stood before the pit of bodies and firing squad, resigned to his fate. Beyond hunger, what would you pay for relief of actual starvation? David Arben resorted to burning one whole bank bag of cash to cook some potatoes, desperately hungering for a much-needed meal. Ever been told you totally lack preparation and qualification to attain a dream destination? The subject of this biography had no passport to leave Germany, no sponsor required of immigrants to America or recommendation to enter the best music school in the country. At this crucial moment, Leonard Bernstein "happened" to write him a strong reference letter.

What friendship and social life can you attain when stumbling over words in a new language, outside circles of opportunity? Before learning English, Arben went by invitation of FDR's granddaughter on a blind date with the daughter of Harry Hopkins, an architect of the New Deal and presidential emissary to Winston Churchill. Want to find the key that opens doors into your ideal position? David auditioned for a seat in the world's widest known orchestra, played thirty-four years and retired at a high post. How best to prove your most vicious attacker wrong? Arben performed in post-Hitler Berlin and received rave reviews from major papers, "a standard of violin playing no longer attained in Germany." All this and more rolled into one person's life, would you care to ride along and have a little David Arben rub off on you? And why not? So, read the book!

Besides affording an interested individual the chance to enjoy an awe-inspiring story, why did we author this book on David Arben? What else would you do in our place, albeit with no background in writing, when practically the whole world could benefit from knowing lessons and perspective gained during a remarkably full life? This work will hopefully expand the circle of those honored to make David's acquaintance, "meeting" virtually through text. And why do we believe that what you are about to read will accurately portray and represent this incomparable individual? Largely because we extensively quote his own words, the same phrases with which he shared his treasured memories during hundreds of hours of interviews over the last ten years.

As he frequently asserted, each person's life is his own experience. Witnesses to the same event will each have their own unique impression and point of view. The account in your hands tells what David Arben experienced, as he himself remembered it. Ours is not a scholarly approach to some of the most dramatic events in recent times. We have, however, endeavored to faithfully render Mr. Arben's verbal expressions and provide some historical context for his remarks.

This book covers the life of David Arben, including his forty-seven months of incarceration in seven detention facilities. No right-minded individual will doubt or quarrel with the reality of what Mr. Arben went through, a man tattoo-branded like livestock and who overcame the tortuous psychological sequelae for years following. Against all odds, David Arben did not merely survive. He overcame and triumphed. Not bitter, nor ceaselessly railing about a horrific past, he focused on the satisfaction of his work, treasuring a day's air and light. To the end, David's greatest pleasure remained time spent with friends, enjoying food and drink together, a profound joy in living. This was the last melodious lesson given, his legacy left to those with a thirst for best quality of existence.

While profound mysteries continue to resist the best analytical probing by world-class geniuses, this master teacher of how to live well chose to lead by example. David never presumed to tell others what to choose or think. At the same time, he never tolerated anyone or anything that would dare attempt to diminish his treasured freedom and cultivated pursuits. To sum up, he was generous, never stingy with himself or others. What he so freely shared with us, bound by happy obligation we presently share with the reader. We believe some, perhaps many, will find herein nourishing thoughts that fill any vacuum of loss with overflowing love and put into words the proven steps that lead to a summit of accomplishment. His groundcrew's work completed, the Arben spirit beckons us to take flight in this life. Freely receive and smilingly share the updraft!

Acknowledgments

For this work, our first experience with book writing, we required and benefitted from the help of many generous individuals. David embodied loyalty and always expressed the deepest affection for his adoptive Swiss family whom he first met in 1948. Respecting his wishes to protect their privacy, we have omitted last names and other personal information. We met Beatrice, a granddaughter, in Flossenbürg when she came with her children, the fourth generation dedicated to their beloved Chaim. She answered questions, provided many beautiful anecdotes and clarified details and chronology of David's visits to Europe, checking with her mother on earlier events that only she would know firsthand. Many thanks to you, Beatrice, Antony, Frederic and Gaëlle, faithful family friends until the end.

We learned much of Mr. Arben's professional history from his close circle of musical colleagues. Friends from days at Curtis Institute of Music, Cleveland and Philadelphia Orchestras generously fielded our questions. All offered their precious, sometimes humorous recollections. Among these, Michael Tree, Ron Leonard, Anshel Brusilow, Luis Biava, and Larry Grika stand out for their gracious efforts. Thank you Margarita Montanaro for providing us personal glimpses, access to private papers and connections to other sources. Your selfless assistance to David, especially these latter years, qualify you for nomination as a true saint.

Two daughters deserve special mention for their devotion to Mr. Arben and touching reflections. Both Suzy, Sam Rudofker's daughter, and Sharon, José Kahan's daughter, remained intimate friends and extended family for David down through the decades.

Annette Jackson, wife to one author, and mother to the other, conducted a number of interviews with Mr. Arben. She transcribed hundreds of hours of recordings, helped compose an appendix, proofread chapters, and recommended improvements. Our daughter and sister, Elizabeth Jackson, helped video documentation of the Arben story, as it unfolded here in Santa Cruz, in Philadelphia and also in Germany. She spent time with him at Cape May, New Jersey, in 2013, later serving as chaperone for one of David's last cross-country air transfers to stay at our California home August through September of 2015. What a family team!

Of course, we acknowledge all the question and answer sessions graciously granted by Mr. Arben. Most conversations took place after he turned eighty, impressing us time and again with his memory for names, of distant events and places. Initial book composition began around Thanksgiving of 2014 with the intent of placing a finished copy in David's living hands. After reviewing first drafts of the manuscript, he commented, "I like it. I trust you."

No writer appreciates more than two novices the debt that we owe to graphic artist Lindsey Sonu, photo restoration by Scot Goodman, German translations by Cecilia Cloughly, editing by Katie Button, and layout and formatting by Marco Rozzano. Thanks also to Lizzy Kate Gray, Jess Lin, Ines Wehowski, Robin Whitehouse, Lynn Kidder, Jolene Woo, and Andrew Thompson. We appreciate all of your support, energy, expertise, and patience on this project. You made possible what originally seemed an impossibility. The group effort made this happen.

Introduction

"And whoever saves a life, it is considered as if he saved an entire world."

— Babylonian Talmud

By Father

During the spring of 2008 David Arben first came to visit us in Santa Cruz, California. I knew of him as a highly-respected musician living in Philadelphia, originally from Poland. The mentor of our older daughter, providing tutelage and encouragement, she had met him at a festival in Puerto Rico in the crucial early stages of her nascent musical career. Even before meeting him, Mr. Arben had already become an important man for our family and someone to whom we would always feel indebted.

The initial extended conversation took place after breakfast as we lingered at a small table in our kitchen. I had heard from Rebecca that David witnessed firsthand unspeakable horrors during World War II in Europe. Due to the subject's sensitivity, I fumbled for an appropriate entree to learn something of his experiences, finally saying, "I wish I knew the right questions to ask." David smiled and said, "That's good because I rarely share much about those times, unless someone asks the right questions." Thus encouraged, I began broaching subjects of universal and timeless human interest. He responded to inquiries about early childhood memories, his introduction to music, incursion of Nazi armed forces, loss of family, concentration camp atrocities, miraculous escapes, liberation, displaced life on postwar streets in Germany, resuming musical instruction and performance, loving inclusion by a saintly Swiss family, immigration to America, studies at Curtis Institute of Music, joining leading orchestras, rising to associate concertmaster with the Philadelphia Orchestra, world travel, famous acquaintances, dear friends, deep affection for students, and abiding appreciation of freedom he felt in his adopted country.

Graciously and thoughtfully, he replied to each and every query. Much more than a source of vivid historical recollections and revealing observations, David Arben, who had changed his name from Chaim Arbajtman (spelling he preferred to the Germanicized Arbeitman or Arbeitmann) after debuting on the American stage, freely shared of carefully considered and seasoned perspectives.

David Arben had come that first visit to our house for the inauguration of Music in May, a local chamber music festival. He returned as a consultant and honored guest each season. The conversations continued and, with his permission, we made recordings. David's life provides precious illumination, no matter what darkness may assail, powerful wisdom that deftly directs, even when death threatens, and such unquenchable inspiration that his story most definitely deserves preservation and retelling. Early on I asked what had enabled him to withstand loss of all his loved ones while yet a boy, to overcome privation and torture, to evade executioner's bullets, to come through strafing by aircraft unscathed, to move forward when he had no food or shelter, to cross borders without adequate money or papers, to bring about self-healing of nightmarish flashbacks, to sail the Atlantic and promptly enter America's premier music school before mastering English, to secure employment and attain lofty positions?! He paused briefly and replied deliberately, "My parents told me that I was a violin virtuoso. They also told me, 'You are special, never let anyone disrespect you.'"

I paused and any thoughtful reader would do well to similarly ponder. Could this possibly offer adequate explanation for the seeming miracles that have occurred serially over many years? Of course, we cannot doubt or question his conviction. After all, David Arben had ample time to reflect on his incredible life experience and come to as deep an understanding as possible. The chapters that follow will attempt to flesh out details of this incredibly special individual's journey and provide a sketch of the profound impact he had on those blessed to know him. This is a written recording of the living testimony that David Arben embodied – an anointing by parents and the enduring love for his family. He guarded and cultivated this legacy within himself, as a sacred memorial throughout the decades. Such commands, even demands respect. Chaim Arbajtman, indeed a virtuoso on violin, the same David Arben chose to live life as harmonious melody in counterpoint to a discordant world.

—John Jackson, M.D.

By Daughter

If one is truly blessed, there is a person who will come into your life and have a profound impact. For me, that person was David Arben. I had the great fortune that our paths crossed in 1999 at an orchestra and chamber music festival in Puerto Rico. Mr. Arben coached the string players. I was immediately captivated by his genuine dedication to helping us. I observed his wonderfully subtle sense of humor. Each day, signature cigar in hand, he would invariably greet me with a kiss on the cheek. His remarkable sense of calm was contagious. I wrote him a card of thanks after that summer and his reply was the beginning of what would become one of my most treasured friendships. I only witnessed Mr. Arben perform once, the Schubert cello quintet. His performance was breathtaking, among the greatest I have ever heard. Nearly twenty years have passed since that summer and I spent countless afternoons with Mr. Arben, gleaning from his wisdom on music and life.

The summer we met I remember another young musician's question. "Have you seen the tattoo on his arm? He is a Holocaust survivor." I was horrified by the thought and even more awestruck by this man. In 2007, I interviewed him for my master's thesis, *What it Takes to be a Successful Concert Artist: Conversations with Renowned Musicians*. He shared his tragic past and how it shaped him. It was a Thursday morning on Spruce Street in Philadelphia. As he began, the street noises through his kitchen window faded. There was a deep aching pain in my heart. I could barely fathom the tragedies he experienced. The grief was overwhelming that someone I cared for deeply had suffered so much. I asked, "What do you consider your greatest musical success and why?" Upon reflection, I believe his response was a touching tribute to his family and their role, sadly cut short, in his greatest achievements.

My family heard of this extraordinary man many times over the years, but it wasn't until the inaugural season of my chamber music festival that they finally met. Since that May in 2008, Mr. Arben came annually to Santa Cruz, California, serving as an invaluable adviser. He also became a part of our family. My Korean-born mother proudly announced, "In your father and mother's combined existence of 130-plus years, Mr. Arben is the most incredible human being we have ever met!" With an added wag of the finger she said, "And we've met a lot of people." My U.S.-born father, who had worked on an Israeli kibbutz in the 1970s, meeting immigrants who fled post World War II Europe, shared an immediate connection with Mr. Arben.

On a Thanksgiving morning, my Father and I began the accelerated journey together with the principal intent of honoring Arben and his family through this book. As we have written and rewritten these chapters over and over again, I cry and laugh and cry all over again. I feel his essence and am reminded of the incredible gifts I received each time I was in his company. This book is a giant love letter to our friend, my mentor.

Mr. Arben, I will miss you forever.

— Rebecca Jackson

The names of ARBEN

Warsaw, 1927 — Chaim Arbajtman
Flossenbürg, 1944 — Chaim Arbeitman
Geneva, 1948 — Haim Arbeitmann
Cleveland, 1956 — David Arben

1
Childhood and Family Life

"Life is good. I am jealous of my life, because I know many people who are so sick and destroyed mentally. Life is a gift. It's not because you live that the Almighty or the world owes you something. Nobody owes you anything. You have to go through the good and bad that life presents. You have to make life."

Chaim Arbajtman's words distill his eighty-nine years on earth. Chaim means "life." In this, his life's story, the number of miracles and successes rises to the uncanny. As he would quickly and confidently add, "I don't have to prove this to anybody, just myself. It's impossible to be happy in life, even with everything the world has to offer, without mentally proving you're worthy. And, fortunately, I proved this to myself a long time ago."

Chaim, born on August 13, 1927, grew up in Warsaw, the bustling city which many likened to Paris. Chaim's father, Abraham, worked demanding hours in Poland's capital as a tailor. He commenced the profession early, already an understudy at age seven in the shop of his father, David. "Everybody working, there were no other possibilities. Poverty was so unbelievable."

Abraham strove for excellence and developed a method to cut stripes, without wasting fabric, that met in perfect alignment at the suit's lapel seam. A pioneer, if not the first to use this technique, his invention created a stir and soon everyone wanted to copy it. "Lots of blue suits had stripes, like you see in old movies." His garments, shirts and even wedding dresses, garnered a reputation for quality and commanded two to three times the usual price. After work he walked home to a four-story building located at Wolinska #9 with courtyard and three entrances, apartment #20 on the second floor.

There the children took up their perch, noses plastered to a full-length window at the front of the apartment. This frigid pane, covered in ice during winter, faced the street and afforded them the chance to detect anyone or anything approaching. Rarely a car passed, but when one did, they applauded. "Only somebody important could deserve such a machine." As the nightly ritual, his children watched intently for the one they expected. A cry went up at first sighting, "Father's here!"

From the street, one entered through a large gate that a guard locked at 11:00 p.m. In the night he would respond to a loud bell that none of the residents could fail to hear, reverberating through their whole building. Across a central courtyard, stairs led to the Arbajtman apartment's front door. A modest abode with tight space, the atmosphere seemed a palace to them. One large room with yellow walls contained beds for everyone, chairs and Abraham's work desk. There were three children in the Arbajtman family: Israel; Chaim, four years younger; and Zysla, eighteen months younger than Chaim.

Abraham, for religious reasons, could not marry a Miriam, his mother's name. His betrothed, three years older and taller than her fiancé, had changed her first name from Miriam to Chaya (feminine form of Chaim). After marriage, starting early in the morning she cooked on a coal-fired stove. It also provided heat, but in colder months all wore a coat or coats indoors. Water ran in a shared sink on the landing outside their door, unless the pipes froze.

During daylight hours, a bathroom in the basement of Chaim's apartment building served for common needs. A descent into the dimness left visual and even more vivid olfactory impressions on a youngster's mind. At night, a chamber pot proved safer and more convenient.

Some days young Chaim accompanied his mother to the market. He bemusedly observed, "She knew how to give a physical examination, more than you get today at the doctor's office, to determine which chicken was healthy." She rejected a skinny bird as maybe sick, preferring a fat bird. The kosher butcher then employed a traditional maneuver, blade to neck, so animals would not suffer. Kids fought over who got to scrape off schmaltz (fat) and spread it on rye bread. Depending on the season, Chaya bought fresh fruits, then prepared jams and jellies. These she stored and stacked in glass jars at home. Nobody made better pies and cakes.

"During the week dinner came at two in the afternoon, the largest daily meal." Among other dishes, favorites included chicken soup and vegetables cooked with chicken fat. They didn't raise their own animals, which could easily be adopted by children as pets. "No room for pets, there was no food for pets."

"For supper, maybe you ate cold cuts and a sandwich with some tea. The gefilte fish my mother made was absolutely superb. We used to fight for another piece. Our family ate more fish than meat. Compared to trout, eggs were expensive." They also regularly ate cheese with bread. Chaya purchased the best pumpernickel imaginable. She served this and, to fill up, different pastas, as well as a considerable quantity of potatoes. Abraham was not a big eater. Possessing an agreeable disposition, he never complained.

Like most other women, "My mother slaved at home. I remember seeing her cleaning dishes and sewing. She often mended and less frequently made new things. Men were out working, not playing cards while the women were cleaning the floor. Everybody had something to do."

"Friday nights, we went to synagogue and sometimes brought back a person to eat with us. There were people traveling around from different cities and villages. There's a mitzvah, to take somebody home to dinner, to do a good deed. This could have been a total stranger you never saw again. Maybe you even invited him to sleep overnight."

"Our house was completely kosher. We couldn't mix milk and meat, and so on. We didn't have any ham or proscribed seafood. I ate kosher food only. We kept tradition out of respect for grandparents who lived with us. We were a very close-knit family." Chaim's mother peeled whole potatoes to make a stew called "cholent." "It was delicious with goose. She would grill it, boil it." Besides goose, Chaya added different cuts of meat, especially duck and gizzards. Not sliced, another layer of whole potatoes covered the meat, some silver foil sealing the dish. At five o'clock she left it downstairs at a bakery overnight to cook. They took it out at eleven the next morning. Some forty or fifty others gave the baker their dishes to simmer all night long. Jews, not allowed to tend a stove or even turn off lights after the start of Sabbath eve, paid a non-Jew to do this.

Every Saturday felt like a holiday. In the morning Abraham took his wife and children to nearby Nożyk Synagogue. After services, they had the stew for lunch or supper. The texture of cholent with uncut potatoes turned brown through and through, the fatty meats, all combined, resulted in a superb and otherworldly taste. Fifteen family members on average would gather in the evening, eat, and sing songs, both religious and popular.

"Very few people had telephones," to call and advise. Relatives from the country might still arrive unannounced before dawn, the next or any other day. Everyone received a warm welcome, life unruled by schedule. "We had a bunch of relatives, uncles, distant cousins. There was no reliable transportation. The train was never on time. To go 130 kilometers, it took days by foot, by hitchhiking, or by horse with carriage."

"When I was a kid my great uncle would walk for three days from Lublin to Warsaw, twice a year. There came a big knock on the door, maybe three o'clock in the morning. My father always got out of bed to talk and mother quietly started cooking. I liked my great uncle very much. He dressed beautifully. Every time he would come, he would give me a silver coin. So, I used to ask, 'When is he coming again?'" Incidentally, the paternal great uncle had three sons: Izzy, Jack, and Lewis. They immigrated to America before World War I.

When groups of family visited, "We didn't have room to accommodate them to sleep. I will never forget this. There were three chairs, put together. They would sleep on the chairs with an improvised pillow. Thinking back, this was one of the reasons families bonded together. There isn't and never will be this kind of family life again. The idea of togetherness was a big force, a big force. I was lucky to be born at this time."

As an annual getaway, June through August, the family stayed at a resort forty-five minutes to an hour by train outside of Warsaw. Attractions included sand, water, and cabins in the pines. A cousin asked Chaim years later, "Did you know of any other family that went on summer vacation every year?" Abraham had to stay in the city during the week, but left in time each Friday to arrive before sundown. His wife and children would wait to greet him at the station. On Monday he returned for work in the capital until the following Friday, then repeated the cycle.

On one such vacation in the woods when he was about two years old, Chaim's mother dressed him in short red pants. This would prove key when he later walked with older children on their way to greet the train from Warsaw. Suddenly, oblivious to the tot, his companions started running. The small kid could not keep up due to his shorter legs. "I couldn't run as fast, so I got lost in the fields." He tried and tried to find his way back, but to no avail. Heart racing, it felt that it might beat out of his chest. "I was very scared. I was crying, crying so loud I was exhausted."

The older children eventually returned from the station. After a few minutes, "My mother realized I was not back, so she started looking for me and became frantic. She looked everywhere. After about forty-five or so minutes, she saw me in the distance. Cows were near me in the field and she saw a tiny red dot." She ran towards it, catching up to the younger son, still moving away from her. Not calling his name, so as to not to startle, she circled around to enter her child's gaze from the front. "I saw my mother. Then I really started to cry." He collapsed in her arms, equally from exhaustion as relief. Even after he mostly recovered from the fright, she thought it premature to give him a lecture on safety. "Every night I kissed and hugged my mother." Later recounted and explained to him, Chaim concluded from her handling of the incident, "My mother was very smart."

Besides other experiences, the woods offered places to fish and swim. During a subsequent summer stay outside Warsaw at age four, Chaim witnessed a boy drown. How horrible to watch the end of an innocent young life when even adults could not rescue him in time! After this traumatic experience, Chaim never quite overcame a fear of swimming.

Sometimes he recalled his dreams. Also around age four, he had an unsettling one, a premonition seven to ten days before the death of his grandmother Miriam Arbajtman, at age sixty-five. This came about as a strange occurrence, impossible to know the meaning. "I never told my parents. I knew she died. I didn't know you don't come back and nobody explained it to me. They sent me away to other relatives," temporarily shielding him from sadness and shock.

Abraham had one brother and one older sister, Ester. Her son, Shlomo, eight years older than Chaim, joined the household. He received equal care and concern as the other children. Ester, attractive according to family, fell in love with Lazaro Morel when he had returned to visit relatives in Poland after living in South America. Before Abraham married, Lazaro and Ester wed, initially residing in Warsaw. They applied for return visas but the Argentine government would not grant their son a visa because of his eye disease. Without him, parents boarded a ship at Trieste, immigrated in 1931 to Buenos Aires and never saw Shlomo again. "They were convinced they would bring the boy over... but they never could." Their family re-expanded with arrival of two daughters, born in the new world.

Childhood days were filled with activities, mundane and special. When sunny, the family might stroll to a garden park, Ogród Krasińskich, not far from home. A picture taken there showed the whole family, the sole surviving image that Chaim retained to remember them all together. Years later, his father's sister sent this photo from Argentina to her nephew. Abraham, prematurely bald, dressed smartly in bow tie, a coat and checkered pants. Sitting on his lap, Chaim had the same eyes and lips, but his mother's nose. Wearing a stylish print dress, Chaya held Zysla, who, in partially laced shoes, appeared anxious to get down and take a walk. She and Chaim, nearly inseparable, went everywhere hand in hand. Israel, next to his brother, had lighter hair. Their parents referred to him as the "brain." On this occasion, quite unusual, he had no book under his arm. Cousin Shlomo in a darker outfit, farthest to the left and perhaps favoring a stronger eye, canted his head to the side (see photo on page 185).

Chaim, not owing to any visual deficit, could sometimes stare at vague patterns on yellow walls in their apartment and "hypnotize" himself. At other times, he would attempt unsuccessfully to break his brother's almost trance-like focus when reading. As the middle child, our subject found himself vying for attention. His baby sister seemed almost too cute for their parents to correct, no matter what circumstance or behavior. If correction came, Chaim received it from Abraham. "When my father wanted to discipline me, I ran and my mother shielded me. My father knew when my mother did this, he could not correct me. When she signaled, he knew he could proceed. It was measured, the best human education. There was no hate, only love and discipline."

The younger son took correction well, when the occasion arose, always knowing he deserved it. Still he tended to test limits. With neither parent present, he would venture out in the city streets to explore. Once he went so far as to nearly lose his way. After finally arriving back home, evading parental detection and a father's scolding, his sister refused to speak with him. They adored each other, almost always together. He called her his baby, his heart, his love. Just so, she couldn't understand why he would go anywhere without taking her.

"My brother being four years older, I could not compete alone. Zysla, my sweetheart, was a year and a half younger, so we teamed up together. 'We will show him who is the big shot.'"

"My father had a first cousin with a fruit stand, a beautiful store at Dzika #3. It was a better neighborhood. Friday night we would go. Every fruit was wrapped separately in special paper, every orange, every apple, every fruit. They were like flowers. My father's cousin would say, 'You want an ice cream?' and I would say, 'Yes,' although my father had taught me to say, 'Thank you, no.'" After the young Arbajtman accepted a sweet, Abraham later corrected him privately. He reminded his son of the more considerate answer during difficult days for business owners, to politely say thank you, but decline.

Abraham, communicating with his youngsters, didn't talk down to them. "When he spoke to me or to my little sister or older brother, he didn't speak to his children like children. Always, no matter what age, we were treated as equals, as far as understanding." He reassured his boys, often saying, "'Nobody can hurt you, nobody can harm you. You're too important. Even though someone might kill you, nobody could destroy you.'" Both parents told all the children, "'We love you. You're special. You're everything good.'" Chaim realized later in life, "This was an upbringing of great wealth. In the first five years, a child's life can be made by your parents. When bad times come along, you are a much better fighter to survive."

In a different way, Chaya prepared her daughter early for coming adult responsibilities. One day, Zysla attempted to bake a cake in the all-purpose coal-burning stove. Smoke filled the apartment. Half choking, everybody saw the humor.

"Father did not have the opportunity for formal, secular studies. Still, he had an appreciation for fine things. He used to talk a lot about beauty in life. He took me to the art museum. As we strolled the galleries, he shared his thoughts. 'Each one of these paintings has a meaning. I have questions, but I don't have the answers. Wouldn't it be wonderful to know the meaning?' He took me to a stage show, to see Molly Picon, who made a career in America," and Ida Kaminska of Jewish or Yiddish theater fame. At synagogues, Abraham purchased expensive tickets for his son to hear great geniuses like Josef

Rosenblatt and Moshe Koussevitzky, the Jascha Heifetz of cantors. Looking ahead, the devoted father wanted Chaim to get a taste and a little bit of understanding. "I didn't understand at that point in life. I would come to understand decades later."

"In the old days, it seemed Jewish families always had a wise man. The wise man happened to be my father in our family. Everybody, especially relatives, would come when they had a problem. 'What is your advice?' They all listened to my father. He was honest, impartial, and very well respected."

"Father had religious training and would go to a big rabbi to discuss the Hebrew scriptures. There were many questions raised, but answers were not always clear. The Torah, I consider it one of the most fascinating books. The beautiful part is, you always have questions and ponder different meanings." Jews consistently emphasized the importance of learning. Excluded from university training by economic limitations and legal restriction, they substituted study of the Tanakh (Hebrew Bible).

"Father was religious, mostly because he was a totally dedicated son." Abraham didn't adhere so strictly to religious practices like David, his very orthodox father, who rose at 3:30 a.m., turned east towards the Western Wall in Jerusalem and recited prayers for hours with "speed like a great auctioneer," all from memory and absolutely verbatim. "He had a big beard and went to the synagogue every morning. He and God were inseparable. So, my father did everything to make his father happy. My grandfather and everybody said, 'Your father was the best son any parent could wish for,' always respectful. Growing up, we learned wisdom by imitating elders. You had respect for the older people."

Reflecting later in adulthood, "It doesn't matter what language. If the brain exercises in Hebrew, Yiddish, in English, Spanish or any other language, you can become a scholar. If the mind doesn't exercise, you have a problem with everything. The orthodox for many, many hundreds of years had to pray most of the day and most of the night. This was a very important exercise to develop the brain."

The paternal grandfather, David Arbajtman, had his rituals and customs. "What he did on Monday, he also did on Tuesday and Wednesday, with no variety. David and Abraham had friends, but they seldom met socially. In the evening they would go out and

Grandfather would take chunks of sugar in his pocket. They would sip brewed tea, very hot and always strong. Grandfather wouldn't touch a cup, always in a glass."

Father and son would go together on Friday afternoons to the Turkish bath. Not so much a mikveh or ritual ablution, "Steam came out from tubes. You started perspiring and needed some cold water to drink." Called a shvitz, common households had no such modern convenience as a warm shower. Besides the steam cleaning of pores and massage, in the public facility they received a thrashing with branches and leaves. This stimulated circulation, provided total body relaxation and cleared the mind. They left completely refreshed, faces reddened, and arrived home glowing before the start of Sabbath. "We three kids would run to the window. We knew, more or less, at what time they would return home and yelled to mother, 'Daddy is coming with Grandpa.'"

"Such a beautiful ritual. The challah was baked, already covered up, and the candles were ready to be lit. Those days you could not buy challah bread in the stores because every woman was too proud to go and buy it. My mother baked everything. She made the best cakes and the best cookies. I have never tasted an apple strudel, apple cake, or anything from a bakery as tasty as my mother's. Maybe because it was my mother or maybe it had something to do with love. Whether I am right or wrong is not important. Everything she made, I loved."

Besides personal religious observance, "My father was going around with a can, collecting money. He was a big shot in the Jewish homeland movement. He made arrangements for a number of Jews to go to Palestine (British Mandate for Palestine), including my mother's sister with two children." Courageous, she had no husband to accompany her on the journey. Despite distant rumblings of trouble out of Germany, Abraham preferred cautious optimism, feeling he could get out at the last minute. "'Let's wait a little longer. This cannot be, this is not right.'" Hoping for the best, he stayed in Poland until all the gates closed.

"All boys had to learn Hebrew. I knew some when I was five or six years old. I sat on the Rabbi's lap. He tried to teach me, but I didn't want to learn. Everybody went to Hebrew school, but I didn't finish it. Did I not like school? I don't know, maybe I thought I was too smart to go. My parents got a couple of private tutors to come teach me."

"Hebrew was the holy language. My parents reserved it for prayer. They would take me every Saturday to the synagogue with a book. I had learned more perfect Hebrew pronunciation. From Poland and Russia, Ashkenazi Jews spoke Hebrew with the accent of Eastern Europe. My father was a perfectionist and saw to it that we spoke correctly with Sephardic pronunciation (like the diction of Jews from Mediterranean and Middle Eastern cultures, thought to be closer to the original). You had to do it right. There was no faking because this was sacrilegious. Hebrew was the language of God. You prayed correctly when you talked to God. Well, they believed in these things. Reverence, this was another important value."

"My brother was with his books morning, noon, and night — hundreds of books. He went his first six years to public school and Tarbut (a Jewish network of educational institutions). He studied all normal subjects, plus Hebrew. He spoke perfect Hebrew. He didn't at home. Yiddish was the language to communicate." Israel spoke Polish with parents and Yiddish with grandparents, more easily understood by them.

"Then my brother was enrolled in a German gymnasium (high school)." Here, Israel studied and attained fluency in both German and French. He possessed considerable intelligence, simultaneously mastering science and humanities at Tarbut. This took two years longer to graduate than with the usual course of studies. He had a flair for languages and took private lessons in Oxford English. "My father didn't have much money, but emphasized education, education, education."

The younger son also entered Tarbut, but never finished. After war and occupation came to Warsaw, this Jewish institution went "underground." Dr. Ezra Eck, who ran the school, survived, later immigrated to Israel, and remarkably, helped found Yad VaShem (the world's foremost Holocaust Museum).

"Among the poor and not so poor, we experienced joy and a special rhythm of life. We didn't have money, but love galore. We were very rich with such an upbringing of importance and dignity. We heard all the street language. My father said to all of us, 'You know every ugly word, but never in your life repeat any.' We loved our father so much, we never, never used such language."

"My father used to sit with us separately and give advice. He would say, 'If somebody on the street asks, "help me," don't ignore him, give something.' Father told us to be the best at whatever we did. 'Whatever you want to do in life, aim for the best. Even if you become a thief, and I don't recommend it, be the best. Where does a mediocre thief end up, but in jail?!' He practiced what he taught. He held himself to the same high standard."

Abraham handled his money quietly and carefully. "They used to have very fancy checks. You could frame one. It was a piece of art with beautiful illustrations." He would sometimes make short-term loans without a contract. "He had handshakes with people. In those days, a handshake meant more than a signature. It was a promise, the holiest thing. It was the honor system and I don't remember any handshake that was ever broken." Abraham had earned trust, loaned to those whom he trusted, and the system worked.

Still, lean times occurred as well. Chaim recalled an occasion when his father had no money to give his wife Chaya. She could not purchase special items to prepare for the Friday and Saturday meals. With prospects of no challah and no traditional family gathering or celebration, the eight-year-old Arbajtman went walking outdoors. The cold and damp paralleled spirits indoors. Suddenly, the glint of something in the snow caught his attention. He picked up two zlotys, enough to rekindle home cooking fires and bankroll the Sabbath. Abraham's younger son received a family hero's reception back at the apartment!

"When I was about seven years old, I fell in love with an eight-year-old girl. Where we lived, there was a courtyard separating our two windows. I was so shy when we both went to look through the glass. We would just stare at one another for an hour. We left. No words ever, I never met her. I always saw her behind her window and she saw me behind mine." This lovingly contemplated vision of a girl, separated by distance and panes of glass, perhaps reflected and augured remaining unattached and free.

Chaim loved to visit his mother's parents. They lived about two blocks away at Mila (Pleasant in English) Street, #24, on the third floor. Grandfather Moshe Knoplich came originally from Russia.

"My grandfather had a glass like a small Coca Cola bottle with spirits, 140 proof, no ice. Nobody drank with ice. There was none, unless you went out in January and chopped it off the window. Every morning for breakfast he had a six-egg omelet with slices of smoked herring, salted fish from the Baltic Sea, and the blackest of bread. He was always smiling and laughing. I had fun with him."

Chaim recalls one particular visit at age eight when Moshe promised to teach him how to drink vodka without getting drunk. "'But you must keep this a secret from your parents.'" With the matter agreed upon, the first lesson commenced. Grandmother Esther Knoplich, a native of Poland, had sponge cake from the store on hand. Grandfather soaked a morsel of it with one drop of vodka. He added two drops the next time. The following week, three drops bathed the piece of sponge cake. Chaim's father soon became suspicious of a new dedication and enthusiasm for weekly visits to the Mila Street residence. He acted decisively and curtailed the frequency. Despite these travel restrictions, Chopin Vodka later in life rose to number one on the grown lad's list of favorite adult beverages.

Around age seventy, or younger, his maternal grandfather died. "In those years, sixty-five was like one-hundred-five today." Such losses begged questions about life's nature and the hereafter. These matters deserved serious reflection. Abraham always looked for opportunities on social outings to nurture and further bond with his son. "Weather permitting, we would have a cup of tea. Father smoked an occasional cigarette." Together they talked and lent support, elder to youngster, even when silent.

"I came from a very close-knit family. You had a sense of strong belonging and it was nice. Every Friday night was like a holiday. Saturday night uncles, aunts, cousins came to sing. It was anything but boring. It was terrific." With orthodox grandparents at home, celebrations followed traditional lines.

Even so, the Jewish festivals brought with them a special kind of chaos, expectation, and hope for weeks. "Holidays were phenomenal. We, the kids, couldn't wait because everybody was involved and something great was going to happen. You were communally involved, everyone in a special mood." Formal preparations might take days and who could resist Chaya's cooking? In a moment with no witnesses, during the day or at night while the others slept, her second son would climb to reach for hidden cakes and pies. His father's homemade wine tasted of fruit. Celebration and revelry lasted from evening into the morning. Even as a child, he "liked all the action."

"Passover came and we had to take away all the regular dishes. We brought out special dishes for the occasion. It was a beautiful life. I used to look forward to Passover Seder. We had to sit for hours. I sometimes fell asleep. They used to wake me up, and nobody minded because the whole family was together at a big table. The participation created such unity and love. We embraced. It was fantastic. We regretted to see it end and it was the same with every holiday."

With family pride in their heritage and Chaim approaching age twelve, his father directed him to resume and complete religious language studies. Within a few weeks, in anticipation of his bar mitzvah, Chaim gained proficiency in reading text with vowel marks. These vowel marks help to take out the guesswork, since written Hebrew consists of consonants only.

"On the streets of Warsaw, before the war, one encountered as many churches as in Rome, one on nearly every corner. Maybe 97% of Poles were Catholic." Walking to school in 1935 or 1936 proved hazardous for young Chaim. Boys his age would attack and beat and punch him for not removing his cap, kneeling and praying when passing a church. He ran, crying all the way home. Abraham gave assurances that he had done right. "Jews do not remove head covering or bow before Christian churches." Together, father and son charted a zigzag course from home to school that would avoid walking past any church. It took three times as long.

The anti-Jewish sentiment prevailed. Though not a Jew, a famous director of radio in Warsaw looked Jewish, and university students set upon him in the streets. He landed in a hospital. Young Arbajtman, observant and thoughtful beyond his years, asked, "Where does it come from and why?"

He later commented, "If people hate you out of inherited and irrational prejudice, you cannot change them." Despite distorted conceptions and unjust street violence, albeit with distinct linguistic and ethnic origins, three generations of his family, counting Chaim, felt rooted in Warsaw. "We loved Warsaw. We loved Poland."

2
The Enchanting Violin

"I had to go on a hunger strike for three days in order to get violin lessons."

From the age of two-and-a-half, Chaim had accompanied his father to a nearby barber shop where he got a shave, just around the corner from their apartment on Wolinska. At a modest price, Abraham went most every day. The youngster noted, "There were three barbers, and a violin with bow hanging on the wall. When one of the barbers didn't have a client, he would pick up the violin and play while the other two barbers would sing." A violin scroll, carved at the top of the neck, reminded him of a human head. Chaim stared at the barbers and the violin, enchanted, not able to understand how this human scroll could make such beautiful sounds. "I was amazed at the sound of the violin. I just couldn't believe this was possible. I was too embarrassed to ask my father, 'From where does the sound come?'" Back at home, from age three to six, he would often take up two sticks, pretending to play and sing "la, la, la." Of course, he dreamed of a real violin.

"Although I came from a family of non-musicians, I was always interested in music." At the apartment he felt drawn to a little radio box, elevated and cemented to the wall. Out of it came the captivating sounds of an orchestra. "I took a tall chair and climbed up to look inside, trying to uncover how it could possibly contain all those musicians." Too shy to ask his parents, the magic box remained shrouded in mystery.

"I was extremely shy and skinny as a kid. My legs and my waist were the same size. People would say when they saw me, 'Here comes the match.' In the old days, if you had fat, that meant you were healthy and rich." Unlike today, carrying extra weight made a person more attractive and eligible, according to the matchmakers. "My family thought I might die because I was too skinny."

Chaya always reminded her son to clear his plate. "My mother managed to get me to finish my food, to encourage a habit." By nature, he didn't eat as much as other children. Taking particular note of his mother's concern, Chaim made a deal with her. He would eat for a price, charging a specific fee for each item of food. His parents agreed to pay him to eat. "I used to have a tariff for every piece of food or fruit that I ate and made some money to buy my toys. My sister and brother didn't do it. I was the only one. Being in the middle was difficult and I wanted to show my strength." He staked out his position and territory, feeling hedged between two other siblings.

"My father was very strict." He consistently followed through on what he said. "My father never corrected me without a good reason. I realized then, right and wrong. He instilled honesty and respect. He was very wise. He disciplined with a nice, quiet voice."

"I was very lucky to have such parents. My mother was a beautiful and intelligent woman, but she was very quiet. She was very gentle, never punished. When my father was upset with me, she was the negotiator. I went to my mother and my mother came to me. My mother would intervene and this was the ritual. She said, 'You know what you should do is go up to your father and kiss his hand. You will see, he will forgive you.' And it was difficult to admit I was wrong, but I knew I was wrong."

Proof of a parent's devotion came during winter, one January or February. With genuinely harsh weather conditions, Warsaw sometimes has snow as late as May. Chaim had fallen ill. "We lived in a poor neighborhood, the ghetto later on, and my father ran a long distance that evening in the freezing cold, maybe three kilometers. He bought me two oranges. They were supposed to take away my fever."

Curiously, another febrile illness helped launch Chaim's future career in music. Late in the summer of 1934 he had come down with scarlet fever, barely seven years old, in the pre-antibiotic era. "In those days, if people had a cold, they might die. If you needed medical advice, people consulted the barber who knew something about medicine."

Chaya's brother had an idea. He knew her son's habit of putting two sticks together as a makeshift instrument and shared the family's concern about their child's prognosis. "My uncle never took a lesson, but when Sabbath was over the family would get together and he would bring his violin to play. The family would sing." The untrained fiddler made his sick nephew a promise. "You get better and I'll buy you a violin." All lent their encouragement. Happily, Chaim did recover and the uncle honored his pledge, procuring an instrument somewhere between quarter- and half-sized. The brash youngster felt ready to start lessons. Not wanting for their son the life of a poor street musician, not confident that even a slightly higher quality violinist playing for bar mitzvahs or weddings could make a good living, his parents said, "No."

Showing steel determination even at the tender age of seven and a couple of months, the boy went on a hunger strike. His mother made futile attempts to bribe him to eat. This clever tactician decided to use the parental preoccupation to get his way. Chaim stubbornly refused to eat anything until they let him study violin. The end of a three-day hunger strike came when his father gave in, and the parents agreed to the beginning of their younger son's music lessons.

Although most any reserves went for Israel's education, Chaim felt confident of his father's support. "I was lucky because he had a deal of his own. He negotiated with me. 'I don't have the money to pay for a good teacher.'" In line with the father's philosophy of always aiming for the best, he proposed inquiring about the most respected violin professor in Warsaw. "Then we would make an appointment for him to examine me. And if he thought I was good, he would teach me for free." If not, Abraham would find some way to pay.

The appointed visit did not include or require a violin. Mieczyslav Michalowicz, professor at the Chopin Academy of Music, admitted to Abraham in Yiddish that he had to convert from Judaism to gain a post. Later Chaim's father repeated to his son the teacher's words, "'I became Catholic in order to be where I am, but my heart is still where it was.'" The professor, who lived at Chopin Street #8, had taught both Ida Haendel and Bronislaw Huberman. The latter urged Polish and German Jewish musicians to immigrate to Palestine, and founded an orchestra there in 1936, which later became the Israel Philharmonic Orchestra.

Michalowicz talked to the child a little. Then he had him sit on his lap in front of one of the room's two pianos while playing different notes. Chaim satisfactorily vocalized matching pitch. "My pitch was perfect, in any range, so my ear was good." Next the professor examined the boy's fingers. "He liked my fingers. 'It looks like he may have talent.'" Chaim thus passed inspection and gained preliminary acceptance into the studio with an offer of complimentary lessons.

"My father said, 'Such a famous man and he doesn't charge any money. Maybe little Chaim is talented.'" Soon began weekly sessions at the studio. On other days, for a total of six per week, a graduate student would come to the Arbajtman home and serve as assistant teacher, working in exchange for a free meal.

Chaim noticed something different about the graduate student's playing, a vibration, but didn't know what to call it. "'When you play, you shake.' He said, 'You want to shake? Go ahead.' I imitated." Quickly and simply, in just a few days of study, the precocious child had developed a vibrato. Positive feedback kept him moving forward.

For a break and reward, "My father used to take me on Sabbath to walk around the rich neighborhoods and plush hotels, just to stand in front of them. I remember the people in fine clothes, the doorman in uniform with a red coat, brass buttons, and white gloves. My father would say, 'Chaim, if you keep practicing, this is all yours. This is where you belong.' I wondered, 'If I practice, how is it going to get me to this place?' It didn't make any sense, but I didn't argue with my father. He was always right. I had to practice."

After just two weeks of lessons he played his first melody. "I remember even now." The Polish folk tune contained a single sharp, G sharp, and spanned one octave. "I was so proud of that sharp. I thought I had achieved greatness." Never mind the six additional sharps and another world of flats to learn; for now, young Chaim virtually soared after conquering his inaugural melody.

"After everything was quiet, I was tucked away to sleep. The lights were off and my father would talk to my mother about me, 'The teacher says he is extremely talented and has a great future. We have to support him.'"

Abraham and Chaya told their son he was a violin virtuoso. "At first, my mother took me to lessons. My father wondered if my mother understood, so he started to take me to lessons instead. In the old days a lesson was not forty-five minutes while watching the clock. There was no stopwatch. Lessons were a minimum of two hours. If needed, he would teach for three hours. It felt long, but I didn't show it. I respected him."

"My father thought I could not digest the three hours, but my mind flourished because I was interested. My father occasionally fainted during lessons. We had to revive him. My father was concerned it was too much for me. Actually, it was too much for him."

"My father sacrificed himself. In a sense, he sacrificed for his family. He would sit next to me while I practiced. He became very knowledgeable about my violin playing. 'You played the wrong note. It's not in tune. Play it again.' He became a big connoisseur."

"I started with the violin young, and I needed help with school. So, we had special tutors come to the house. Michalowicz's assistant teacher would practice with me for three hours. Even on the Sabbath, after sundown, I had to make up the hours I didn't work. And I didn't resent my parents for making me practice Saturday. No, I respected them. Respect."

After three or four months the student lapsed on regular exercise with his instrument. "I wanted to play like other kids, and not practice." Abraham said nothing, but picked up the violin and without explanation started out the front door. "'Father, where are you going?' 'To the shop where the violin was purchased.' 'Why?' 'To sell it back, since you aren't using it.' I started crying. 'I didn't insist that you practice. You wanted the violin. And now, you don't want to practice. You have had enough? I have had enough too.' He was very smart." All nonchalant and polite words from Abraham, but Chaim immediately committed to more regular practice. "I practiced three hours daily and made good progress."

"After six months, the graduate student gradually stopped coming to practice with me. I had learned how to practice by myself." Sometimes Chaim went alone to violin lessons. In the wintertime, no matter the many layers of socks, gloves and coats his mother put on him, he felt stone cold after a forty-minute walk. "Twenty-five degrees centigrade below zero, like Siberia with snow up to the ears" made travel in these temperatures a formidable undertaking. It caused his violin to "go kaput" and resulted in a major chore to tune upon arrival.

After just nine months of violin instruction, Chaim performed his first recital, which included Vivaldi's Violin Concerto in A Minor, at Chopin Academy in Warsaw. "After ten months with Michalowicz, my father took me to a violinist by the name of Ignatz Weisenberg, a pupil of Auer in St. Petersburg, as were Heifetz and Zimbalist, among many other greats."

Arbajtman's new teacher, of sterling caliber, tall, strong, and handsome, seemed less civil. "He was a great teacher, very disciplined. I learned a lot from him. But he was very tough, if you played the wrong way. He expected perfection right away, no matter what."

Chaim studied with Weisenberg for two years, a typical lesson consisting of scales, arpeggios, etudes, a sonata or concert piece, and mock performance for the professor and his wife. At age ten, he spent six months under the instruction of Mr. Kleinmann. This man previously taught Michalowicz, Arbajtman's first instructor. It seemed everyone knew everyone in the small world of classical music. "The best of the best education, no money can buy this kind of foundation."

"I had a cousin and he was thirteen years older than I. He was a big man and he used to come three times a week. He liked to hear me practice, especially Tartini's Violin Sonata, so he would sit down in a chair and listen. We created a close bond." Wolf Tuchmann's father, Abraham's first cousin, had the nearby stand on Dzika street with fruits, sodas and sweets. The store owner would also visit the Arbajtmans with some frequency.

"I remember playing when relatives visited. My parents expected me to become the next Heifetz. I noticed the smile and joy my father had when I played." Both parents showed a marvelous dedication, not just to their younger son, to each of their children. This love and devotion proved paramount through the impartation of an incredible inner strength Chaim would require soon and utilize throughout his life.

"My father was interested in everything about music." In 1936, he read and announced to his son a great violinist would come to the city for a concert. "'Do you want to go?' 'Yes!!' I don't know how many buttons my father had to sew to buy the tickets for both of us. We went together."

Anxious and excited, at age nine Chaim already knew of this famous artist, and accompanied his father to hear a very special Warsaw Philharmonic performance. They played at home in the capital, near Chopin Academy where Arbajtman first took violin lessons. A Russian, soloist Efrem Zimbalist came on tour from America. His performance of Beethoven's Violin Concerto brought the house down in a sea of clapping hands and stomping feet. "The audience would not let him off, with flowers like a whole garden" thrown on stage.

Chaim felt swept up by the electrifying thirty-minute ovation. "I just remember he was there forever. So taken, I was shaking." A daring vision occurred to him. "This was the night I promised myself, one day I will study with this man. I knew this dream was ridiculous. Knowing how this would sound to my father, I never mentioned it." Giving no verbal indication, thereafter he steadfastly dreamed of instruction with Zimbalist.

Some interval afterward, "There was a big, elegant nightclub that invited me to play regularly. They offered me a fee, an amount that meant that I would be making more money than my father." He said, "'No, I will not use my child.' He just wanted me to continue learning."

"My father always found me the best teachers." Such dedication he faithfully invested in all his family. "I have two sons and one day the world will know about them."

3
A Jewish World Falls Apart

"The 'solution' had a beginning, a middle, and finally the end
— death."

"In just four months I was scheduled to debut with the Warsaw Philharmonic as soloist, playing the Mendelssohn Violin Concerto." Abraham had made arrangements for his son to take instruction from Szymon Goldberg, the former concertmaster of the Berlin Philharmonic. This eminent violinist, through advocacy with Hitler by the widely regarded Conductor Wilhelm Furtwängler, remained longer in Germany than other Jews. The temporary stay ended with his forced return to Poland in late 1938. Goldberg had contacts all over the music world and had studied with Carl Flesch, now living in London, to whom he sent a letter on Chaim's behalf. Chaim received approval to come, the grant of a scholarship, and word to start lessons with Flesch in a short while. The plan developed for him to go there accompanied by his father. Another several months, and the two would have made it to England, avoiding so many inexpressible troubles.

Like our young musician, his parent had the gift of prescience. "My father had a horrendous dream six weeks before disaster started. He wouldn't talk about details, but cried many tears. The nightmare was of total destruction of the family. It came true."

"The Jewish world fell apart. When I was twelve the war started." The Nazis invaded Poland September 1, 1939. "Air raid sirens screamed. In order to go to the shelter we had to run across the street to another house." For the first time, he saw German warplanes overhead. "As I ran for safety, a fire bomb in front of me exploded. The safe place collapsed, completely destroyed. Flames were everywhere. Warsaw was burning. I wondered, 'How can I escape?'" He ran back to his less damaged apartment building. "Life suddenly changed, becoming more and more difficult. There was uncertainty and talk of World War."

In October, the whole country fell into disorganization. Normal tutelage in music proved impossible. "I practiced, but had no lessons. I lost a lot in these critical early years, but had a good solid beginning that could propel me afterward." One person for whom Chaim frequently played, "My grandfather David, in the middle of the day he would get a chair, sit down, and watch me practice. I felt very close to him. He had such joy." How much, the grandson grew to appreciate even more fully when older.

Attaining age thirteen in August of 1940, the time for bar mitzvah arrived. This ceremony took place in a small synagogue near the apartment. Not a formal event, just close friends and family attended. Plainer and simpler under the stark conditions of occupation, such an event could not attain the grand scale of today's celebrations. "My paternal grandmother had passed away, but Grandpa came. I remember all the kids, my father and other relatives. The thinking at that time, better do things today, not knowing what tomorrow will bring. The way we pulled together was so great."

Before hostilities commenced and loss of sovereignty occurred, Abraham's passport showed his place of birth as Poland, his nationality as "Israelite." "This was long before the war. Wherever you went, you were a marked man, a Jew." Distinction between Gentile and Jew had long gaped wide. Often this gave rise to unprovoked trouble.

Under German occupation, separation occurred between the "master race" and the subjugated Poles. Only Germans could enter certain shops, attend better theaters, eat in the choice restaurants. When food rationing commenced, the resident population received much less. This fueled the black market as everyone tried to combat starvation.

Against such a backdrop, SS Chief Heinrich Himmler allowed some Poles with "good" racial characteristics to register as Germans. Some Polish children moved to Germany, others even kidnapped, for rearing as Aryans. None of this applied to known Jews.

Chaim's brother, called Israel since birth, appeared light blond and didn't "look" Jewish. He perceived certain possibilities to navigate around prejudice and social stigma, assuming the name "Staszek," which was short for Stanislaw. This prompted people to assume him a Catholic.

Staszek, with his consummate command of German, helped people write professional letters for submission to authorities after arrival of the Germans. He possessed a gift for literary turn of phrase, even catching the attention of Nazi officials for such. "A very strong mind, my brother was like a poet. The writing was too good, and because the intelligentsia were the first to go, he knew he had to stop."

The younger Arbajtman son felt estranged from his own brother; Israel seemed barely one of the family as he began to move outside Jewish circles. He habitually frequented social gatherings, ingratiating himself with non-Jews, closed societies friendly to the Gestapo. His language skills and physical attributes allowed this. Often, he did not return home until midnight or later. Abraham and Chaya would have doused the lights around eight o'clock to avoid drawing unnecessary attention to their residence. Still, like all good parents, they waited up until Israel arrived safely back home. Approaching the apartment, he carefully looked over his shoulder to exclude the possibility of someone following. "Sneaking in at midnight, then they could breathe."

Staszek had already told them about the people he met. He would not obey curfew, and refused to wear the Star of David label required of Jews under occupation. Fiercely independent, proud of heritage, but hardly reassuring his parents, he promised to "'never work for a German (in a camp) or they can kill me on the spot.'"

A non-Jewish, influential and prosperous Pole hired Staszek to teach English to his eighteen-year-old daughter. Complicating matters, the young lady fell in love with her tutor who ended up practically a member of this household. "My brother ate well, but the rest of our family didn't. Conditions were getting worse. One incident still gives me goosebumps when I remember it."

Staszek attended a party at the rich Pole's estate where he encountered an invited VIP, the regional Nazi governor, Hans Frank. At midnight, their host proposed a toast to his uniformed German guest and asked what he would give for killing all local Jews. The Nazi offered, "'I'll give you a special reward, a big gold medal.'" Taking courage, and knowing that love of music could sometimes temporarily shift focus from nearly constant racial bigotry, the closeted Jew quickly thought of a possible overture. This could have more fundamental benefits, again just temporary, calming of hunger on the home front.

He casually commented that he had been walking by a poor neighborhood. Hearing beautiful music from the apartment building, he walked upstairs and encountered a young "Israelite" (actually his own younger brother), playing the Mendelssohn Violin Concerto. Would this prosperous head of household care to have the lad invited to give a home concert and hear for himself? Staszek offered, "I would like to bring him." "Yes, get the boy," replied the Polish man.

Israel told his brother of the arranged performance and confided with their parents about a plan to possibly bring home any extra food. Mindful of the ever-worsening shortages, they agreed, but could not relax until both sons re-entered their apartment door.

A day or two later Chaim went to play at the large residence, feeling a bit overwhelmed by the unfamiliar surroundings. Escorted in, suddenly he stood up straight and had to rub his eyes in amazement, transfixed by how well his brother blended in with those others in attendance. "This is not my brother, but he looked like my brother. I thought he was my enemy. I was so young and sheltered. I didn't understand." He sat in the big room, on a stately chair, with double breasted suit, legs crossed, postured as if he owned the place. After a foreshortened performance of some mazurkas, a polonaise, and a Chopin nocturne concluded, everyone applauded vigorously.

Afterward when given a little plate, the dainty morsels did not necessarily impress him. Of course, this thirteen-year-old took all that was offered to share at home where the cupboard too often remained mostly bare. Much more than any temporary reprieve from prolonged hunger, his parents would feel much greater relief after embracing both sons, food foraging operation completed. Chaim arrived first, his older brother quite a bit later. When he finally walked through the apartment door, Chaim kept looking at him and wondered, "Is this really my brother or someone I no longer recognize?"

As time progressed, home felt a lot less secure. Here in bed, late one night, the younger brother had yet another unsettling dream, involving his father's father. Approximately four weeks after this premonition, Grandfather David Arbajtman died at age seventy-four. Though never superstitious, his peculiar visions marked early instances of a kind of instinct or intuition that would follow Chaim in future years. He did not disclose the dreams to others and, for the time being, did his best to shift attention from sad inner thoughts.

The Germans followed a very organized plan. Construction of the Warsaw Ghetto wall had commenced April 1, 1940, on order of

District Governor Ludwig Fischer. On October 16, a formal announcement of Ghetto formation came from Governor-General Hans Frank, with gate and district closure on November 15, just thirteen months after the invasion. Nazis officially established Warsaw Ghetto as a place to deposit and detain all Jews. They numbered four hundred thousand, and represented 30% of Warsaw's total population. The Ghetto amounted to less than 3% of the city's land mass. This heartless decree brought about horrendous disruption and displacement. Compounding matters, an influx of Jews from smaller outlying villages multiplied the bodies competing for limited space and diminishing staples in the capital.

"Where we were living became part of the Ghetto. We didn't even have to move." There, Jews had an average of one hundred to three hundred calories to eat per day, starvation rations, about 10% of normal. People felt desperate and trapped. Small children furtively hurried to help sustain their families and keep them alive. Many were shot dead for attempting to smuggle food across the wall, or merely moving about after hours. Occupation forces performed brutal searches, tossing babes in arms out of second and third floor windows for no infraction at all. Ghetto residents, including those who had at first found such shocking rumors and reports unbelievable, eventually came to realize the deadly seriousness of their detention.

"Before we were rounded up, we came together. After Sabbath we sang and danced. Family was what kept the Jewish people hopeful. Without hope, you didn't have life. No matter what the situation, without hope you didn't have a future." Perhaps twenty to twenty-five Arbajtman extended family members lived in the Ghetto.

"There was no food. There was no money. I went to Catholic families, pretending to be a Catholic." He went for whatever he could obtain by nearly any means. "People were starving and dying. We had a God with no ears. His 'chosen people' lost a lot of lives. Why didn't God choose somebody else?"

Conditions steadily worsened. Most everyone felt desperate. A smaller number wanted to defend themselves and fight. The Jewish resistance had their first hideout at Mila Street #29. When discovered, they quickly moved into Mila #18. Smugglers with whom they collaborated had a "bunker" at the second address. This became headquarters for leadership of a valiant Warsaw Ghetto Uprising.

Chaim's maternal grandparents had lived at Mila #24, just steps away from the cauldron that would later come to a boil.

Before the Uprising triggered final destruction of their neighborhood by Nazis, swift currents had already enveloped whole families. Ghetto walls physically confined them and even retarded social intercourse. Chaim sensed the tension in his parents' words when they quietly discussed their narrowing range of choices. "As days went along, life slipped away."

One option, taking into account Poland had been divided between Germany and Russia, occurred to Wolf Tuchmann. Son of Abraham's first cousin, he still came each weekend to the apartment on Wolinska. He still loved to listen when Chaim practiced violin and to get advice from Abraham. After the invasion, Wolf took his young wife Karola, whom he married in the Ghetto, and fled to a Russian occupied zone in the east. There they heard an offer, or demand to sign papers and accept Russian citizenship. This declined, authorities took them prisoner. "He thought he was doing the safer thing and ended up in Siberia."

"You couldn't freely leave Warsaw because they already had gates to the ghetto closed." The Arbajtmans hatched an alternate plan. Abraham's cousin lived around Lublin, 180 kilometers away, and invited them to join him. "When my father left Warsaw, the only way to leave was through sewers. We all went together." They entered through a hole in the street January 17, 1941. "Inside were Polish men you had to always bribe; otherwise…" The family resurfaced outside the ghetto wall. Near the city, at a safe distance from the center, they would board a train. "This was illegal. Jews were not allowed to buy tickets and were not allowed to ride the train. You had to wear the Star of David when outdoors."

"My father looked Jewish. My brother with green eyes appeared Aryan, according to Hitler who had brown eyes." Israel had stealthily exited the family fold already, and had gone into hiding outside Warsaw. "I was a blond, and all curls. The ladies thought I had a special barber. I didn't exactly look Jewish. Mother was too nervous. My parents designated me to buy the tickets."

They carried practically no belongings to the station on January 18. To avoid exposure on the train, "My parents devised a disguise, the towel. In the old days, for toothaches you wrapped yourself with a towel." Abraham wanted to conceal Jewish features. With a "schmatta" or rag about his head and face, nearly covering one eye, he feigned a dental condition. Getting onto the train camouflaged, "We surrounded my father, so nobody could get close to him. We were a shield." Standing between cars, "We kept him near the toilet like he was waiting to go. We avoided talking." He turned this way and that way, facing away from any conversation. Not sitting, lest a German should approach to take his seat, thus they avoided drawing unwanted attention.

Sadly, cousin Shlomo had not joined them, having previously drifted away, disillusioned by the seeming abandonment of his parents. He never reappeared. Close by in the train, Chaya watched over Chaim and Zysla. Against incredible odds, they made it to Lublin.

When Abraham arrived, no ghetto had yet formed. Unfortunately, this soon changed by German decree. Created on March 24, 1941, Nazis later slated the Lublin Ghetto as one for earliest liquidation in occupied Poland. Meanwhile, at nearby Lublin Castle imprisoned Jews continued to direct underground activities, an added dimension of conflict and danger. "We were there for a couple of weeks and it was not safe." Abraham's cousin, who served as President of the Jewish community, looked for less conspicuous housing. "He helped with where to go. So, we ran."

Shortly after Germany invaded Poland, Hitler had devised a so-called territorial solution to the Jewish Question. He came up with a concept, deportation of European Jews to the "Lublin Reservation," with help from Nazi chief ideologist Alfred Rosenberg, Heinrich Himmler, Hans Frank, and others. Reports characterized this area as "swampy in its nature." Advocates proposed that it would serve well as a reservation for Jews. "This action would cause their considerable decimation." The territorial solution proved less efficient than anticipated. Better suited to their aims, Nazi Germans later switched plans and implemented Operation Reinhard in Poland. A staggering tally, the gruesome statistics would amount to a lion's share of the infamous "final solution" for Europe's Jews through mass murder in death camps.

Meanwhile the Judenrat, or Jewish Council, which was foisted on local leaders by occupation authorities to carry out Nazi orders, had essentially no support when advocating for Jewish community interests. Commanded by local non-Jewish police and Nazi SS under threat of death, Jewish Order Police served as tools to control their own populations. Eventually, Germans walled off fifty-seven ghettos in Lublin district towns and villages to accommodate the influx of displaced Jews from elsewhere. Synagogues closed for services and served as housing units.

"We ended up staying in a two-story synagogue on the corner with many refugees. As was custom, women and children stayed on one floor while males stayed on the other." For whatever reason, Abraham didn't stay at the synagogue, perhaps going in search of a not so obvious and less vulnerable shelter.

"We were gypsies, running from place to place." They ended up in Lysaków, a small village nine kilometers northeast of the big city Lublin. "I didn't see my brother much. His hiding place was a mystery. He would come to our place occasionally. My family had no food and no income."

"Every day seemed like a lifetime. Every day was very bad. From the village I would take a train around 5:30 a.m. and ride, maybe for ten minutes, to neighboring villages. I managed for my family because Jews were not allowed in the trains. I would go as a Catholic boy, going from farmer to farmer. I pretended, crossing myself as Catholics do, to bring some food. On good days I got a piece of bread, one or two potatoes. Hours later, as I came back to my village, seven-year-old Polish kids called 'Jude! Jude! Jew! Jew!' They were wanting to alert Germans to pick me up, but I would run. Boy, could I run."

"In the village we wanted to avoid problems, staying away from any Catholic neighbors who hated the Jews and would tell on us to the Germans. The Jewish police, too, were forced into working for the Nazis."

In the countryside around Lysaków, a shelter for partisans who hated occupation, Nazi police came to search for weapons, and summary executions occurred. The Arbajtmans remained here a few short months, still intent on evading trouble, if humanly possible. "There was no ghetto here yet. Eventually everything was bad for the Jews, everything. It was only a question of time."

During these days, Nazi officials directed police to commence rounding up males, ages seventeen to forty-one, as forced laborers. A search for seventeen-year-old Israel had proven unsuccessful. "My brother was tipped off by somebody. He pretended to be Catholic, a refugee from Schlonsk (a village in central Poland village populated by many German immigrants). The authorities got smart and figured out he was a Jew. My brother took off, always saying, 'A free man until I die.'" Circumspectly, he kept moving in and out of family contact, to limit Jewish connections and reduce the likelihood of his own detection.

"Looking for Israel, the police came at two o'clock in the morning. My parents may have had an idea where he was. The children weren't given details because we might give them away, if interrogated. So, they took my father and said to my mother they would keep him for twenty-four hours. If my brother came, they would let my father go." Abraham was taken hostage early that morning. Born in 1900, according to German law, he had passed the upper age limit of forty-one to enter a work camp. Nonetheless, local authorities decreed release could only come when the older son appeared and took his place. Still, Staszek refused to surrender himself to the Germans and enter any camp.

Without Israel's cooperation, Chaya had little time to formulate her desperate gambit. She told Chaim, not quite fourteen and still wearing a pair of short pants with long socks, that he had grown almost as tall as his older sibling. The young impostor heard instructions to don his brother's blue, white-striped high school trousers. Chaim should stash shorter pants in a sack. After presenting himself as ransom and gaining the father's release, Chaim could change back to his own short clothes. This, at least, was his mother's daring strategy. If it went as planned, he would have to be released because of his youth. The other family members would go to a prearranged hiding place to reunite there.

"My mother wrote to the neighborhood police station about an exchange. My father got out and they took me. Then an hour and a half later I changed the pants to short pants. I told them, 'I am thirteen.' They said, 'We will only let you go if your brother comes.' My mother had talked me into going. If I had known that they would keep me, I would not have gone."

Chaim had obtained his father's freedom for the moment. Unfortunately, those in power would not let this frightened youngster go until they had his brother in hand. Israel never reappeared or rejoined the family. Something or someone likely unmasked his Jewish identity which led to fatal consequences. Chaim remembers last seeing him that first quarter of 1941.

Despite his disqualifying age, he was detained for three weeks in April at a labor facility close to Lysaków. He didn't stay long enough to remember the name. Contrary to strict interpretation of Nazi law, they kept Chaim. "I will never forget my job in the camp. There were no concentration camps in the beginning, only work camps." His job in a gang of eighteen to twenty proved heavy labor for the lad. "I was working with hammers to break stones to make them smaller for the road. It was about five kilometers from where we lived. At that time, your parent could visit. My mother came and visited me from twelve to one, every lunchtime for one hour. She would bring me food."

On such a visit, Chaim told his mother he wanted to escape. She objected, "'No, don't escape, you will be shot, they'll kill you. Your father is doing everything to get you out,' but nothing was happening. I cried my heart out, wanting to go home with her. My mother cried with me because of her pain seeing me cry." His parents later sent three letters, telling him of orders they report to Lublin's Umschlagplatz. Rumors circulated about transport to Treblinka.

The shocking realization he could no longer depend on the intervention of others spurred the youth to take action. He spied some hay, stacked next to a section of barbed wire that encircled the camp. "The hay for horses was like a big mountain. I thought, 'During a big downpour I can hide there.' A skinny kid could get through the wires which were not electrified, but the problem was how to bury myself without anybody noticing. Rain made the ground muddy." The soft ground below left possibly just enough extra space to wriggle his way to freedom. "And that would happen one day."

Five to six days later, "I escaped, at three o'clock in the morning. It was a nightmare. I jumped into the bunch of hay and buried myself. I got through the barbed wire and walked five kilometers. I knew where my parents were staying. I got there a bit before five, while it was still dark. My parents were shocked."

His family departed immediately, knowing the Nazi police would come on motorcycles within the hour to search for their son, even more enraged that the whole family escaped. Seven to ten days prior,

Chaya had arranged temporary refuge for Zysla with ladies back at the large two-story synagogue ten kilometers away, isolated on a corner. Chaim rushed to fetch her, taking a short train ride part way, then walking another four kilometers.

He arrived and climbed to the second floor where females hid, mothers and kids. "She was crying, I was crying. She was so furious with me. Not that her parents left her, but that I left and didn't stay with her." After hugging his sister, they ate a little bit of food, their emotion-filled time together lasting merely minutes.

"Suddenly, a pair of policemen burst through the door and shouted at me, 'Come!' 'Can we finish our sandwiches?'" They closed the door and waited outside, atop a wooden staircase. Teenage Chaim had shrewdly asked for precious extra moments to quickly come up with their escape plan. "I said to my sister, 'You must go that way. Never stop until you see our parents, never stop, never stop. No matter how tired, do whatever it takes. I will go this way to try to escape. I am going to jump from the second to the first floor, open the windows of the synagogue and run for it.'" Chaim instinctively acted quickly, calculating that departure in different directions would divide their pursuers and increase chances for both to survive. He didn't know if Zysla completely understood, but their hasty reunion had come to an end.

"Landing in the yard, they got me." Surrounded by officers, two Jewish police — cooperating with the Nazis overseers, in order to survive — immediately grabbed and handcuffed him. Cold metal on skin in the early morning hour, his wrists felt the shock even more.

"I let out a cry. This was my first time getting handcuffed, at thirteen. But only bad people were arrested. I wondered what I had done wrong. I didn't understand." Shocking and painful, these collaborating officers shared Arbajtman's ethnicity.

By force, Chaim was returned to confinement at another nearby camp, still in Lysaków. In the confusion, he had lost track of his precious Zysla. Last sight and last sound, "At age thirteen, my family and I were separated. We had tried to run away, to hide. I never saw my family again. I had a younger sister, a brother, parents, grandparents, uncles and aunts. Tragedy happened. We were all sent to different concentration camps where my entire family was murdered."

4
Nazi Camp Life

"Even at the worst times, in some concentration camps, occasionally there was music. Before they might kill you, and after they might kill you, but not during music."

"When you don't know how you are going to live, it's miserable. It's a horrible thing to wait for death at any moment. No human being should ever live with the horror, whether they're going to see the next day, the people you care about, or whether those people are going to see you again."

Two officers deposited Chaim in a second Lysakow facility. They didn't know exactly what to do with a thirteen-year-old, as Nazi law specified sixteen as minimum age for detention. "There was a spot to sleep near the gate. Two policemen who took care of the camp stayed there, and one other, the chef of the camp's kitchen."

"I was confined to the cot above, late at night, starving. The three Jews, the chef and the two police, had lots of meat. Instead of cooking for the prisoners, they took the meat and ate it all." They never offered an underage boy in the upper bunk a single morsel, and he started crying.

The kitchen chief took out a long knife and said, "'If you cry any more, I'll cut off your head!' As when the Jewish policemen arrested me, I was so confused. I was taught by my parents to stay away from anti-Semites, but never to stay away from a Jew. This I could not understand."

From his cot, he overheard talk of freedom fighters and coordination with a partisan movement. The chef again threatened, "'If you say anything you've heard, I will personally...'" They frightened the youngster, while plotting resistance to what soon proved an inevitable onslaught. After the favor of special status and free access to food for a short season, the Germans eventually killed them all, chef and police.

Any additional day of life carried no promise of adequate sustenance. "They got us up early in the camp. Breakfast consisted of one piece of 'straw' bread." Work details started by 7:30 a.m. They kept going until around 4:00 p.m. "For supper, we received one cup of 'soup,' a horrible liquid without barley or anything solid. The trick was to wait until the end of the soup line." Chaim discovered that at the bottom of the pot he might find something thicker than water, perhaps a few grains to consume.

In contrast to the fare at home through his childhood, "It's not a soup, and the same every day. I was used to a slice of bread with marmalade. This was the most precious memory of my time while starving, total starvation. It's a luxury to dream for a second, but you dream and don't have it. Then you wake up to the bitter reality of more pain and suffering."

The stay at the second work camp lasted considerably longer than his two or three weeks at the previous facility. "My first real job was to take a bunch of geese out of the camp site, near the pond water, and to bring them back to camp at a certain time. The geese were smart. They could become aggressive and take a bite out of my leg. I didn't know what to do, so I ran and they came after me. By the lake the geese took a rest. I did too, and fell asleep. Suddenly, I awakened to the sound of a motorcycle. The SS came up and right away put his gun to my head. Every lapse, it was a gun to your head. I took the geese back to finish my day's work."

"I was taken young at age thirteen and things were getting bad for me in the second camp. Nobody was coming to visit me now. I couldn't understand. When growing up, I was so sheltered by my parents. My parents said, 'You are very special and we love you.' I thought, 'My parents must have lied.'" He could think of no other explanation. "'If I'm so important, if they really loved me, they shouldn't have left me in this place.' I was too young to understand the circumstances. I was mixed up and, for a while, I hated my parents and blamed them for letting this happen to me."

Chaim had no way to mark dates, but estimated. "After maybe six months, already in two different camps, I thought my parents were still around to come and fetch me to safety." He didn't realize, or couldn't face yet, the likelihood they had already died. "It took a year to accept. When I was fourteen, I understood that it was unlikely that they survived. It was not that they didn't love me or care for me. Everyone went to gas chambers. We found out from people coming into the camp, though no one knew about my brother. I heard he was posing as a non-Jewish intellect and they found him; so, he had no chance. He probably was shot to death."

"We wanted to know, and also we didn't, because it was so painful to dwell on it." Should his father and mother yet live, "They would be in pain, not to be able to help me. If even one of the children had been killed, my parents never could have survived. It would be something like one for all, and all for one. It kept changing, what you believed was true and what was wishful thinking. You had to sort it through which took a while. Some sorted faster than others. We needed time to grow up, and some never did."

Time went on with little to mark its passage, one day blurring into the next. Adult inmates did not talk to Chaim, simply lacking the energy, or perhaps judging him too immature for adult conversation. This added to the nearly unbearable isolation. On the other hand, "The younger you were, the better chance of surviving physically and mentally. If you were older and had a family with kids to lose, it was more difficult to survive."

"When I came into camp so young, separated from parents, I became an orphan. Many children were either killed immediately or sent for medical experiments. They injected all kinds of poison to find out how they would react." Wanton violence and murders occurred daily. The randomness and unpredictability kept everyone on edge.

Nazis routinely moved prisoners from one camp to another to serve as forced laborers on needed projects. From his second facility, Arbajtman was sent by train in late 1941 to further detention at Janiszow, nine kilometers southeast of Annopol. Jews had been transferred here from Szydlowiec in August 1940, and from Ryki as early as 1939.

Chaim's assigned work included dam building on the Vistula River. The malnourishment, fatigue, prolonged immersion in water, and exposure to cold posed risks to health, especially to skin. "I carried loads uphill with no shoes. Fall and winter were very cold, below zero. With no fat to eat, my body was deprived, and could not heal. With no circulation, my feet swelled and had multiple wounds." One open sore on his right leg showed signs of infection and would not close. They seldom had a blanket to ward off freezing temperatures in bed. An undeserved consequence of inadequate rest at night and merciless beatings at work by day, those too weak to keep up with demands found themselves taken to the river and murdered in a birch forest.

Walking the grounds, he spied some grass and picked this for later use, hoping to aid his infected leg sores. "In springtime, there was one kind of green leaf, name unknown, which I decided to try. I washed by whatever means I had and put the leaf on my wounds. Unimproved for a long time, the next morning it became less inflamed. It started healing. Nobody told me how to do this. In Stone Age conditions, what did I know?" It would take more than five years for his lower extremities to return to normal.

"In this camp, there were Jews in the forest, fighting against the Germans. They liberated the camp where I was. In the middle of the night there were lots of Jews that escaped. I did not flee because I thought to myself, 'I don't know where I am. I don't know where to go and they can easily kill me on the way.' Mine was the best choice. Those that escaped were caught and shot dead. I was one of those that remained, and we were transferred to another camp." They walked back to Annopol and entered cattle cars destined for Krasnik.

From these experiences, Arbajtman found himself frightened and suspicious of guards, camp kapos (fellow prisoners assigned as overseers by the SS), partisans, police, Germans and Poles; everyone. Besides Janiszow, other facilities around Lublin saw escapes. Himmler closed thirty-eight out of forty-two smaller, less secure installations. Rather than deportation, Nazi regime heads had already begun opening larger concentration and death camps, with greater efficiency by means of extermination, to resolve what they termed the "Jewish question."

In November of 1942 Chaim landed in a fourth camp, Budzyn, his largest thus far. The prior summer, various groups of Jews first came to a village, five kilometers to the northwest of Krasnik, as slave workers. Occupying Germans converted a former munitions factory to the Heinkel Company aircraft plant. On entering, an overhead sign read, "Jedem das Seine" (To Each His Own). Laborers tediously, wearily assembled parts for German war machines, bombers. Two other former Janiszow detainees who made it to the new facility had something remarkable to say about Jews already there. "In their eyes we were free, and they were imprisoned."

This latest in a series of internment sites for Arbajtman, he later sardonically called them "all winners. Every camp was like a different country. All camps looked like hell because they were hell. Nothing was the same, except death. The end result was death." Chaim remained here some nine months before the forced labor facility received reclassification as a concentration camp, with many more months to follow.

Shortly after arrival, the fifteen-year-old Arbajtman learned of one special "Polish prisoner of war, captured by the Nazis. He was a Jewish man from Poland who was a high-ranking officer, which was unusual. The Nazis charged him to count the Jews and he reported the numbers to the German authorities. To be a Jew and a high-ranking officer, he had to come from an important and very well-educated family. In his early thirties, blond and Aryan in appearance, tall and handsome," Noah Stockman (also transliterated as Leib Noach Sztukman) originally came from Brest-Litovsk, later Końską Wolą.

Of further historical note, Samuel Jarniewski relates in his memoirs that he and fellow prisoners traveled by train to Budzyn on October 15, 1942. SS Unterscharführer Otto Hantke quickly attached their "comrade" Stockman to the Jewish camp leadership already transferred from Lipowa camp in Lublin. Taking him as a key individual to meet, Chaim searched for the man.

"The first day, the first hour I came to this camp, I asked, 'Who's the head of the camp?'" In their Warsaw apartment he learned early to respect authority figures, both his father and grandfather. More critical in a camp, "I wanted to analyze who is the powerhouse. Whom can I talk to, to save my life?'"

Chaim learned his identity and, within an hour ran to this Jewish man in a Polish army uniform. "I told him 'Herr Commandant, I am a violin virtuoso,' because this was what my mother and father used to say. This man talked to me. Not a violinist, but a violin lover, he was already on my side. My luck was that this man knew a lot about violin playing. He asked me with whom I studied and what I had played. I didn't know how he knew, whether he played another instrument or if in his family were musicians. Right away he started taking care of me. I, and others, called Stockman commandant, but he was not. The real Nazi commandant appointed this man as camp elder."

"The next day, he sent an assistant to my barrack, early in the morning before we went to work at seven o'clock. He said, 'The camp elder wants you to go to "kompania" (company or work group) #7,' not barrack #7. What I found was unbelievable, all older Jews, maybe 20, in fur coats, shaven, elegant suits, shiny shoes. I went to their beautifully dressed capo, and said, 'The camp elder elder asked me to come here.'" This unit leader, speaking rather disparagingly, told the youngster his age hardly qualified for inclusion in their company and to go to another one. Nearly ejected, Stockman suddenly came up and said, "'Take the boy.' And of course, 'Jawohl,' like Germans, he saluted and obeyed the command of his superior officer."

Another prisoner, Daniel Freiberg, corroborated that certain Budzyn prisoners "appeared well. Their dress was Polish army fatigues and civilian clothing that were tailored in that style which were also quite fine with respect to the local conditions. Their shoes were also good – for the most part boots that were in good shape."

A day later, Mika Bruk, the Polish officer's assistant found Chaim. "He showed me where to take a shower and dump all my clothing. Then, he took me to the warehouse to pick fine clothes like the others wore." Then they went back to company #7. "I had to register. They took me in, all Jews, scientists, doctors. So, the rumor among other inmates in the camp was that Stockman found a nephew in me. His favor got me some privileges."

In approximately a week, "I got the call in the morning by his assistant. I came to Stockman's office. On the table, there was a violin with a bow. He said, 'Play.' I picked up the violin and my fingers wouldn't move. I had not played in over a year and a half of hard labor. I could see the expression on his face. He thought I had pretended to be what I was not. He became angry."

"In my condition, the violin didn't feel right. This was how bad it was." Near panic and adrenaline quickly spurred him to a desperate plea. "I said, 'Give me some time, I need more time.' 'Take all you need,' he said, 'but play.' So, after three hours the fingers started to move a little bit." No small relief came when he finally heard better clarity and tone from the borrowed instrument.

Subsequently, Chaim received assignment to the camp kitchen. Unfortunately, his early morning tasks included washing, peeling, and cutting frozen potatoes. Wintertime, inside of days his hands and fingers became stiffer and more swollen.

He complained to the camp elder. "'Look at my fingers. I will never be able to play the violin.' People were hung, tortured, dying, starving, and here I was concerned about my ability to play the violin. He said, 'You come with me.' He took me to the kitchen. He told the chef, 'Let him warm his hands by the ovens. Whenever there is an inspection by the Nazis, we will alert you, then you make him peel the potatoes.' Relieved of the cold chores, I kept my hands warm. From time to time, I snuck a frozen potato into the oven to bake it. You have to live a little bit," he said with a satisfied smile. Thereafter, the kitchen work involved warmer cooking tasks. This special dispensation lasted two months or so.

Stockman had received permission to continue wearing a Polish uniform and to select his personal companion from the separate women's facility. "He picked Regina, a beautiful Jewish girl in her early 20s. They lived together in a bungalow outside the fence." As a privilege, "Twice weekly, occasionally three times, I would be called to play for Stockman. I used to be invited after hours. Because you were not supposed to leave the barracks after eight, a Nazi with a machine gun would come at nine to get me. I followed him to fetch my violin from the office of the camp elder; otherwise, in my barrack it would have been destroyed in no time. So, there was no such thing as practicing."

"Wherever you walked, lights and reflectors showed your every movement. You couldn't be out on your own or you would be shot. The Nazi took me to the camp elder's bungalow and I would play mazurkas for him with Regina, a friendly girl in a nice dress. A way of life for weeks, I couldn't believe it, candlelight, steaks, French wine, and cakes. I would get a little bit of the lavish food after playing for them. Between ten thirty to eleven o'clock, dinner with my 'friends,' I had my own chair and ate at a separate table." In camp, if one noticed steaks on a table, the thought occurred to squirrel away a piece, but immediately the fear of attack by another detainee in the barrack quashed any such idea.

In December of 1942, a new German commandant at the facility, Reinhold Feix, came from prior duty at the Belzec death camp. A heartless murderer, he would shoot Jews in front of his six-year-old son, who reportedly committed suicide as a teenager. Executions occurred daily, usually at evening or morning roll call, sometimes for the most minor of misdemeanors. Undressing too slowly might provoke Feix to shoot. Discovery of money and his wife's jewelry concealed in a soup dish with false bottom prompted the grisly punishment of a prisoner from Warsaw named Bitter. Feix commanded the assisting Ukrainian guard to place a rope around the inmate's neck, intending to hang him. They dragged him before an assembly of more than two thousand of his fellow prisoners. The sadistic commandant demanded they beat this Jew, but not heavily enough to hasten an end and foreshorten the suffering. Contrariwise, blows too light could arouse suspicion of sympathy and result in one's own demise. If Bitter lost consciousness, pails of cold water awakened him for more torture. According to a witness, death mercifully supervened some thirty minutes later.

After such horrific murders, the order could come for enforced singing and dancing to a point of exhaustion. Feix often chose the Polish tango "Marianna," Yiddish songs, and repeatedly demanded the melody, "Highlander, have you no regrets?" He played violin, talked quickly, and if someone failed to obey at once, he beat him and screamed to the high heavens like a madman. A camp orchestra could play both before and after executions. Sometimes they played when prisoners left for work in the morning, and again on their return.

"Nobody saw a clock." According to this camp's routine, days started with prisoners rousted from their bunks for inspection and body count at 5:00 a.m. They remained standing until the SS officers finished eating. Around 6:00 a.m., work parties departed for the aircraft factory. They paused for lunch, cabbage "soup." In the evening, workers returned for supper, cabbage soup, and a slice of "bread." All entered the barracks, converted horse stables, by 8:00 p.m. Lights went out at 10:00 p.m., with four or even six bodies alternating heads and feet in bunks of three or four levels.

"It was like in the army. To give you a picture, the mattress was some little thing pulled over straw. There were four guys in a bunk, two heads and two pairs of feet on each end. And there was something similar to an American army blanket, green or brown. The moment the lights went off, the blanket was stolen, but you could not catch the thief. It was pitch dark. I never robbed anyone, not once. You froze to death all night long. Kapos would beat you up if you complained. So, you didn't. I think I must have fallen asleep some, or maybe I died during the night and then came back; somehow, I lived through it."

Night and day, "We were too busy surviving. From minute to minute, it must have been subconsciously with me, we were trying to live every moment. You tried to do all you could, to become clever, to hide in case of emergency, to foresee bad things, to fight smarter to survive. All these skills were not normal to learn."

"If I spoke of hope, they would think I was crazy. We never talked about hope. How can you talk about hope in the worst existence ever? It was an instinct to survive. When you try to kill a mosquito, it runs away. It's an instinct."

"Even in the concentration camp, there was a system. The younger and more alert you were, the quicker you learned the system. Because of my quick reactions, I learned to jump and duck, to not get hit as much as others. When we were walking five abreast, I noticed the first one on the side was smashed for no reason. Unless they missed you, you were clobbered on the other side too. It wasn't easy, but I was fast and always managed to be in the middle."

"Nearly skeletons at eighty pounds, we used to make jokes. We used to see a guy and say, 'The way you look, you are not going to live tonight.' The one you talked to, he was laughing too. Jews would laugh at themselves. They would joke about you the more they cared about you. This was the eastern Jewish heritage. This kept us alive."

While still at Budzyn, Chaim came to work on a plum project. "There were about fifteen people that didn't have any assigned job, so we were left alone. Any German could come in, needing a work detail for this or that project and say, 'I need three guys.'" According to Arbajtman, "A different job every day, where you were beaten or killed and, of course, for no reason." The risk remained random and always present. "After some weeks in the 'leftovers' group, a Nazi came in, and wanted four gardeners to plant a garden." Though not an obviously preferred position, Chaim dared not decline this draft assignment. "What did I know about gardening? I didn't know how to grow an onion. So, I went. Without the other guys, I would have been dead."

"This was a good job, in front of the Commandant of the camp, Oberscharführer Feix. Outside the camp, he had a nice big house in the trees and nothing but acres of forest. The first time in my life I became a kapo, in charge of twenty-five people to cut and dig out small trees. It took around five months. Feix told my friend and me, 'Follow these blueprints.' I was fifteen, what did I know? Misread the plans, make some small mistake, and here comes a bullet. Fortunately, one of the guys was a gardener before entering the camp." The older man, in his 30s, reviewed a couple of blueprints for gardens. "Yellowing prints, he managed anyway."

"We built a garden. In the middle he wanted a swastika of plants, which we hated, but my friend did it. On one side it was '19' and on the other, '43.' It was in 1943. Besides a flower garden, he wanted to grow vegetables. After some months, everything was accomplished and growing."

"While others were stuck in the barracks, we went out to gather fresh produce. Someone was assigned to go to the yard, pick, wash, and deliver vegetables to the kitchen. That was our daily job. We were not being killed because the Commandant needed celery, radishes, and carrots." It felt like only a few weeks, not months, before the planting, cultivation, and harvesting assignment ended.

On a June day in 1943, according to ex-prisoner of war Daniel Freiberg who wrote for the Yizcor Book Project, Noah Stockman fell under suspicion. Accused by prisoner Samos of extorting inmates and secreting valuable properties, the beloved camp elder and another supervisor named Zoberman disappeared. At the end of three suspenseful days, just one mutilated and dismembered body required disposal. After this interval so nerve-racking to inmates, Stockman had reappeared with his body badly beaten and extensive facial contusions, apparently exonerated through violent interrogation. Three thousand detainees broke into song. As if on cue, they all sang Hatikva ("The Hope," Israel's future national anthem), to the man so loved for his many brave and selfless acts of kindness.

Forced to transfer, Feix left in August of 1943 and Werner Mohr assumed command of Budzyn. During the winter of 1943-44, Budzyn's classification changed from ZAL (Zwangsarbeitslager or forced labor camp) to concentration camp (Konzentrationslager). In accordance with German law, six years later Arbajtman would commence filling out what eventually amounted to a series of reparations applications, distinguishing between ghetto or work camp confinement and time in concentration camps. All total, he cited seven facilities, counting Budzyn twice, I and II.

Chaim's "Budzyn II," qualified as a genuine SS camp, with machine gun armed Ukrainian guards in positions elevated at each of four corners. These anchored the barbed wire enclosed rectangle. Evergreens could be seen beyond a bordering strip of bare land. A cluster of pines and bushes stood opposite the main entrance with a guard house on the right. Inside the gate, a row of barracks preceded a large open square.

The atmosphere and backdrop could not help but raise fears for prisoners. The case of an older man stands out, maybe sixty-five years old. You couldn't grow a beard. "The Nazis would light a match to singe the beard, just horrible." Chaim noticed this religious Jew. Any spare moment he would pray, pray, pray. Yom Kippur, the holiest day on the Jewish calendar, started at sunset on Friday, October 8, 1943. "He said to me and a few others that he's not going to work. Our thought, 'You're not going to live tomorrow.' How can you say to a Nazi with a rifle, 'I'm not going to work?'"

The next morning, this religious Jew assembled with all others in the central square. "He stood in the line to go to work. I was watching him being counted. We started marching. I saw him get out of the line and go back to the barracks. Nobody bothered him. And the Nazis saw him. This was real nerve. The SS acted as if somehow blind and let this religious man get away with it on Yom Kippur. Things happened that no one could understand. I saw it and never forgot this."

"We were too stupid to know it wasn't possible to work so hard without decent clothing in the winter, eat so little, and not die. Stupidity was the lifesaver, a blessing." Prison dress year-round, day and night, amounted to nothing more than pajama tops and bottoms. For "shoes," they scrounged German newspapers discarded in the trash, tied them with string on their feet. This arrangement didn't last long when working in puddles and wet ditches. "Half an hour and it's gone." Most of the time young Arbajtman's legs felt swollen, and festering sores continued to appear on his feet. He had fevers for a year or more, non-stop.

Relieving yourself at night meant you had to leave the barracks and a man in the tower monitored an inmate's movements by lights. "You had to scream at the top of your lungs, 'I'm going to the toilet!' Going back, you had to scream again, 'I'm returning from the toilet!'"

In late January of 1944, detainees moved three kilometers to an enclosure closer to the aircraft plant. Civilian guards disappeared and just SS remained. Obersturmführer Josef Leipold took over command from Untersturmführer Fritz Tauscher. All POWs donned striped uniforms. With a 50% reduction in the workforce at Heinkel, sorting and selections of prisoners intensified in spring and early summer. Weaker individuals were murdered onsite, while others were taken to factories elsewhere, and to death camps.

Some testified of slightly improved rations, bread, a dab of margarine, and the soup with maybe a couple of potatoes. In the spring of 1944, reportedly Stockman even obtained permission and provided for Jewish inmates to celebrate Passover, starting at sunset on April 8. "He was a genius of a man, trying to get special care for sick people confined to the barracks."

Some weeks later, Arbajtman played for Stockman at 10:00 p.m. "The next day, at six thirty in the morning on motorcycles, SS stormed in to inspect every inmate. We all had to step out, and I realized that the Nazis were directing some people to the left and others right. After a while you realized that going left was not so good because you saw young people, old people, and sick people. At the end, about 500 were marching off to work. I was in the left group. They had collected 105 people, including me. We were marched outside the camp into the woods, to a spot in the forest."

"This was ugly. There was a grave ready, humongous and deep, a firing squad behind us. I counted seven Ukrainian guards. I realized when I saw the grave, this was the end of life. They had a dozen tall inmates, also later shot, with shovels ready to bury us. Though I reasoned that everybody would be shot to death, no matter how hopeless things appeared, it was only human nature to imagine that maybe the bullet could fly off course and miss you."

"We were told to line up, three abreast. We had to put clothing, if we had any, on the side. You were almost naked. I took off my pants and shoes, laces tied together. I knew at one particular moment that the next bullet will be for me. It was such a horrible feeling. You knew in the next few seconds you would be buried. Either somebody shot you dead or you were buried alive because somebody missed. When this went into your mind, you stopped living at that split second. You could have chopped off an arm and I wouldn't have known the difference."

Chaim closed his eyes, "I hypnotized myself." His brain raced through his earliest memories to the present horrific moment. "All my life since childhood, like lightning, came to my brain. And then the brain stopped. I went blank." In his mind, he had already died.

Without warning, "This prisoner of war, the Jewish camp elder, grabbed and took me to the Obersturmführer, for this camp the highest rank of the Nazis." Stockman said, "'He is a violin virtuoso' — This is exactly what I told him when I met him — 'and we need him.' The German didn't know why they needed me. He probably thought I was playing for the officers. Whatever his thinking, he said, 'Okay, take him back.'"

Despite his sudden reprieve, Chaim continued in a stuporous state. Instead of returning directly to camp, he "zig-zagged" in a circle and stumbled back into the line of those condemned! "I was dizzy, I happened to step on a foot of the man who took me out of line at first." Forcefully, the camp elder pinched tightly and lifted him up by the left ear. "He said, 'Get out of here!' This woke me up from a nightmare. He saved me twice." In this mental state of shock, Chaim finally returned to camp. "Because of the violin, I was the only one that came out alive, from 105 people who were shot to death or buried alive."

Arbajtman later learned that Stockman had also tried to save a seventy-year-old Jewish doctor who was still in line for execution. "This physician went to the camp elder who would get medication for people who couldn't get it otherwise." The Nazi commandant had had enough and angrily cursed Noah Stockman, the would-be angel of mercy. Leipold screamed, "'You want to save every Jew.' The SS whipped the Jewish officer and made him blind in one eye. I was one of two that Stockman tried to save that day." The dedicated doctor did not survive. Something of a miracle for Chaim alone, this day the Nazi granted a first petition, but not the second. "All dead were buried. Those with shovels to bury others were also shot."

Back at camp, Chaim had already entered the kitchen where he worked. Stockman appeared fifteen minutes later with his eye bloodied. "He said to the startled chef, 'You always have food for yourself, but sometimes withhold food from others, which is not right.' I will never forget when he said, 'You see this eye? This will be alright.' He pointed to me and said, 'You see this kid? It would not have been right to kill someone so young.'" He did not mention the unutterable torture of innocent adults, or seek sympathy for the loss of his eye. Beyond dispute, but all eclipsed by the mitzvah, in a moral deed of immeasurable human kindness, at great personal risk, he had redeemed the adolescent musician's life.

"The day after, I was called to play for him at the cottage. I didn't see his girlfriend. It was not my place to ask where Regina was. He gave me some food, but seemed very serious. Later, an SS guard accompanied me to the barrack."

"At four in the morning, three Germans with guns came into the barrack. With German shepherds growling, ready to eat me up, they put a gun to my head. It wouldn't take much to pull the trigger. 'Where is Stockman?' According to the SS, I was the last one to see him. They thought that I knew where he was. I didn't know. I had to recount all the details." Nearly frozen with fear, Arbajtman denied any knowledge. As unpredictably as the episode began, it concluded, not a shot fired...this time. Further sleep would elude him the balance of night.

"Stockman left a note of resignation, admitting the massacre. They shot 104 people under his administration. He took responsibility on himself and disappeared. We didn't know what happened. There were rumors he escaped. I wanted to believe such rumors. There was no easy way to flee on your own, but there were possibly some collaborators. I hoped he was alive. I owed my life to Noah Stockman."

After Leipold's assault and the blow to his eye, Stockman may have doubted he retained residual favor. A prisoner, Morris Bergman, later testified that he had approached the Polish officer for help in going together with his nephew on an anticipated camp reassignment. The camp elder said, "I can't help. I wish I knew where I was going. So far, I don't know. I can't help myself."

David Crowe, in his 2007 book on Oskar Schindler, placed both Leipold and Stockman at factory facilities in Wieliczka, followed by Brünnlitz. Another researcher said the Nazis ultimately murdered Noah Stockman, possibly at Auschwitz. Who can explain such injustice to him, and all those he attempted to save? Arbajtman would add, "Anyone who says they understand, I don't trust them. If they say they don't understand, I believe them. I was there, and even I don't understand."

Absent a patron, Chaim's special privileges stopped. "Same camp, different situation. No nice clothes, food, or baked potatoes. Now I had to cope with no access to the kitchen chef. I had it good one day, then the next day I was loading coal, wood, work, or death."

Despite a changed administration and new regimen, which was really an existence of renewed torment, he quietly clung to hope. During a wonderful family upbringing, as children, "we had lots of hope." Now, even without a violin, he pretended that he had one. "The violin itself became part of my body, my soul. I would play silently. Imagining my parents, I played in such a way, wondering whether they would like it or not."

"Without the music, I don't think memory of my family could make any difference. I would not be here. I would have been buried alive, or shot to death in front of the grave with 104. The violin kept me alive. As I said before, very few people ever thought of their families in a concentration camp. Thoughts were occupied with survival, most every moment of your existence."

By late spring or early summer of 1944, Budzyn completed its closure, with evacuated inmates going to other facilities. In late April, Chaim had moved with his same assistant from the garden project to Wieliczka, a satellite of the camp at Płaszów. Entry took place through a tunnel with the usual "sorting" process to eliminate those weak and lame. Arbajtman received an identifying tattoo on his left arm with letters KL, abbreviation for Konzentrationslager (concentration camp in German).

The two new arrivals pitched a plan for fresh food to their commandant. He liked the idea, but it never came to fruition. Arbajtman soon lost track of his associate with the green thumb.

"You went through it all, blurred with so many camps, but each one was the same garbage." He went to work in a salt mine, compounding the seemingly endless suffering. "That's why I don't like salt." More bitter than salty, despite a natural desire to retain hope, slowly the truth hit him. "I began to think I would never come out alive. I saw reality, I saw how many people were killed. I didn't believe anyone would survive, including me."

Germans planned for Heinkel and other war-related industrial operations underground, inside the salt mine at Wieliczka. Approaching Russian troops precluded a full ramping up of activities. The time remaining barely allowed for removal of essential equipment and work force for use elsewhere.

After approximately three months of subterranean work, Chaim moved by train again, destination unknown. All wore thin shirts and pants, tattered from hard labor. "Here taking a transport, we were eighty to a hundred people in a locked cattle car. There were only holes on top of the car where air came in and we had one bucket, to pee or do anything else. The bucket was filled in the first ten minutes. You went on the floor. You stood because there was no place to move. We were standing many hours, sometimes overnight, with all the smells and no fresh air. It was inhuman. And you survived. How one survived I cannot understand. What I learned over time is human beings can be stronger than a tank. I never gave up struggling, how amazing!"

His train stopped en route for one day and night. Peering out, detainees read the station sign: Auschwitz. "In a closed-in car with so many people, you could not sit. We were like animals looking out the little windows. People got sick. Because they didn't have enough room at the camp to kill us, we had to move on after twenty-four hours. We had no food, no water, nothing." Suddenly, the locomotive lurched forward once more.

At their next and final destination, a Bavarian village, the townspeople had appreciated an economic boost after the nearby camp's opening. Many took advantage of prison labor at a granite quarry and in other local industries. Some rented out rooms to Nazi officers, and even accepted invitations to view movies in the SS casino next to headquarters. Later they would resent any insinuation they knew much of internal camp activities. Still, an easy fifteen-minute stroll led civilians to the nearby hilltop where they could readily observe goings-on, and the deadly means employed to enforce detention.

Entry to Flossenbürg concentration camp took place on August 4, 1944. From the train station, prisoners marched uphill in plain view of residents along a winding street of the small German town. Ruins of a twelfth-century castle dominated the skyline. Sounds of gunshots and a pungent odor carried far on the wind.

A contingent of inmates soon reached the camp's main gate. An inscription on the left post read, "Arbeit macht frei" (Work makes you free). Detainees continued through an open square, the Appellplatz. Zugangslager, a screening and temporary holding area towards the rear, contained four large barracks inside a barbed wire fence.

Chaim arrived here for initial evaluation. Randomly, Chaim received a forceful "welcoming" application of a club to his forehead. The resultant concussion rendered him partially amnesic to what came next, a strong smack at the front of his chest. Event markers, two lumps remained for life on cranium and sternum.

As part of his intake interview, he gave name and date of birth. "We were not human beings. Not a name, we were a number. My number was 14088. They recorded information in a large Bible-sized book with all the names that ever passed through Flossenbürg. I saw Chaim Arbeitman. My birthday was August 13, although there, it was the 15th and I'll explain. When I came into camp there was a Nazi (inmate secretary under their authority). You had to give them your name and birthdate. I told him August 13, 1927. I saw him write out 15, and so it remained in their book. I'll never forget. I was not going to correct the Nazi secretary because it could have cost me my life." A third blow that same day might have proven fatal.

Clothing surrendered, sun-exposed by day and freezing at night, for three days they remained essentially naked for extended scrutiny. The old and weak, as well as leaner kids of lesser stature appeared less viable candidates. "They wanted taller people able to work. If you were young, short, or skinny, you were no good." After complete examination by Dr. Heinrich Schmitz and four assistants, with rectal probing by pencil to exclude contraband, a coded number painted on one's forehead rated physical capacity. Number one indicated capable of regular outdoor work. Two meant lighter duty. Three signified limited indoor labor and also applied to women. Four signaled diversion to a special barrack and the crematorium. Rounded up and herded into an adjacent laundry building, prisoners descended the steps into a large basement. Forced to shower under the streams of water as powerful as that from a fire hose, merciless kapos then beat their naked flesh with rubber hoses and sprayed disinfectant that burned the freshly wounded skin. Now stripped of their clothes, dignity, and identity as humans, the time had arrived for final processing and induction into Flossenbürg.

Detainees were identified by color-coded badges on their prisoner uniforms, striped pajamas. Jews wore a yellow triangle. Superimposed inverted triangles formed the Star of David. Each color had meaning. These included a red triangle for foreign forced laborers and political opponents. Green signified convicts, criminals. Any letter on the triangle indicated a non-German country of origin, such as "P" for Poland. Colors and letters determined camp status. Career criminals from Germany ranked higher, with Eastern European Jews at the bottom. Flossenbürg's concentration camp had about 11% Jews, and others from all over Europe: Soviets, Poles, Czechs, Slovaks, Hungarians, Belgians, Dutch, Italians, French, British, American, even Germans, all nationalities, and different faiths.

Immediately inside Flossenbürg's main gate to the right, stood barrack #19. Chaim resided there with other youths up to eighteen years old. Their housing unit leader, a notorious German from Hamburg, Karl Gieselmann, had committed criminal acts before the war. He made life miserable for all those under his charge, beating and molesting inmates. Late after hours, past midnight he would awaken everyone to do a body search for lice. By 1944–45 the population had jumped and each barrack, originally designed for 250 inmates might house 600, 800, or more.

A laundry, kitchen, detention camp, or "prison within the prison" and crematorium comprised the only stone structures in the camp. In the Appellplatz, roll call took place early each morning and evening, with inmates standing at attention for hours under a burning sun or in the freezing snow. Other times of assembly included mandatory witnessing of executions.

"Most people did not last a long time in the concentration camp. They were killed both methodically and by whim. That's why they didn't last; otherwise, they could have lasted longer. Giving up mentally, this was a different story. When you gave up, your life span shrank, the opposite when you were more positive. I had a strong mind. My parents eventually wanted me to achieve something and this was always on my mind. I could not give up, because I wanted a violin and my parents gave me the violin. My parents would not have approved of my giving up, so, it kind of propelled me."

Within a few days at Flossenbürg, Chaim learned of a chamber orchestra. "I wanted to play in the group. This sent life to me."

Arbajtman later recalled his initial impression that the maestro had a political prisoner's red triangle. Hearing him conduct, surely youth and naiveté crushed by now, Chaim still thought, "'He is going to be good to me.' He was detained there, a German against the Nazi party and regime."

"I went to this conductor after they finished and said, 'I play violin.'" Of note, in 1944 to save cloth, a stripe was sewn above the yellow triangle on a Jewish inmate's shirt. "And he saw my yellow stripe." His terse reply, "'I don't have any Jews in my orchestra.' He was against the Jews. This burned me up because he was a prisoner and what he was telling me made no sense. It shocked and confused me. I quickly learned you could be 100% anti-Nazi and hate the Jews at the same time."

One of the Nazi commandants at Flossenbürg, SS Obersturmbannführer (Lieutenant Colonel) "Killer" Max Koegel would visit camp two to three times a week, and shoot people dead each time he visited. "When the main gate opened up around noon, I was standing outside my barrack with two other kids, chatting. It was a nice sunny day. I started shaking. I didn't realize then what I was about to do. I was sixteen."

"I ran up to him." Like David facing Goliath, but without a slingshot, Arbajtman caught this Nazi between the eyes with a zinger. "I must have lost my mind because I said, 'I am a violin virtuoso,' as my mother used to call me. 'I want to play. The conductor of the concentration camp orchestra won't let me. He told me I couldn't play because he did not allow any Jews in the orchestra.' The commandant scowled, looked at me intently and said, 'You come with me.' We finally found the conductor. He gave him hell and screamed, 'Put him in. He is going to play in your orchestra!'"

Two of Chaim's friends saw everything, and wanted to beat some sense into him. No Nazi commandant ever showed sympathy. Indignation on Koegel's part from perceived usurpation of his authority, as sufficient impetus to overrule the conductor, seemed a fool's bet. "They thought, 'Are you crazy, you want to commit suicide?' The two boys punched me twice, afterward in the barrack, simply wanting to teach me a lesson. I used to do strange things, even risking my life for something I believed. I didn't do it to die or to become a hero. It was just something that meant so much to me. The violin meant more to me, more than my life."

"Flossenbürg's orchestra wasn't a regular thing, but we were available whenever they wanted music." Perhaps their performance schedule amounted to no more than a small handful of dates in a year. Music had incredible power. Confined where death visited daily without provocation or seemingly any chance of escape, the talent to play violin saved young Arbajtman's life on two occasions, already at Budzyn and now here.

The maestro of the orchestra (forty-five members at most with many good musicians from the Prague Philharmonic) did little to conceal his contempt for the newest violinist. "Convicted criminals usually wore a green triangle, and the conductor had a record. He made my life miserable. I had to load and set up the stands, carry all the music for everybody. After the concert, I had to carry and return everything."

Another day, "They needed four musicians. They took us to a small house with narrow winding stairs and a Bechstein piano." The instrument weighed considerably more than the inmates at eighty-five pounds or less. "If we scratched the piano, we were finished. A winding staircase, when you tilt the piano, it becomes heavier. Not piano movers, we had little time to learn. Four of us managed. We didn't scratch anything. Highly motivated, we wanted to live a few more seconds. I don't know where we got the strength to carry this monster."

"Lazarett" or "revier" in German meant hospital or infirmary. Some prisoners called this a waiting room for the grave. "They had a clinic in the camp. It was unwise to go." Concerned so long about his legs and feet, Chaim eventually paid a visit. "I decided to take a chance and go see. They said, 'Yes, we have to amputate your right leg.' But I knew, if they amputated, I would only live for hours, if that. Of course, I didn't do it." Inability to work on one leg would render him hardly useful and subject to prompt execution.

At certain jobs, inmates earned camp credits. This could serve in exchange for sexual services. Nazis provided prostitutes to some prisoners, while killing others. "Who could analyze their thinking? They didn't treat us like animals, they treated us worse than animals."

The lean, fifteen-year-old Abajtman paid calls to what he referred to as a "whorehouse." The oldest of human urges drove him there. He theorized German officers sometimes gave the women extra bread. "I reasoned that young, beautiful ladies were taken from other camps, both Jewish and non-Jewish. The Nazis made love to them at night and the next morning indiscriminately shot some of them. Intuition told me that the Germans, before they made love, brought food. I wanted food. Nobody taught me to go get food from the prostitutes."

"One of them, a nice blonde in her twenties looked at me. 'You must be kidding, you didn't come here to…?' I asked, 'Can you give me some food?' She gave me a bag with all kinds of food. I was right, and never told anybody. I kept it a secret, thinking everybody would get in line and nobody would get any food." Chaim went once a month. "I stood in line, but not for sex." Food remained the object of his constant desire, wherever and however it could be acquired.

Arbajtman's days passed slowly, sleep quality at night ever more fitful, but not owing to the freezing cold. He saw his future dimming. For a space of three months, he contemplated running and throwing himself on the fence, here electrified. "I didn't want to live anymore, life was unbearable. I knew, all I had to do was run to the barbed wire, be electrocuted, burned."

After analyzing things, he decided against that rash course of action. One question made him wonder: if not strong enough, the current might fail to kill him immediately. "If I don't succeed, I am injured or crippled. My death will be much worse. Then I thought, 'Maybe some fences are not electrified. Then, if somebody catches up with me, they will shoot me, hang me, kill me, and I would suffer.'" The prospect of a painful death held no appeal. "I didn't want to give

Nazis the opportunity to punish me more. If I would have known that when I went and grabbed the wires I was finished, I might have done it at that time. But after three months, my thought of committing suicide left."

Did the psychic outweigh the physical for Chaim? "Hunger was a tremendous pain." This made one morning's incident unforgettable and incomprehensible. A fellow inmate somehow acquired a Pall Mall cigarette. He cut it in two and offered the halves for "sale," trading for a couple pieces of bread. Imagine everybody starving, but at least two prisoners craved the passing pleasure of a smoke more than food essential for life. "This is what smoking meant. Somebody gave up life for a cigarette."

He and his fellow inmates never had the resources or time to just sit and contemplate life; all were concentrating on survival from moment to moment. "Trying to stay alive, you didn't know because one hour later you might be dead. And there was nothing you could do about it." The common desire was to live long enough to see Germany defeated, and then die happy with a smile. "We were angry that Americans didn't come to bomb the concentration camp. We wanted to see Germans defeated, to pay the price for what they did, and we would gladly have given our lives for it." No matter the exact circumstances, each assumed death approached, likely without escape.

Contrary to subsequent legal defenses of the indefensible, Nazi murderers did not just follow orders. Sounding strange after the fact, not all German soldiers would kill Jews. A few would not. Their only penalty, they failed to get promoted. Alternatively, SS who shot prisoners dead could receive a special three-day holiday. Regarding the question of nature versus nurture, "The environment and beliefs were the same. Abnormal behavior in an abnormal society was normal. Still, some Germans couldn't kill and some could."

Daily roll call for bread distribution came not by your name, but according to the number on your left chest patch, spoken in German. A group of fifteen to twenty, seventeen-year-old Italian Catholics who had opposed fascism didn't understand their captors' language. They fell prey to repeated beatings for not responding when called by number. "I heard German in the camps. You were young. You picked it up in no time. If you didn't follow their orders, you might be dead." With no advantage to himself, the Jew from Poland, who by then understood and spoke German perfectly, took on the task of learning numbers in Italian. With his translation provided while the Germans barked numbers to move forward for bread, beatings of the Italians could be avoided. "It was the right thing to do." In the same barrack, his popularity among these teenagers soared.

"This is the way we lived. It was beyond mental anguish. You had so much pain from so many things. Your body was frozen. There was no way to warm up. There was no time, day or night, when you felt a little warmth. The stomach was empty. A skeleton, that's what I was. If we had been adults, we would have been dead in no time, knowing we could not live like this."

Playing an instrument was hardly his main assignment at Flossenbürg. The Germans knew they were losing the war, with so many aircraft shot down daily by the Allies. Camp manufacturing operations took on special urgency. Some riveters drilled extra holes, hoping to weaken structural integrity. Chaim worked fast to assemble Messerschmitt Bf 109 airplane wings. "And I was very good at it. If I made a quota, by five o'clock, I got extra soup or an extra slice of bread. I was competitive." Significantly, the greater need for slave labor translated into fewer killings. "You had the feeling, maybe they wouldn't kill you because they needed you. Somebody had to work."

There occurred notable exceptions. Within the German military intelligence service, Abwehr, members of a secret group of plotters against Hitler failed in their attempt to assassinate him on July 20, 1944. They then found themselves convicted, imprisoned, and later moved to the special detention camp within Flossenbürg. "I tried to look through the barbed wire. I heard some English spoken by American Jews, caught while visiting Polish relatives."

On April 4, 1945, a diary of Admiral Canaris, who headed the Abwehr, came to light, and an enraged Führer ordered the death of all co-conspirators held at Flossenbürg. Four days later, they faced a mock SS court martial without witnesses. Prominent Lutheran minister and theologian Dietrich Bonhoeffer, who had long opposed the Nazis, came to judgment too. He had spoken in radio broadcasts against Hitler two days after his election as Chancellor in 1933. Bonhoeffer wrote of disaffection from a church too complacent, despite dictatorial government abuses and rampant atrocities. Links to the July 20 conspiracy at the Abwehr led to his arrest and confinement.

One sympathetic guard at a less secure facility had offered to help him escape. He declined with fears of retribution against the family, including his Jewish brother-in-law and a brother also imprisoned for underground resistance activities. Transferred to Buchenwald and later Flossenbürg, his trial took place two weeks before Russian troops assaulted Berlin, and three weeks before Hitler committed suicide. The resistance fighters and Bonhoeffer were hanged on April 9. As he went to execution, a witness heard the minister say, "This is the end...for me, the beginning of life." A plaque at the site now commemorates these events.

Chaim declares, "Without my parents, I definitely would not be alive after what I went through. My parents said, 'Nobody can insult you, nobody can harm you, you are too important.' Hearing this, when you grow up, you have inner strength and wealth. Yes, somebody can come and shoot you, but mentally, nothing could destroy you."

"Even at the worst times, in some concentration camps, occasionally there was music. Before they might kill you and after they might kill you, but not during music. Just imagine the world without music. Music is the greatest peacemaker ever."

"My devotion and love of playing the violin persisted even under the most unimaginable circumstances the world has ever known. The reason I am alive today is because of the violin."

5
Liberation, April 1945

"Liberation was a shock. Here I am alone. Worse than loneliness, you get sick in the head, thinking 'I'm not worthy to be in the camp anymore.' It's another war to fight."

On April 16, it came as an ominous sign when Jewish prisoners were ordered to stand at the railroad siding. Rumor had their final destination as Dachau. "We didn't know for sure, but we had an idea. When you were in the camp, your destiny was written in big letters — DEATH."

Assembled inmates began surging and crowding into cattle cars. "I was seventy-five pounds, a dead man walking. A cold April, it was going on nine months and nearly as long as I had been in any camp." Arbajtman would later muse, "Did I have a coat, any sweater, a hat, shoes? We didn't have anything but rags and newspapers. We put newspapers on our feet and attached them with string. How did we survive through December, January, and February, working outdoors? I got frostbite. Sub-zero killed when you were naked."

Chaim had a quick choice to make. Which train car should he enter? On previous transfers, with hot and sweaty bodies crammed together, "We would have given an arm for a glass of water." The only air came through narrow vents up high. Not just for those plagued by weak lungs and heart conditions, air made a merciful difference for everyone, especially with no bathroom facilities on board. Looking for fresh air, "The first car from Flossenbürg next to the locomotive didn't have a front wall. Instead, it had a deck for stacking wood." Support poles allowed space in between for air to enter. "And I jumped on this one because I figured, if it rained, I would have something to drink." Thus, he picked an open carriage to the rear of a fuel car and the locomotive. Concealed behind their gaunt faces, each person on board had a vague knowledge of the fate awaiting them at Dachau. Their train began to move.

Little more than fifteen minutes out of the Flossenbürg station, allied aircraft swooped down, mistaking Chaim's train as a military transport. The low flying fighters, obviously not knowing of so many innocents inside, strafed the cars accurately. Large caliber bullets ripped through the wooden walls, and in a body-piercing flash, killed half of the three thousand occupants. Incredibly, Chaim's carriage was largely spared. He exited the disabled train amidst screams of the wounded and orders shouted in German.

"The planes came and bah, bah, bah, bah, bah (imitation of gunfire). I ran through and couldn't see anything through the thick smoke. I thought maybe I was dead. Pinching my body to check, I was still alive! The smoke left and a lot of dead people appeared. Some of the SS ran away."

Arbajtman ran with one other young person. They raided a little house where this jar of lard caught immediate attention. In their emaciated state, "nature was calling for fat." The lady owner then came upon them and promptly called to a nearby German officer. "I heard 'Halt! Halt! Halt!' There was an SS on the ground in the grass by the trees with a rifle. He said, 'Don't move! Come back here! Who is in charge of you two?' He kept us until the bombardment calmed down, then we went back to the train. They reorganized. The train was finished moving, so we started walking towards Dachau."

Other Nazi guards also remained determined to prod and herd their prisoners to reach the original destination. All of those who remained alive, including walking wounded, started on what became known as a "death march," one among several in the vicinity about this same time. They moved forward six or seven days, and entered forest which served as cover, concealing their movements from allied aircraft flying overhead.

"On this march, they gave one slice of bread a day. In the evening, we got soup with nothing in it. The walking was done mainly at night. We didn't have shoes, so you found paper and garbage for wrappings. Both my feet were like swollen balloons. In the daytime we would try to sleep, but couldn't sleep. You didn't want to lie down, because chances were you'd never get up and then they'd kill you. If you couldn't walk, you got shot. Many were murdered on the road. I never forgot the scene. Not even deadly sick, one man just couldn't walk because of a blister, and the cold-hearted German shot him in the head. A blister was unacceptable. You had to be perfect."

"I was in the woods with the SS, marching to Dachau for seven days. We marched five abreast. After a day or so, we were three abreast. I looked at the stars or the sun to figure out whether I was going south or north? The forest became a little thicker, with less space between trees. Suddenly, I was lost." Maybe at the back of

Chaim's mind, the memory returned from a day of panic on family summer holiday outside Warsaw, again lost in the forest.

"I tried to remember the last time I saw something recognizable, a break in the tall trees, an open space." He had the rudiments of a plan, if only free of the group now blindly herded ever farther over uncharted ground. The bunch clinging together came to a halt. Decision time, "We stopped for about an hour and a half. We didn't know what was happening. We wondered why Nazis up front were throwing away their uniforms and rifles. There was a little celebration."

A group of younger persons, maybe twenty or so, had stuck together amidst all the chaos. They already knew each other from barrack #19, ages eighteen or younger. During three hours of moving, then rest and discussion, "You saw the leaders being born. Whoever spoke louder, they followed. To me, there was no need for a leader. You should go according to your senses, right or wrong. One guy convinced them to go straight. I said, 'This is the wrong way to go.'" Germans chose this direction for their own reasons, most likely to evade American forces. Chaim recalled a clear area they passed, around one kilometer before stopping. "They wanted to go the same direction the Nazis were going. I said, 'No.' Soon, I was by myself. I decided not to go anywhere."

Shortly after the others pushed on, a bombardment commenced. "There was a big tree with an indentation. I tried to bury my body a little bit and backed into it. So, if bullets flew, I might have had a better chance." He cautioned those passing nearby, "Don't go there. The Germans are over there. All I had was my instinct and it told me, if the enemy goes there, do the opposite."

Chaim had decisively elected to part ways with the other youth. He didn't trust their leadership's advice to go deeper into unknown territory, with limited visibility and unseen dangers. He favored retracing his steps to an open field noted two kilometers back, concerned about going in circles without clear reference points in the thick woods. The bombardment, lasting two hours, concluded and cautiously he began moving again. The others hadn't gotten far. Ten or fifteen minutes later he came upon more discarded uniforms and rifles, as well as the bodies of those in the group of young people who didn't attend to his counsel. "Nobody listened. Those that went ahead were all shot to death by the Nazis." Again, his instinct for life guided a course from unseen danger to safety at the moment he most needed it.

Later and still navigating through trees, encountering a few straggling Nazi soldiers who feared the allied forces approaching even closer, one officer reached to assist Chaim. He noticed a Red Cross armband on the dissembling German's sleeve. "'Do you need help?' When I saw the Red Cross emblem, I didn't trust him and thought he would put a bullet in my head." The man gave him chocolates, kindness quite out of character, but deception all too familiar. Tired and weak, Chaim knew to keep moving and get away from his tormentors. Finally alone, he carefully made his way forward. "I ran through the woods and escaped to another village."

"Every village had civil police." Suddenly a different Nazi ordered him to the ground. Arbajtman instantly obeyed, planting face to dirt, expecting a gunshot. "A guy in uniform saw me with the concentration camp uniform and came up with his gun. The reason he didn't shoot me was because Allied planes came in to bombard, and he ran. I ran away again." Alone at that point, but wanting to avoid any possible detection, in silence he took internal inventory, involving eyes, mind, and heart.

Slowly finding his way back to the clearing and a road below, Chaim concealed himself in the crevice of another tree. "I watched from above, and after several minutes I saw a tank." He had encountered a line of U.S. armored vehicles. "I thought, 'No swastikas, so they're not enemy tanks.' I went towards them and also saw low flying planes."

Liberation took place on April 23, 1945. These forces represented elements of General Patton's 3rd Army, 761st Tank Battalion, better known as "Black Panthers," currently supporting the 71st Infantry. Out of a hatch of the lead tank, a large black man emerged with the most beautiful sheen to his skin. Arbajtman noted, "He was as black as coal, humongous, and very tall. I wanted so much to go touch this chocolate man."

"An untouched mind could not be spoiled with prejudice. I was enchanted." Besides his skin color, the American's prominent lips and repetitive cheek motions captivated Chaim. Could this be a habit peculiar to Africa?

Then a white face emerged from the tank. He made the same facial movements. To help explain the teenager's puzzlement, a reader must realize that Eastern Europe had yet to discover the pleasures of chewing gum. Before any real attempt at conversation, aircraft passed overhead, close enough to recognize Nazi insignias. Soldiers shouted for Arbajtman to dive for cover under their tank.

"I was under the tank, but I could see through open spots. The black man was preparing the bullets and the other was grinding - dah, dah, dah, dah. They were whistling. Was it a joke to them? They must have known something I didn't. At a short distance away, I saw they shot down one German plane. Now I can die happy. I lived to see the Germans lose. Then I thought to myself, 'This is not real. I must be dreaming.'"

The air war in Europe had diminished by this time, but Nazi units still flew a number of sorties with 150 aircraft in March, attempting defense in the southland where Allied bombers hit nearby Berchtesgaden and Pilsen on April 25. Small numbers of the new Messerschmitt 262 put up a last ditch effort as late as May.

After the brief strafing run, an all-clear signal sounded. "American planes flew as low as they could, protecting their own tanks." The white GI spoke a little German. He asked Chaim where he came from, the youth answering as best he could. Reassured that he had so far done well, his American liberator advised to keep going, course unchanged. "'This is the middle of war, you cannot stay here.'" He needed to continue another five kilometers to reach a better secured area.

This same white tanker offered Arbajtman the option of a firearm to protect himself, "'If some German comes up…' But I didn't want the gun after so many killings. I had never even owned a pocket knife. I said, 'No.'" Soldiers shared chocolates with him and said farewell. "They came to liberate Europe. Fierce war continued. The war was still raging, big time. Supposedly liberated on April 23, war really ended May 9. There was a lot of killing between April 23 and May 9."

Confirmed by these GIs as a safe route, Chaim continued his path, noticing that U.S. tanks had ejected metal canisters on both sides of the road. "The countryside was filled with cans, meant for people like me to eat. I thought they were explosives." He dared not touch them then, fearing a new type of grenade, but later learned of their healthy contents. "Each can with a key had food: chocolates, cakes, meats, corn beef. But I had never seen anything like this. I suspected, if opened, you were dead. Everybody was hungry, but for fear, nobody touched the cans." Who had heard of putting food in diminutive metal containers?!

About four kilometers later, in another small village he observed from the distance of one block an American tank moving slowly, and barely negotiating the narrow street. "They had to use not only the road, but the sidewalks on both sides." An older German woman stood on the second-floor balcony, inexplicably firing a revolver at the tanks. "I stood there and the tank stopped. It turned around and 'dah, dah.' The whole house was mashed potatoes. And then he continued, as if nothing happened. I saw the whole thing, thinking it a nightmare."

"As my journey continued, I would pick up potatoes in the fields. That second day, I didn't know how to bake them, and drifted into a village. There was a bank, doors wide open and unguarded. I entered and picked up a sack full of money, then burned it in the field. The potatoes might have cost half to three quarters of a million (Reichsmark notes)."

After four and a half years of deprivation and detention, starting in the Warsaw Ghetto, continuing through the indescribable horror of seven slave labor and death camps, Chaim found himself free. "Where was I going? There was no place to go. Subhuman, they threw me out of the camp. The idea of a locked gate didn't bother me anymore, because at least in camp I had friends. Now, I had no home and no money. I didn't have anything. You couldn't trust anybody. I certainly didn't trust any Germans. I was all alone, no family. Everyone was gone."

On Friday, April 27, he reached Schwandorf. Chaim approached local authorities and obtained a document in German, signed by the mayor's office, attesting Arbajtman had come some 65 kilometers south from Flossenbürg, and was traveling through town. "Germans offered help. I didn't accept. I would run into a barn after dark. Every night I slept in a different barn. Early in the morning, when someone came out of the farmhouse, I ran."

For eight days he saw nobody familiar, and then spotted some fellow refugees. "I met a young guy. He asked, 'Where do you stay?' I said, 'I stay in different barns. What about you?' He said, 'I found a nice German family that gave me a nice clean room. Come with me. They have an extra room.' I said, 'They'll kill you.' I was convinced."

"My instinct made me careful. I didn't trust the youth even though he was still alive after nine days living there. I reluctantly went and this old lady gave me a clean room. She was very nice. Being tired, I went to bed, but could not sleep. I had not slept in a bed for more than four years. So, I got on the floor and fell asleep in five seconds." He stayed several days.

"You would get up in the morning with nothing to eat, nothing to hope for, nothing to do." More pointedly, he had no pre-designated place to stay longer term, no bread or soup lines, no clothing other than ex-concentration camp rags, and no country. He would have preferred the camp, having no choice but to live off the land in southern Germany. He could not trust in the benevolence of a recently vanquished and shamed populace.

Confirming his suspicions, subsequent reports came of cases in which other displaced persons accepted a meal and room for the night, whom they murdered in their sleep without provocation. All this kept him on the move, ever looking over his shoulder. "I am all alone in a strange place outside the camp. I felt worse than in the camps. In the camps we wanted to be liberated and free. Now that we had it, we didn't know what to do with it. It was a shock to the system for a few years."

Within a couple of weeks, he met up with other young ex-detainees who also sought companionship and greater safety in numbers. "You met them in the street and formed a group. Instantaneously you 'knew' each other. We spoke Yiddish and Polish." In plain attire, they sometimes entered homes and appropriated items. This proved easy, as practically nobody locked their doors. Group members only took what essentials they lacked, not valuables, leaving behind no traces.

They formed a gang of eleven; nine boys and two girls. At seventeen, "I was the oldest. The youngest was an eleven-year-old boy. The two girls were fifteen and sixteen. With no outside law enforcement, we confiscated a German Inn that had a few rooms.

Among ourselves, we had an orderly way of doing things. A vote the first day at the little inn, we elected the president of our group. It went by votes and nobody was allowed to change. If I got the majority and accepted, they had to follow my direction. It was genuinely democratic." Unanimous, all voted for Chaim.

"I made a rule. 'They are our sisters, our mothers, our flesh and blood. If any of you touches them, including me, with no exceptions you will be beaten.' Nobody dared to touch them. Their names were Anika and Sara. I had a great love for my own sister. After I lost her, they became my sisters."

"Some of the kids still had uniforms from concentration camps," of which local Germans seemed wary. "We needed food. We held a food acquisition meeting." President Arbajtman announced at midnight, "'Go into the villages and raid whatever you can: eggs, a chicken, live or dead. Whatever it is, bring it.'"

"Wherever you saw food, you rushed to grab it. A single sardine would get cut five ways to share. We thought scarcity was going to continue forever. Actually, we didn't know what was coming the next hour. Because the stomach was small like a baby's and our eyes were so hypnotized by food, people overate and ate the wrong things. A lot of people died. One kid brought a bucket of lard." Early on, they knew nothing of potentially fatal hazards from eating calorically rich fat too rapidly.

"Another problem was that we were all self-appointed doctors. Because of poor nourishment, if we got a cut, the wound never closed. I had some skin sores on my legs and never went to a doctor. After the war, I was like an animal living in the wilderness with no doctors. Sometimes a problem took care of itself."

"A few days after forming the gang I realized that I needed a violin." A galling amount of lost time since the Warsaw Ghetto, "For six years I didn't play. The best years were taken from me. I told Joe (Josel), 'Search the homes for a violin and bring it to me.' One year younger than I, he brought me a red violin with strings, a bow, and a case. I played things recalled from memory." The proof positive results of this violin search can be seen in a photograph taken near Schwandorf, May 1945.

"Right after the concentration camp, I didn't know whether I wanted to go back to the violin. Then I remembered my parents.

When I first wanted the violin, they said, 'Yes, provided you promise not to become a street musician.' Knowing their thoughts helped me. I felt very strongly I must continue what they hoped for me to do. After the war, there were bad moments of not feeling right. I would always pick up the violin and play. I felt so much better afterward. Music was my medicine."

"This was the first part of May. I usually got up at ten. The sun was out and weather was nice. Every day was like a lifetime. Still, you were busy surviving. If you went to stay at these ex-POW (prisoner of war) and now DP (displaced persons) camps, you had a bed, breakfast, lunch and dinner, all free. Though I didn't have a coin in my pocket, I managed without having to go back to any camp."

Looking into options for himself and the gang, reconnoitering bigger communities, "I would get up, find someplace to steal or sell somebody's clothing to get breakfast. Then I would go to an autostop on the main road and hitchhike. The Germans would ask, 'Where are you going?' And I would say, 'Wherever you go, I'll go,' because it made no difference. I didn't know where I was, so, I went to the next city."

"I had a paper from American authorities written in English, which I couldn't understand." Surviving paperwork read in part, "This person was in a German concentration camp for some time... For any consideration you may offer, we will be greatly appreciative." His impression was that, "There was a law that displaced persons like me should go to the city hall, which had to provide a room and give a ration card for food; otherwise, you couldn't get food (without a lot of money on the black market). Each city hall I went to gave another key for temporary lodging. Eventually, I had twenty keys. If I met other Jewish kids who were liberated that needed housing, I said, 'These are keys. Take them, maybe one of them will fit a place you find.'" Paperwork indicates Chaim had completed the process described by summer of 1945. To help quantify need, authorities carried out a census. After some months, because people registered over and over again, they counted more Jews than before the war.

Statistics could only tell part of the story. "In my case, we were living in an abandoned house. There was nothing in this small town." His group of eleven souls elected to move from Schwandorf, 45 kilometers south to Regensburg, where a contingent of the Allied Expeditionary Force with U.S. troops took up occupation.

"We were not normal, not after what you went through. You were not a human being, so how could you behave like one? The junior Joseph, not Josel, got a little bit out of hand." On a different hunting trip, this youngest group member, those less mature tending to think less carefully before taking action, audaciously stole a bicycle in front of the police station. "The police came at 5:00 a.m. in a jeep. Two Americans with rifles asked for IDs. We had a little idea of what they wanted from their written note that read, 'One person took an item…' They promptly returned IDs and put us in the jeep. They gave us the back seat and got in up front. The motor started and we jumped. We were young, could jump fast, and had learned to escape."

"They came again the next day and tried to scare Joseph. I went to the police. Speaking German with the big shot, I said, 'I give you my word. Tomorrow I promise to come back to the police station and personally deliver the bicycle. I will be here, one o'clock in the afternoon.' They said, 'Okay.'"

"I got them to surrender the bicycle, but it took a lot of convincing. I had to be a wizard at talking because the gang were already street smart and knew how to spot a trick. 'Look, I am going to help you steal another one.' It was wiser to say I was going to help them, not that I was in trouble and needed their bicycle. They would have jumped all over me. We all went to the police and gave back the bicycle. We never saw such gigantic people as the American military police. The MPs embraced us, their arms around our heads. Suddenly happy they said, 'Wonderful, good boys!' We understood 'Good boys.' We got oranges and chocolates because we kept our word."

Afterward, in a group meeting, to avoid another brush with police, he reminded them of who was boss. "If you're thinking about stealing, remember, you elected me to be your boss. When I say, 'steal,' you can. When I say, 'You cannot steal,' don't."

The eve of summer after liberation, Arbajtman had another fortuitous encounter. Near Regensburg, the small community of just a few dozen Jews decided to organize. They appointed as president for the newly constituted Hebrew association a man possessed of some fluency in English. Many of the Americans didn't speak German and needed a translator. "I used to play for them on weekends." A week or so later the recently married fifty-two-year-old president spoke to Chaim, "'I'm having an American medic come to my house next Friday night. We don't have much to eat, but why don't you come? He's a violinist and maybe he can help you.' I accepted saying, 'Wonderful!'"

The other guest, a twenty-three-year-old soldier stationed in Regensburg and part of the occupation forces, apparently shared an interest in music. After three hours of conversation in English, their host helped by translating. The GI asked Arbajtman about any plans after winning his freedom, whether to stay in Germany or not. "I want to study violin in America." He still clung to his dream of learning from Zimbalist.

The soldier's mother had encouraged him to study violin. He played in a big city symphony a couple of years, later switching professions to psychology. The service man asked whether Chaim knew any family or other contacts in the U.S. "My father's father had a brother with three sons who went to America, between 1911 and 1917. One went to New York, one to Philadelphia and one to Chicago. They got jobs and all sent money to their father. The amount of money, maybe not much in dollars, was a fortune in Poland. He lived quite well." This great uncle used to come to Warsaw from Lublin and each time gave the young Arbajtman a coin.

The medic commented, "'I'm from Chicago. Do you recall the address of the one who went there?' 'No.' 'What was the family name?' 'The name was the same as mine: Arbajtman.'" The GI, nearly shaking, lept to his feet and exclaimed excitedly, "That's my name!" The only difference was that he had shortened it to Arbeit, Joe Arbeit. The soldier soon made contact back home with his father, Jack Arbeit. This man felt overjoyed to find a long lost relative. "He wanted me to come right away, had signed papers and done all the things needed to help with immigration. Joe's father started sending me care packages which had good, canned stuff."

"I didn't want to be a burden or feel indebted to anyone else. I didn't want to be helped by relatives. I wanted to see them after I was established." Chaim thanked him for the kind offer of help to speed a move to America, but declined. He wanted to make his own way and not take any shortcuts.

"There was no such thing as government sponsored programs. There were aid committees, Jewish and and non-Jewish, Red Cross for example. Most refugees didn't get anything. The American Jewish Committee sent clothing for young people like me. These were a priority, but I never received anything of value. I got two razor blades every week from Gillette. When I came out of the concentration camp, I didn't grow any beard to shave. Every week I got another toothbrush. We didn't need one every week. People gave good things that were shipped from New York to Genoa in Italy. Better things were sold on the black market. We only got the leftovers. I needed and was supposed to get some shoes. When they came, I opened the package and there were two left shoes. One was too long. One was too short. I was not upset. This was just what happened. People gave a lot, but we got nothing useful."

"You had to go out and constantly hunt for what you needed. After three-and-a-half years, I spoke German like a native. I picked it up by necessity."

Meanwhile, some of the "gang" members did well, some not so well. "The youngest, an eleven-year-old boy, was impossible to control. When he got to the camp, maybe he was seven. At that age, either they killed you or did 'research.' They made many cripples, then killed them to leave no evidence. I didn't know what kind of shots Joe got. He survived and became wild."

"I tried to work with him, but he wouldn't listen. He was a sick boy. At twilight near a lake, he pushed an older couple in and ran. I said, 'You cannot do this. If you forced the man to give his wallet and ran, it would be better than drowning somebody who cannot swim.' Of course, I didn't say he should do either!" One catches echoes of the father Abraham Arbajtman's advice in this counseling session with a boy.

The American medic, Arbajtman's aforementioned cousin, would only remain at his post another five days. He inscribed a picture of himself on October 15, and gave it to Chaim. Also, he knew his relative obviously needed more to eat. How about a creative idea? The Officers' Club needed some live music while they consumed and imbibed heartily, always with abundant leftovers.

"'Do you know how to play a piano?' 'I never tried. When would I start?' 'Tomorrow night.'" Arbajtman appeared in the club, strode to the piano, looked at the keyboard, and started plinking with one finger. "Then I tried making a simple chord with the other hand. I had learned a song, 'You Are My Sunshine,' listening to American radio, trying to learn a little English." The familiar melody caused the officers to join in singing, some patting the young man on the shoulder to encourage him. "I am not used to strangers putting an arm around me, but this was the American way. They were so tall compared to us. I had to look up and my neck started hurting. I ate way too many leftovers." Regensburg had an "arbeitsamt" (the employment exchange program), but this ideal inside job didn't last.

One morning, the start of an early winter, Chaim's personal footwear turned up missing. "In a small room, I had a roommate, his little bed on the other side. It was snowing like crazy and we had no food. Our only choice was to get up early and go searching, but one morning I didn't see my shoes. They weren't very good, but they were something to protect against the cold. I couldn't make a move until the thief came home late at night. Again, it was Joe. 'What did you do with my shoes?' 'I woke up, saw your shoes and took them to trade for breakfast.'"

"This abnormal behavior in abnormal times was normal. It became our way of life. Joe tried to make amends and offered, "'I'll give you the bicycle I stole yesterday.'" Chaim wanted to know what Joe would ride. "'I'll steal another one.' I traded his stolen bicycle for my next pair of shoes."

Of note, after reaching the U.S., Joe did quite well in business. Remembering and regretting the affair, years later at a reunion of the "gang of eleven," he told their president he regretted this shoe caper and offered "reparations."

"After the war, people gave their names, looking for missing relatives. There were so many organizations searching and mostly nothing came of it. The Red Cross tried to look for my family. I tried to look for them in many different places." Once, Arbajtman saw someone with his same last name on a printed list. The person from Belgium, on further checking, belonged to an unrelated line.

"You didn't like to accept that they were gone. Every day you kept looking, for months. You looked through new lists that appeared. The lists were posted everywhere. The effort was made to help the people who survived to find their relatives. You didn't quit looking so easily. Giving up was hard. There was no easy turning of the page, not in a few seconds, a few minutes or a few days. The page turn took three months, six months, or more."

Finally accepted, he concluded, "Everybody perished, but crying wouldn't bring them back to life. No tears, but I had a broken heart. And even if my parents had survived and could not find me, it would have destroyed them. It would have been death by torture."

Knowing no better way to honor his parents, living or dead, he felt compelled to seriously pursue violin, and could no longer live in an abandoned house. "These ten kids were my family, but I couldn't and didn't want to live like this. How could I leave my family? But I dared not talk to them, because they would not understand what I wanted, what I needed, what I had to do. So, the only way was to run away in the middle of the night, and that's exactly what I did."

Early one day at 4:30 a.m. and before daybreak, he left the group of eleven without saying goodbye. "What did I have? The violin Joe stole, a very thin briefcase, a toothbrush, some clothing, and shoes." The distance to Munich, 125 kilometers south of Regensburg, would take some time. He had but one means of quick transport, hitching a ride. When cars or trucks stopped, they routinely asked, "'Where you headed?'" Chaim always answered, "'To wherever you're headed.'" He paused at points, even playing in some local bands or orchestras. Still, he kept moving. His main goal was to find a serious violin teacher.

Somehow, he found his way to an abbey in Emming. St. Ottilien, converted by the American military, served as a holding compound for care of former concentration camp prisoners. "From May to October, Jews were staying there. You couldn't get out with walls and barbed wire. They wouldn't let doctors in, and when Americans arrived with truckloads of food, those in charge would not let the military distribute supplies. People were dying from a lack of both medical care and food."

Army privates Edward Herman and Robert Hilliard, stationed in Germany at the close of World War II, found horrific treatment of displaced Jews in St. Ottilien. In an effort to alleviate suffering at the facility administered by the American personnel, these two GIs stole food from their own mess and smuggled it into the camp. Then the two soldiers started a letter writing campaign. When nobody seemed to listen, they wrote to the New York Times, posing the question whether prisoners who had survived privation imposed by the Nazis would now succumb to neglect by their liberators.

This caught the attention of President Harry Truman, who ordered an investigation that led to the end of such terrible neglect. Conditions had improved significantly by the time of Arbajtman's arrival, the end of October, 50 kilometers from Munich.

"In July, I heard about the St. Ottilien Jewish Orchestra and wanted to belong. Later I auditioned. They were very nice and gave me the job. It wasn't too far away from where I was with the ten kids." He would not see either of the two Joes, Sarah, Anika, or any other of the gang until nearly twenty years later. Chaim lodged at Emming from what remained of 1945 into 1946, a total of seven months. "I wanted to make music."

"To me, music represented life, hope, and peace. So unique, not only that it saved my life in the concentration camp, but music had the incredible force of gravity that pulled all kinds of people together from different cultures, different nationalities. Phenomenal!"

6
Displaced Life in Germany

"I will not pay you seven cigarettes a month for rent. What I will pay, if you'll accept it, is ten."

Seriously ill, walking wounded, and recently liberated prisoners entered the monastery at St. Ottilien in April of 1945. There, one month later, displaced persons had already formed an orchestra, first performing on May 27. They played for U.S. military personnel, and subsequently took their music to patients of neighboring sanitaria, and residents in other DP camps.

Chaim came with his violin in the late fall and gained admission, the youngest of a seventeen-member ensemble. On road trips, they billed themselves as the Jewish Orchestra of Bavaria. On Wednesday, November 14, they performed at a town theater in Landsberg.

"We played a concert, and my cousin who survived the war was at the concert. The last time he saw me, I was twelve years old." Wolf Tuchmann used to go to Chaim's home in Warsaw and listen to him practice. "After six years, he didn't recognize me. The difference between twelve and eighteen, I was another person. He didn't see my name in the program, but some days later there was an article about our group in the paper. He saw my name in print, and this is how we found one another. He sang Tartini Sonata for me. It surprised me how he remembered. He was the son of my father's first cousin." Wolf and his wife spent the war years in Russia, later making their way to Germany. "Yes, they walked home, all the way from Siberia. It took five months."

"He told me the story. They were in a displaced persons camp after the war. She could not come to the U.S. due to a medical restriction. They could have gone to South America, but didn't want this. The first time I met him again, we had dinner. All he had was a twenty dollar bill. He took it out and begged me to have it, because I didn't have any money. He wasn't thinking of himself or what he could spare. I never took the cash, not wanting to owe anyone. Still, we were very, very close. He was just so happy I was alive and breathing." His wife fell prey to pulmonary TB and required treatment for five years in a sanitarium at Gauting, outside Munich.

At the end of 1945 in Munich, Arbajtman had the pleasure of meeting Michael Taube, who received an invitation to give concerts in the displaced persons camps. He served as concert director, assistant to Bruno Walter at the Municipal Opera in Berlin before World War II, and in a nearly identical conducting position at the Palestine Philharmonic (later the Israel Philharmonic). "He was a terrific pianist. I told him, 'I'm staying in the camp at St. Ottilien.'" He managed somehow, despite paltry conditions and means, to make these exploratory trips. Munich supported an obviously higher level of cultural expression and freedom. Chaim and the others knew they could accomplish greater things here.

Before year's end, the Jewish community knew where each survivor lived. "Suddenly, I was drafted to fight for Palestine which became Israel. I was young and still naive. Many young people went to fight. Actually, the Jewish community didn't have authorization to sign up soldiers, pass out a machine gun and uniform, then send you to serve. I told them, 'I am studying violin. I need to learn, so let me out of the draft.'" Fortunately, he received a student deferment.

The first formal Congress of the Central Committee of Liberated Jews took place in Munich on January 27-29, 1946. David Ben-Gurion, the future first prime minister of Israel, attended and the orchestra from St. Ottilien played. Continuing their musical mission, the orchestra ventured again to Munich. They played on Sunday, March 17, at a Young Men's Hebrew Association Soldier's Center. This Purim Festival performance quickened their yearning for fuller schedules and grander venues.

On May 7 came a special honor. Fifteen musicians donned striped prisoner uniforms and assumed the stage name Ex-Concentration Camp Orchestra. "We were invited to give a concert at the Opera House for all the international judges at the Nuremberg Trial." Prosecutors and staff attended at the facility where only too recently, Nazi elite had listened to Wagner's operas. As onstage scenery, barbed wire and two large Stars of David served as backdrop to the concentration camp uniforms worn by musicians. In front of orchestra members' seats, large block Hebrew letters spelled from right to left, "The People of Israel Live."

The first part of the program included works by Meyerbeer, Rossini, and Offenbach, while the second half featured Henny

Durmashkin performing songs from the Vilna Ghetto. It seemed artistic justice. Having formerly performed to placate their Nazi torturers, now they played an encore. In a sort of swan song at the criminals' final curtain, before their sentencing judges and a worldwide audience via covering media, what human being could fail to stand and applaud approvingly?

Shortly afterward, group members all decided to move long term from the Benedictine abbey in Emming to an urban environment with the broader range of activities. "We received a few more jobs playing than before, and also more rations to eat."

On the first of July 1946, they moved to Fürstenfeldbruck. "I was staying in a hotel. There were seventeen of us living on the second floor. I was not happy with my room. We had to share a toilet with eight others. I decided to find my own place."

Chaim needed a stable living arrangement and a top-notch instructor. "I could walk free in the streets. Here the Germans were tolerant because they felt guilty about what was done to us." Passing through the streets of Fürstenfeldbruck, a comfortable western suburb of Munich, he noticed a rather imposing home just six blocks from where the orchestra rehearsed.

After climbing stairs at Pucher Strasse, #51, he rang the bell beside a card with the name, Richard Tischler. Presently, a tall and rotund individual appeared in lederhosen and bellowed, "'What do you want?' 'Herr Tischler, Do you have an apartment to rent in your house?' 'Well, I wasn't thinking of it. There is a room, not really set up for rent. Do you want to see it?' 'Yes.' 'Come upstairs.'" They encountered Richard's wife Maria in the kitchen and continued further to inspect a possible space to let.

The huge room seemed nearly as large as a whole barrack in the camps. Stained glass windows and a beautiful view of trees appeared almost perfect. "'Will this be sufficient?' 'I think it will do. How much are you asking per month?' 'I don't want money. I prefer that you pay me in cigarettes. I will be very pleased, if you can pay me seven cigarettes a month.'" Chaim replied without missing a beat, "I cannot do that. I will not pay you seven cigarettes a month for rent. What I will pay, if you'll accept it, is ten."

Richard Tischler's face veritably beamed at the offer, and he promptly agreed to rent the room. "I won him over when I did this.

He knew I was a Jew, probably the first he ever came to really like." Tischler couldn't do enough for his new boarder, and even warmed hot water bottles to put in his bed on cold nights. "Tishler made a fire in the fireplace. He gave me a key to lock my room, but I refused to lock it. I was no longer in prison."

Tischler didn't know the source of his cigarette windfall. Chaim performed at musical events, sponsored by an American Jewish agency that paid in commodities and smokes. "We were paid a little bit of money for playing certain concerts. Also, we were given a pound of coffee per month, one pound of sugar and, the most valuable thing, maybe half a carton of cigarettes. If I had known an American to get thirty or forty cartons more, I could have bought the best violin. People don't realize, one cigarette on the black market in 1945 after the war was the equivalent to what a German made in a whole month. Cigarettes were like gold."

"Tischler was away during the day. His wife would show me photographs from Belgium and Holland. When I saw the pictures, I got goosebumps. In Amsterdam he had a limo, chauffeur, and ceremonial sword." What a drastic downturn in fortunes! "When I was looking for a room, people in Germany lived on rations. The only way to have a good meal was to spend a month's salary."

Tischler, formerly a "big shot Nazi," adopted the violinist as his favorite "Jew boy," but called him by a typical German name. Chaim became Heinz. "I let him call me anything he wanted." Names meant nothing, as long as killing hadn't resumed. The relationship seemed oddly jovial and cordial, but, "Tischler didn't want his friends to know that I was a Jew, even after the war."

Arbajtman and his Ex-Concentration Camp Orchestra colleagues played at Landsberg, one of the American zone's two largest displaced persons facilities, on August 25. Chaim found it of interest that, when confined to a nearby jail in 1924, Hitler had written Mein Kampf. For lack of more traditional venues not already retained and scheduled, the orchestra performed in converted Wehrmacht barracks. Their program included Meyerbeer's "Entrance March," selections from Verdi's La Traviata, and Bizet's Intermezzo and Farandole from L'Arlesienne.

Chaim and his fellow players could not move freely to perform outside their immediate locality because of poor road conditions, expense, and lack of gasoline, among other challenges to travel. With no other convenient vehicles available, they used ambulances. In 1946, a bus came into their hands, through the offices of the American authorities. This facilitated travel to more distant venues, other DP sites, and elsewhere.

Despite gratitude for comfortable lodging where he could rest between jobs, one day Arbajtman returned to a discovery that demanded his response. "After two months living there, I came home, opened drawers and found things missing. I always knew exactly what I had. Sugar, coffee, and a couple of cigarettes were gone. I went into the kitchen and there was Tischler with his wife. I said, 'I am leaving now and I am coming back in one hour.'" He finished in a stern voice, "'Everything you took must be back where you took it, or else.'" Within an hour, everything had been returned. "'I am not locking this room,'" he declared, putting them on the honor system. Years later, in a different city and context, he would change his practice. "I do lock my room now."

"A detective, I would analyze. When I was eighteen, I used to bet where things might end up with other people. And most of the time I was correct. People had a hard time lying to me, because I would see it."

A perennial pursuit, Chaim scanned the horizon of opportunity to make contacts for advancement musically. On September 26, he attended a concert by Herbert Aumere, associated with the national theater and opera, so likely a capable pedagogue. The ambitious young violinist took mental note.

Saving some money each month, Arbajtman continued living with the Tischlers in Fürstenfeldbruck. "Then came New Year's Eve. They had a telephone, which was unusual in those days. I heard him talking on the phone. They were invited to their German friends' place. He didn't see me in the other room and said, 'We have an auslander (foreigner) staying with us.' Suddenly, Tischler was calling me an alien. In Germany, this was not a nice word. He didn't say a Jew or non-Jew, but added 'a very nice foreigner.'"

Soon, Richard Tischler began inviting him to parties which other high ranking ex-Nazi party members also attended. What a difference a few months had made in social life. It still felt strange, listening to the content of their conversations, knowing that the same ilk had killed his whole family! He knew to listen carefully, ask very little, say nothing about himself, and to speak only when questioned.

"I could never talk to him about politics. The few times I tried, his neck veins would pop out when talking about Nazi matters." Chaim first went to live with the German couple about fifteen months after liberation, and stayed two to three years. Later, he moved to America, but returned to Munich on many occasions. Chaim never failed to see Richard Tischler. Their unlikely relationship, Jew and Nazi, transformed remarkably over time. "Whenever I went to Munich, I always went to visit. I don't know if I would call us good friends, but they were good to me."

Postwar Germany hardly threw out the welcome mat to a displaced musician from Poland, Jewish at that. Therefore, in the spring of 1947, he first contemplated a move to the freer atmosphere of Switzerland. "I saved enough money to bribe somebody to take me across the border. I went and checked into a horrible little place near Lake Constance. I was there for a few days and found a smuggler, a Russian Jew. When we met, he was around twenty-seven years old, a good-looking guy who played cello."

The fellow had a remarkable background. He had ended up living in Paris, eventually obtaining French papers. There an announcement came, "'All the Jews must come to the police precinct.' He went and they put a big stamp, 'Juif,' on his ID. Back home he realized his mistake. If he had known they were going to place the stamp, Jew, he wouldn't have gone. Later, he went to another precinct and said he lost his papers, hoping to get the replacement without any stamp. He got it and continued living in Paris."

"Once the war reached Paris, things got bad. The cellist saw an ad for a small Hungarian group, auditioning a musician who played two or more instruments for a two-year contract to play in Hamburg. He auditioned and got the job. The year was 1943. No Nazi would ever think a Jew would go from Paris to Hamburg at the height of war. He was a genius. I wish more Jews dared going there. Sometimes you had to do something brave to stay alive." Jumping into the fire, he defied logic and swallowed fear, running straight to the heart of enemy activity. From 1943 to 1945, the Jew hid openly in a major Nazi industrial center, and lived to see Germany defeated.

This fellow knew about risk taking; nevertheless, "He felt sorry for me, was a decent human being, and set me straight. He said, 'I can take you across the border in no time. Within twenty-four hours, they will pick you up, because every Swiss person is a self-appointed police officer. So, when they see you on the street and you don't look like you belong, they call the police. Once caught without papers and deported from Switzerland, you're blacklisted and can never get legal papers to re-enter. I suggest you go back to Munich and find a legal way to go.'"

After returning to Munich, Chaim frequented a dance hall, some twenty minutes away by streetcar. "I went in the afternoon around four o'clock tea time. In spring, the sun was out, the weather was perfect. I never took a lesson. Dancing three times every week, I won second prize in a dance competition. I was quite good at the foxtrot, tango, and waltz."

The local Jewish community, maybe sixty, all from the camps, organized a live theater group. The Ex- Concentration Camp Orchestra supplied a small combo to play as part of the productions. Though the youngest musician, Lithuanian manager Jascha Gurewitc asked Arbajtman to conduct. He briefly wielded a baton, but would never claim this amounted to actual conducting experience.

In suburbs of Munich, Gurewitc continued to manage the seventeen-piece orchestra. "One rehearsal, I was a few minutes late. Jascha got up on the stage and said, 'Chaim came in late. He will pay a penalty.' It was not much money, but if you didn't have any, it seemed a lot of money. 'Next pay period I will deduct two hundred marks.' The day before payment, I approached Gurewitc. 'Jascha, tomorrow you are not, by any chance, going to take out two hundred marks?' He said, 'Oh yes, I am.' I said, 'I didn't give you permission. It's my salary. You cannot take it.' He said, 'Oh yes I can.' It became an argument."

In the hallway, Arbajtman pulled out of a pocket two hundred marks of his own, tore them in half and threw everything in the manager's face. Hearing an argument, the other musicians came out, picked up pieces and pasted them together to give Chaim. "I never paid Gurewitc a penalty. The loss wouldn't have bothered me, but more the principle." He felt it unfair and unjustified to dock his salary without prior specification of penalties or any warning. Standing up for himself bore fruit. "And what happened, after this Jascha liked me even better."

The orchestra manager later helped fund Chaim's pursuit of serious violin instruction. Every Saturday, the local Jewish association, "rented one large room where sixty people of all ages gathered. They hired four musicians, including a violin and accordion. I went there to play and see my friends. Everyone brought their own bottle of vodka and sat at a table. So much smoke you couldn't see anybody and so noisy you couldn't hear the person next to you. There was a German wanting 'more dance music.'"

Gurewitc urged Chaim to play a solo instead. At this particular club date, alcohol-fueled revelry defied any serious desire to listen. "It was about one o'clock in the morning, and even louder. I didn't want to play over the noise, so I made a condition. I said, 'If you can get everybody silent, I will play.' This seemed impossible, but after about an hour he finally managed to get everybody quiet."

"In those days, when you got up and played, it was for the pleasure of everybody who came. No matter how you sounded, they reacted with the same joy, as if you had been Jascha Heifetz." They lavished their affection without conditions.

After sustained applause, Jascha motioned to Chaim. "Around 3:00 a.m., Gurewitc says, 'Have another vodka with a little salami. Whatever I can do for you, I will do it. You have my word.' The moment I had an opportunity, I grabbed it." Arbajtman replied, "'Thank you. What's the earliest time we can meet Monday morning?' He said, 'Eight o'clock.'"

Monday morning, right on time, came a knock at the door. Arbajtman thanked Jascha for committing to help him with whatever he needed. Encountering no argument, he became more specific. "'Playing in the Ex-Concentration Camp Orchestra is not my future. I have an idea about some teachers, concertmasters in Munich at the Opera or the Philharmonic. I want to study but I cannot live without getting paid. I want you to give me the salary without working, so I can study.'"

"He says, 'You are crazy. You're asking me to do the impossible, the musicians will never accept it.'" Chaim pressed his point, "I am crazy because I want to do something? They will kill you only if you let them. You can do it. You're the manager. If you exercise your authority and keep your word to me, then there's no problem." Arben's considerable talent for negotiations displayed, Gurewitc concluded by saying, "I promise, I will try."

"He proposed it to the group and they all screamed at him, 'We're talented too, not as young as Chaim, but….' He said, 'Chaim has talent. He is young and cannot achieve greatness here. We, everybody, must help him to achieve this.'" He withstood resistance, went ahead, and honored his promise. "After three weeks I got paid, and was able to go study with the best teachers."

"The concertmaster of the Opera in Munich became my teacher." Also, the concertmaster of the Munich National Theater Orchestra, Hubert Aumere, came from Estonia. "A wonderful man, he invited me to his house and I played for him. After accepting me as a student and learning I didn't have money for lessons, he said not to worry about it."

"He didn't say anything to me about plans to leave Germany. I later learned he got an offer from Colombia and became the big professor in Bogotá." Incidentally, while there he acquired a student, violinist Luis Biava, who would years later play with our subject as a colleague and friend in America. Aumere didn't fit well in Bogotá, and subsequently returned to Munich.

Undiscouraged by his earlier failed attempt to cross into Switzerland, Arbajtman still searched for a safer route to freer society. "I found out during that year the only way was an international music competition. But I wasn't ready." He developed strategies to enter legally, contacting Jewish refugees who had preceded him there and local organizations for help to extend his stay. He was granted a spot at the Geneva fall 1947 music competition. "I went to the Swiss consul in Munich and showed them my letter."

"I told him, 'I want to go to Switzerland for the competition.' 'Let me see your passport.' 'I don't have a passport.' 'If you don't have any documents, I cannot give you a visa.' The only way was to become a Polish citizen, which I could have become. The only way was to become a Polish citizen which I didn't want." As a displaced person, he had no official papers that qualified him for international travel.

His efforts to secure a visa stalled, for the lack of a passport. "I wanted to get out of Germany. They killed my family. They destroyed my life. I wanted to get out the moment I could, but I couldn't, because I didn't have a pfennig (penny). If you didn't have a passport and no visa, it was impossible, as simple as that. It took another year to get some kind of travel document from the American forces."

Fortunately, Jascha Gurewitc kept the support checks coming. "Right after the war, he had little money." Gurewitc and his wife, during lean times, used to stay with Arbajtman in Munich. Summer weekends, Chaim used to stay at their cottage by the sea. "We bonded over those years (late 1945 to 1948)."

Focused on profiting from the present for future possibilities, "I was practicing. Within six months (from start of pay without working), I auditioned for Bavarian Radio Orchestra. This led to many recitals and solos. I still have a letter from them (dated September 18, 1947)."

His ex-concentration camp musician friends tuned in the station and listened. "When they announced on the radio in Germany, 'Chaim Arbajtman,' I gained the respect of my colleagues." Jascha had gambled and initially disgruntled orchestra members had invested. All won. Chaim's success provided a source of pride for the entire Jewish community.

Chaim communicated through music, a universal language that touched hearts in the listening public. Playing on a Bavarian radio show as resident soloist created considerable attention and excitement. Against this backdrop of greater name recognition, late in 1947 Michael Taube contacted the local Jewish community again. His wife Elsa Jülich-Taube, a Wagnerian soprano from the Munich Opera, had converted to Judaism. Already, "They knew me. So, I met and played with him. We decided we were going to give concerts. He would play a solo and then accompany his wife. A shock to me, she started singing Schumann and Schubert in Hebrew. Then I would play and he would accompany me."

Like so many others before and after, Taube sensed something special about Arbajtman. "Once he said to me, 'Chaim, I am sorry what you went through in life, but it was the best thing for your violin playing. When you play the violin, you don't just play, you have a certain cry, a certain sadness. It comes with the experience of life.' I don't know whether I would agree with him or not. I had seen posters of Michael Taube conducting the Berlin Philharmonic before the War. Now we went on tour."

A promoter arranged the series of engagements for Arbajtman, Taube, and his wife. Performances generated big ticket sales. After profits of more than ten thousand in Reichsmarks, by a calculation that made no sense, the violinist's share came to a paltry two hundred. With eight dates set in Berlin, skepticism arose over the contract arrangements, and it sounded like a long way to travel.

Taube called the minimum of days ahead of time to finalize concert details. "But in January of 1948, I went to Berlin mostly to look for a new teacher." The trip via Leipzig by train and on streetcars, even before the Russian blockade of West Berlin in June of 1948, could not have contained more twists and turns. Landlord Tischler did offer him the name and address of a female friend, known as his secretary to wife Maria, who could put Chaim up for a few days.

Arriving exhausted in Berlin and entering the right building, nobody answered when he rang. In the adjacent apartment a woman, maybe thirty-one years old with an infant child, didn't know where her neighbor had gone or have a guess as to the exact hour of return. She agreed to watch Chaim's things while he looked around Germany's capital. Having already purchased a return train ticket and saved adequate funds, but with no feeling of loyalty to the promoter who had cheated him on earnings, he decided to boycott the arranged concerts. This assertively "off-duty" musician returned at five thirty, but Tischler's "secretary" never appeared.

Chaim did find a music professor, but the blockade would soon get in his way, impeding travel between West Germany and Berlin. After returning to Munich he felt no guilt, despite the promoter's incomprehension over his "no shows," and forfeited his salary. Taube was also angry with Chaim, but a declaration of independence by Israel on May 14, 1948, called him back to the Middle East.

Before parting ways, despite their strained relations, Arbajtman boldly asked a parting favor: his collaborator and colleague's written recommendation. "I still have the letter from Michael Taube, the stationary printed, Palestine Philharmonic."

Still seriously focused on his long-term goals, Chaim learned the Germans let some promising students leave the country on musical scholarships to attend school in Vienna. He opted for instruction at the Mozarteum in Salzburg, and studied there briefly.

His teacher and concertmaster of the Vienna Philharmonic at that time, Wolfgang Schneiderhan, "had a big reputation as being a Nazi." Every day boys and girls from all over Europe would attend his masterclass. They all had to be there ten in the morning until five. "We all played and listened to each other. I was always the last one, and he used to take me apart, used to make mashed potatoes of my playing. The non-Jewish kids came from Yugoslavia and Czechoslovakia. I was the only Jewish boy. They came up to me and said, 'You play beautifully. We don't know why he is tearing you apart.' They knew there was something wrong."

"I knew it was because he was an anti-Semite. Everything I did was wrong." After class, all the students would go out together. They recognized their teacher's racism, that he didn't pick on the others who played less well than Chaim. In the final masterclass, Schneiderhan said to him, "You are a very fine talent. If you accept, I will give you a full scholarship to Vienna Academy of Music." Chaim accepted, but then offers came from elsewhere. He elected to leave Austria for Munich again.

Also in May of 1948, Leonard Bernstein came for his first visit to Germany under the auspices of U.S. government and occupation authorities. Georg Solti, a Hungarian Jew, had invited him to conduct the Bavarian State Opera Orchestra. While there, much interested in the tragedy that happened to Jews in European concentration camps, Bernstein inquired whether any remnants of Jewish presence remained. His chaperones, an entourage of German Jews, shared that some survivors yet congregated locally. He asked whether any musicians could be found among them. Informed about a small group of seventeen musicians that included Chaim, calling themselves the Ex-Concentration Camp Orchestra, Bernstein asked to meet them. Jascha Gurewitc served as liaison.

After listening to the musicians at a rehearsal, some 50 kilometers from Munich, he spoke in German, and they understood that he wanted to conduct two of their concerts. Rehearsals commenced for performances in Feldafing and Landsberg. Musical selections included Bizet's L'Arlesienne Suite and Gershwin's Rhapsody in Blue, with Bernstein conducting at the piano. Members of the "Nazi Orchestra," as he termed Solti's orchestra, came to attend these concerts. Bernstein called it "a kind of expiation...like Yom Kippur." When they covered the stage with a shower of roses, the young American conductor felt they "wanted to atone somehow."

During one intermission, Bernstein looked around and spotted Arbajtman. He approached Chaim, not concertmaster Borstein. "He said, 'I want you to pick a piece. Do you have the piano part to it? I will accompany you.' When they heard Bernstein picked me to play with him, it turned into a riot. It was unbearable. Bernstein understood the tragedy of these people. So, he said, 'Whoever wants to play, I will accompany everybody...' and he did. I played Tartini G Minor Sonata and a Brahms Sonata."

"I never took advantage of someone's fame to help myself. I tried to stay on the other side of the room," wanting to distance himself from insider politics.

On this same government sanctioned visit, Chaim had watched Bernstein conduct the Bavarian Orchestra and heard him play a Liszt concerto. Georg Solti, the Hungarian conductor who would later become conductor of the Chicago Symphony, sat in front of Arbajtman.

Though he would see the manager Jascha Gurewitc again, a reunion of the Ex-Concentration Camp Orchestra never took place. "I kept in touch with most of them. When immigration started ten months later, the group disbanded. Most went to Israel or to the United States." Gurewitc moved with his wife to New York. He lived to the advanced age of eighty-nine, and maintained friendship with the violinist for whom he took a risk.

During Chaim's time in Munich, a childless Canadian couple of considerable means heard him play. They fell in love with his musicality. Learning of his plan to go to North America and why, mentioning the paperwork hurdles and long waits involved, they made an unexpected offer to adopt Chaim after their return with him to Canada. Obviously sincere, their plan made eminently good sense. He thought but for a second and respectfully declined, explaining he, "already had good parents."

He rejected another "shortcut" from some matchmaker, a rich Jew from Mexico. The man had a daughter who needed a husband. "I didn't know how she looked. I never saw her... No, I didn't accept." In practical terms, Chaim knew he could not yet support a wife in the Americas. Besides, he still needed substantial work to ready himself for a move to the new world. He felt acutely aware that he had been robbed of instruction during his early years, the best and most critical to formation of his technique. No less deleterious and of potentially more long-term detrimental impact, he struggled internally with what therapists today would describe as a post-traumatic stress disorder.

Once again, Arbajtman applied for the Swiss international music competition and received acceptance. At this point, intent on satisfying requirements, "American authorities gave me a temporary travel document." He showed the document along with the Geneva acceptance letter to the Swiss consul, who asked, "'Do you have any sponsors in Switzerland?' I didn't know anybody."

"I was invited to go there for twelve days, but I needed sponsorship. Some people helped me. It was a ten-person chain, one talking to another. The one who lived in Paris, I never knew. He apparently used to arrange letters for people. I received a letter from some Swiss bigshot, and he would help pay for expenses."

The breakthrough had come! "It took me a year to figure out how to get to Switzerland, with much difficulty." Though nothing about these ongoing trials mitigated an intense bitterness of soul, or built back any spirit of trust in his fellow creatures, Arbajtman remained resolute in the pursuit of greater violin proficiency. The ultimate goal was to find Zimbalist. The immediate stepping stone was crossing the border with a temporary visa sometime in September of 1948, destination Geneva's Concours International d'Exécution Musicale.

7
Switzerland

"They brought back my sanity. They made me into a human being again."

He rang the bell at a late hour, not knowing the family, his only connection a folded piece of paper with the scribbled name and address. A Swiss woman, Hedy Salquin, who had agreed to accompany him in the competition, had suddenly cancelled, describing her schedule as now too busy. Responsibly, she referred him to another young pianist, who lived with her parents. At 10:00 p.m., how uncivilized he felt, showing up unannounced. Had they already gone to bed?

Only a day or two in the country by this point, Chaim had previously gotten off his train at Etskin, loading site for the export import business of a Mr. Perlini, who lived outside of Zurich. Around 2:00 p.m. on a beautiful day, he located the man's house, and maids told him Mr. Perlini would return at 9:00 p.m. Arbajtman waited without any offer of food or drink. Their meeting took place punctually at the designated hour. "I showed him the letter he had written. He was supposed to help me. He took me down to a hotel and told the hotel woman to give me a meal. He said, 'I help many people come to Switzerland, but I don't do everything myself. The man who asked me to write a letter lives in Paris. I never know details, only names. Go to Geneva tomorrow. Call me in two days, and if the friend of mine in Paris tells me to give you money, we'll give you the money.'" Chaim started his journey with a mere $5.00 American in his pocket, and the modest hotel that first night charged $0.75 for a room. "Something to eat, already it would have cost me $1.25." Fortunately, Mr. Perlini paid for the hotel, arranged a meal, and gave Arbajtman 50 Swiss francs before departing.

Chaim boarded another train the next morning, arrived around noon, and walked the city streets. "When I first entered Geneva it was a garden. I've never witnessed a place that was so spotless, so clean in the streets. I had less than $4.00. If I ate, with little left over, this would be very bad. Dollars went fast in Switzerland. It was always more expensive." A room at the station cost $1.20. "I didn't know what to do next." Subsequently, he again counted what remained and quickly concluded that, despite such a late hour, he must act, and pulled out from his pocket the folded piece of paper with scribbled name and address. By this sequence of events, he found himself standing on the apartment landing of his substitute pianist's parents, two hours before midnight, in primal desperation. He rang their bell.

A smiling woman in her red velvet nightgown opened the apartment door and greeted him, "'Do you speak French?'" He answered, "'No, do you speak German?'" This woman, approaching age fifty, replied, "'Ja, wir sprechen Deutsch.'" The family spoke four languages. "I said, 'My name is Arbajtman.'" After a brief explanation on his part, she invited him in to meet her daughter, also dressed in what he took as matching red velvet, though actually flannel. The nineteen-year-old, like Salquin who recommended her, was a collaborative pianist for Geneva's music competition.

The immediate visual impression struck him, on all the walls an extraordinary number of crosses and paintings of the Virgin Mary. Not suspicious, just a little uncomfortable, he wondered what might come next. "If they find out I am a Jew, they will send me right back to Auschwitz. I'll be crucified on the spot." The exaggerated count of wall hangings bespoke his hypervigilance bred in the camps. The reference to Auschwitz, simply a ghetto sense of humor sharpened on the same grinder's wheel. Speaking in German, he felt it best to start explaining that, despite his last name and recent arrival from Munich, he originally came from Poland. Likely taking him to be Catholic, the mother interjected reassuringly, "'We love the Polish people.'" He continued and disclosed his ethnic origins as Jewish. Without so much as a brief pause, she added, "'Oh, we love the Jewish people.'"

This sounded too much to believe after everything experienced in a short but eventful life. "I didn't trust them. I had friends who hated Jews. Because they admitted it, I trusted them. Someone who said they loved Jews was dishonest. They must be hiding the truth." He couldn't fathom them, these ladies in red.

With introductions made, the charitable and courageous family quickly checked room availability, guaranteeing payment to put Chaim up in a hotel for the next two weeks. Such seemed the most practical and proper arrangement for this aspiring musician whom they had just met. A weight dropped off his shoulders. What incredible "luck" again, now with lodging procured when earlier the same night, his money reserve had run precariously close to bust.

The family knew a secretary at the Mensa Club. "I went to meet her. Here was a card with my name. I was a Mensa member, a group for geniuses like Einstein. I could eat meals for free and mix with intelligentsia. Enormous IQs, they were busy learning. I didn't realize how smart they were, young girls and boys from all over the planet. For me, it was somewhere to go eat."

In the coming ten days of "observation," returning to their big apartment, he and the daughter rehearsed for their upcoming performance. Initially, "I didn't devote myself to music. I was wild, so I didn't practice much. They knew and didn't approve, but didn't criticize me. If I had heard one hint of criticism, I would have been gone. They knew that I had a lot of anger and hate. They didn't say I should do this, but gave me the space. I didn't understand then what they were doing. They were smarter and never said, 'Chaim, let it out, you are angry.' No. I would have held back. I had the pain inside. I had the burden. No questions came, absolutely none."

Undoubtedly the family liked his playing, but this hardly explained a raft of kindnesses. "They invited me for dinner." The mother prepared their meal in an apartment where they moved and took up residence in 1940. She encouraged him to call her "mother." "'I'd like to, but I cannot. My parents raised me well. I had a wonderful mother. May I call you Aunt?'" She assented to "Tante" (Aunt in German).

"Life began again when I moved in with them. One morning, they woke me up at nine. Our next stop was the most expensive store in Geneva. I needed clothing, and hadn't even thought of it." Naturally, Chaim appreciated that they took him to a topnotch tailor to be fitted for proper attire. "He brought out all kinds of suits I should try. I tried on silk shirts, but didn't like anything. 'Don't worry, tomorrow he's going to bring new selections.'" The best of cashmere creations, a store representative carried everything to the apartment. Arbajtman's preferences resembled that of royalty, not the humble tailor's son. How could he have displayed such an attitude, insisting on the best coat, costly pants, etc.?! Tante and her husband were both supportive. "Uncle was especially phenomenal." They paid for everything with no hint of disapproval.

After the scheduled competition, a most urgent issue remained. His temporary visa would soon lapse. The matter of how to stay in Switzerland longer term quickly came to the fore. One option was to somehow gain acceptance to school. He then could obtain a student visa. As soon as achievable, in October they helped him enter the Geneva Conservatory of Music, where he remained until the following June. Voilà! "Permission to stay a year, my life changed drastically."

At the Conservatory, Arbajtman learned about a world of opportunities in music. "I found out that Zimbalist was the Director of Music at a school called Curtis and taught there. So, now I knew where to go. I saw him in Warsaw before the war. In those twelve years since, I had become an old man." The desire to take lessons from such a famous violinist, conceived at age nine when Chaim's father took him to see the visiting artist from America, would not abate.

"They just wanted me to be the happiest person, nothing else." The Swiss family liked to go for a picnic or walk on the Salève, a mountain very close to town, but in France. Tante's husband, a very powerful man in Swiss business and military circles, whose family dated back to 1425 in Geneva, contacted a good friend. Xavier de Gaulle, brother to Charles, served as French consul in Geneva. Basically, the conversation went, "'We have a boy from Poland who is struggling. He went through hell.' 'Okay.'" Xavier tried his best with the French authorities, but was not able to get papers for Chaim to go to France.

"Onkel (uncle in German) had a lot of businesses. First, he was selling British parts, from bicycles to cars and airplanes." Notwithstanding the financial abundance, Chaim remained baffled, just not understanding why they seemed pleased to take care of his every need.

Once secure with resident status and now moved from hotel to the family apartment, his time had come to resume focused music studies. He began devoting longer hours at home to practice, wanting to "catch up" after so many years lost to the ravages of camp life. The interruption in his progress on the violin caused a churning inside every time he thought of it. No better remedy, he practiced and practiced. "In 1948, my Swiss family knew important people, arranged for me to play a recital and found some sponsors. One was a Rothschild."

Chaim and Tante's daughter performed recitals in homes. "I invited her to go to the movies, but I didn't have money. The mother gave me some money. She gave me much more money than the movie cost. At the theater I asked, 'Do you want chocolate?' During the movie I bought some for her. Afterward the family made such a big thing out of it, 'What an incredible human being.' Why all the attention? It was their money."

Chaim preferred playing to eating. "I was so skinny when I came to Geneva." Tante was not happy about this. Due to her concern about his gaunt appearance, she tried to fatten him with rich foods. "She would cook so much and, for a few weeks, I ate everything. My stomach hurt with so much rich food. I couldn't digest it all." She also somehow knew what doctors subsequently discovered about patients with starving nervous systems, as in the case of anorexia. You must feed the brain cells before working to heal the psyche.

"She mashed bananas, added lots of orange juice and some sugar for me to eat. Instead of a normal amount, I got three big mashed bananas. She would fool me by preparing it in the kitchen, so I wouldn't see." The young man did his best to please her, despite a "baby stomach." When his system rebelled and no progress could be detected, she even secretly consulted a rabbi to learn about kosher foods that might appeal more to his tastes.

The family displayed a special kind of humanity. Tante herself exuded unqualified love. Many examples could be cited. One freezing night in November, at an hour even later than when he had first arrived, came the sound of a knock at the front door. Chaim opened it so she could talk with a caller standing in their hall. The itinerant peddler offered trinkets for sale. "'Can you use this?'" She said, "'Oh, yes, I can.'" She surveyed his wares and "finally said, 'If I buy the whole thing, how much would you charge me?' He gave a price and she said, 'Okay.'" Tante went for her purse, gave him the money, and took all his wares.

"After closing the door, I looked at her. 'Tante, do you need this stuff?' 'Not at all.' 'So, why did you buy what you don't need?' She said, 'It's raining like crazy. It's cold. The weather is so bad. It's late and he would have to go many places to finish his sales. This way, he can go home to enjoy his family.' I couldn't comprehend such dignity. This was kindness, simply incredible. Where did she get such a heart?"

Incomprehension, yes, but no reservations remained about her saintly character. "Onkel used to come home late, maybe eleven thirty. We were still up talking. He didn't scold me, but he was surprised. I wouldn't let them sleep because I couldn't sleep. The moment I fell asleep I was being killed, over and over, so I kept the conversation going. I kept everybody up, so that I didn't have to go to bed. I became a night owl. Being polite, they didn't want to interrupt. Only later, I realized they were trying to help me." Rising early for daily activities, and to attend church on Sunday mornings at eight thirty, they made it their habit to turn in early. Onkel left the room. Ever patient and attentive, but with challenges of her own, Tante would finally give another hint and turn out the light.

Hours later, gentle as a feather, Chaim felt the ministering movements around three thirty in the morning. He suffered continually with terrifying dreams. Nazis tortured and murdered him every night. Alerted by his cries and shrieks, Tante immediately came to investigate. "My bed was like a bathtub, the pajamas, pillows, blankets, sheets, all soaked from sweating. This angel came in with a bottle of water and glass, gave me fresh pajamas, sheets, and changed my whole bed." Quickly and quietly, not saying a word, she made it all fresh and clean. "Then I could really fall asleep." She did this, each night, for thirteen months. "If such a thing as an angel exists, this woman had to be one."

With thyroid, blood sugar, and heart issues, "This sick lady showed me humanity I hadn't known for years. Christmas time, the table was extended a mile long. She had a few apartment buildings from her inheritance, and only rented to poor people who couldn't pay rent. These people had children and couldn't buy toys. One Christmas, the table was full of toys. She was wrapping them. 'What is going on?' I asked. 'Poor people cannot afford to buy. It's not the children's fault.'" There seemed no end to her compassion.

The process of releasing so much darkness and pain took time, ultimately more than five years. "I had a lot of hate in me after the war. I was a big mess, and I knew it. My Swiss family didn't know anything I was thinking. I never told them, but the thinking machine ran all the time."

"They never asked me to go to church." Chaim accosted them, wildly. "'You go to church on Sunday morning. What for? Why do you go to church?' They smiled. I criticized their Catholic religion, 'What good does it do?' They smiled. I didn't want them to go to church. I was unreasonable. 'You believe in God, really?' They smiled. I didn't have their patience. How lucky I was they didn't throw me out of the apartment. I was wild not only to myself, I was wild to everybody around me. I had all this hate in me that needed to come out after so many years of abuse in the camps. Who received it? The people who loved me, they understood. My luck was that they were smart, wise, and compassionate."

Sometimes we hurt those closest to us, the ones who love us. "What I did was terrible. I think what they saw was beneath the surface. They understood more deeply. They understood the hell I went through, and they knew that I had a war inside of me. They knew I had to let it out, and they made it possible for me. Once the pain was out, there was hope and an opportunity for healing."

The Swiss family never argued, never criticized or questioned his feelings, always respectful and sensitive to his wounded soul. "They brought me back my sanity, back to life. Before I met them, I was a tortured human being. The beauty was, not once did they say that I was 'right' or 'wrong.' They set examples and I started to realize myself. It was too hard for me to try to ask for forgiveness when I sometimes wronged her. I never said that I was sorry. I wrestled with myself. This was what I was at the time. 'I am what I am.'" He lived in each moment's reality.

Contrastingly, Tante approached Chaim to ask forgiveness. She had reflected on one of their outings to the countryside. He requested something to eat, food already prepared and placed in a picnic basket. She refused, and told him to wait until they arrived at the campsite. Later she regretted her decision. "She said to me, 'I apologize for not giving you something to eat. If something would have happened to you, and I didn't give you something to eat when you wanted, I couldn't live any more. I should have given you food.'" One can only speculate on what influences shaped this saintly woman's character.

"This was an incredible family, God-sent. You cannot picture how wild a man I was. To me, I was normal. But living with them more than a year, I calmed down and became a different being. They were very clever, in the examples they set. People who knew me before said, 'It's impossible. You are so nice, so civilized, elegant, and sensitive. What happened?' In two years, how can one be unrecognizable?"

"We always had wonderful fun." Tante noticed her daughter's life changing after Chaim showed up in Geneva and they began to spend time together. They would cook pasta after concerts, late at night, and have what they called a "Nudeln Festspiel" (noodle festival), things the daughter would never have done alone. "I adopted the family and became like them. I am so lucky. They made me into a human being again. The beauty of it, they made me who I became. Every time I think of it, I owe so much to them."

Onkel and Tante loved for their daughter to spend time with Chaim, and he with her. "She was everything phenomenal. Her father wanted me to take over the big business. I loved them like my own family. They loved me. It was wonderful. An Orthodox family in Poland and this religious Catholic one in Geneva, I was lucky to belong to both these worlds. In between these two, I went through hell in the camps where I became a member of the dead, another part of my life. I lived through it all."

What the parents saw in him, besides his musical talent, remained unexpressed. Six or seven months after Chaim arrived, Tante asked Geneva's chief rabbi, "How is it possible for a Polish young man, a Jew, to marry a Swiss Catholic woman? How can it be done?" The rabbi responded, "It can be done if the man, the Jewish man, agreed to raise the children Catholic. Then it's possible to marry her.' And he can continue as a Jew. The children and wife continue as Catholic. It's possible."

Chaim's Swiss aunt had introduced him to Mieczyslaw Warm, a prominent Jewish lawyer from Warsaw, who moved to Geneva early in the war. Tante hoped Mr. Warm might help Chaim. She also asked about the technicalities of an interfaith union. "I found out she asked my new friends, 'How can a Catholic and a Jew… Is marriage possible?'" The lawyer shared his opinion.

Tante's whole family absolutely adored Chaim. Surely, the parents had looked ahead and beyond, seeing something special. "I don't know whether it was something special or if they felt sorry for a young Jewish boy who lost his entire family, life destroyed by people without humanity. I didn't know. I never asked. I never questioned why they approved of me. My thought, 'Don't question anything that is good.' They accepted me and I was grateful."

The Swiss family never faltered. Notwithstanding, the young Arbajtman always ruled out marrying a rich woman. He believed a man should support the woman, and didn't want to owe anyone. "Another reason, I couldn't raise my children Catholic. It had nothing to do with my own feelings about having Catholic children, but I would never disappoint my Jewish parents, never. They were the most important thing in my life." Truthfully, perhaps he didn't have time for getting serious with a woman while focusing so intently on his violin.

During this time, Chaim mostly stayed in Geneva, but made one visit to the north of Switzerland, to La Chaux-de-Fonds. "I found my teacher." He visited Professor Ignatz Weisenberg, his second instructor from childhood days in Warsaw. "I finally tracked him down, got his phone number, and called. We made a date and I rode the train two-and-a-half hours. Now twenty-one, I hadn't seen him since I was eleven years old. I rang the bell. He opened the door, asked me to come in and his first words, 'You look the same as you always were, you did not improve.' I said, 'Thank you.' This was how to get reacquainted? He then moved aside, letting me into the house. His wife was sick. Because of the war, his career went down and he was working in a watch factory. Nobody knew he was a great violinist."

"Once, some doctors arranged for musicians to play chamber music. Weisenberg was invited and everybody was astonished. In 1936, before the war and before I met him, Ignatz Weisenberg and Vladimir Horowitz went on a South American tour for six weeks playing sonatas. This was the caliber of Ignatz Weisenberg. Ernest Ansermet, music director of Geneva Symphony and internationally famous conductor, invited him to play the Glazunov Violin Concerto. He was a great violinist, but the war did something terrible to him.

He was very bitter about what happened. His family was destroyed. Never wanting to leave his wife's side, he couldn't take a break."

Chaim studied with another Polish Jew, Michael Schwalbe, at the Geneva Conservatory. This man studied and played in France before the war, fled south after the fall of Paris, and in 1942, hid in the back of a furniture van to reach Swiss asylum. Impressively, he won first prize at a major competition and joined the Suisse Romande Orchestra as concertmaster under direction of Ansermet, all before age thirty. Schwalbe complained people did not pay the proper recognition owed him, blaming it on his relative youth. Hearing this, his new student thought silence was all he could muster as due respect.

At a subsequent concert recital, one untactful reviewer wrote in French that Arbajtman played with a maturity beyond that of his teacher. Chaim went on to win the Prix de Vituosité (Virtuoso Prize) in June 1949 at Geneva's Conservatory, performing as soloist with Orchestre du conservatoire.

Schwalbe came to visit the Swiss family's apartment with one of his own students, a friend of Tante's daughter. This grown-up woman in her thirties taught youngsters music. "She wanted one child to play for my teacher." The pupil played something, but not well. The kid and the woman left. "I was staying at the apartment, but my teacher didn't know. I picked up the violin and started imitating the child," playing badly on purpose. Schwalbe commented, "'The young kids today, they play out of tune.'" Arbajtman threw his door open and made a surprise entry into the room. "He saw me with violin in hand and shouted, 'You! You!' I used to play these tricks."

Onkel and Tante found a few rich Jewish families in Geneva willing to give money each term, to help Arbajtman in his studies. He didn't remain in Onkel's apartment during the whole Swiss stay. At some point, he lived with another family, Mr. and Mrs. Luthi.

When the time came to seek a higher level of music instruction, Tante and the rest of the family hoped their adopted relation would choose Paris or London. They offered every help to make this possible. Still, Chaim already knew, and could not get out of his mind, the Curtis School in Philadelphia where Zimbalist worked as director and taught students. Though he hated leaving his loved ones behind in Switzerland, he kept his focus on going to America.

Chaim, more courageous than ever, shared particulars of a dream from age nine to study under the man whose performance had so electrified him in Warsaw. Without any chance of success, short of a miracle, his goal had served as the fixation point when utter darkness threatened to choke every fantasy to death. A subconscious yearning to study with Zimbalist aided in pulling him through the camp years. Now, his ambition propelled him forward to a fonder hope in life than any other he could imagine. He shared all this with those closest to him and who cared the most.

"When I was to leave for the U.S., I asked my aunt if she could do something for me. She said, 'Yes, anything.' 'Could you give me an army blanket?' She asked, 'Why do you want this?' I said, 'It's possible I will go to America and be sleeping in the streets.' I never had to sleep in the street, but I had the blanket for a number of years. I don't know what happened to it." Onkel gave him his own best overcoat to protect against the cold. Tante concealed and sewed gold coins in coat linings.

"When I was in Geneva, I started working towards going to the U.S. I was young. The energy was there. When I became focused on something, which could be good or not, nobody could talk me out of it."

Despite short cuts worth considering, he listened to all offers and said, "No." He desired no help and didn't want to feel further indebted. Immigration law dictated terms which required he return to Germany in order to seek U.S. admission. On departure from Geneva in November, 1949, Chaim Arbajtman felt an excitement over his big next step.

8
Immigration to America

"I was nine years old. One day I will study with this man. And I knew this dream was ridiculous. Knowing how this would sound to my father, I never mentioned it."

Chaim made arrangements to temporarily move back in with the Tischlers at their Fürstenfeldbruck home outside Munich. A picture of him taken there, sporting Onkel's coat, survives. "They saved my room, I saved some cigarettes." There he applied to have his name placed on a waiting list to go to America. "Since I was a child, everybody talked about America, the land flowing with milk and honey. I registered as an immigrant. Following all legal requirements, my turn came."

Depending on the document and government, spelling of his name varied. Germans "messed up my name completely...they put double 'n' at the end, like Thomas Mann." Chaim Arbajtman and Haim Arbeitmann look different, but sound the same. Notwithstanding any potential confusion over his identity, this one person faced a pair of oral exams at the American consulate in Germany.

They asked lots of questions. "If somebody tells you, 'I want to kill the President of the U.S.,' what would you do?' I said, 'I would call the police immediately.' He said, 'Very good.' Sometimes two different people talked to you in your own language." Most particularly, why did he want to immigrate? For entry into the U.S. at that time, depending a person's place of origin, various quotas applied. "I was under the Polish quota, maybe not as desirable as someone from Belgium."

Prospective immigrant Arbajtman offered explanations, all answers presumably as forceful and resolute as his nature. A woman, Bella Maiksing, helped organize his planned departure to the U.S. She had helped many Jews leave Germany. Additionally, "You had to have a sponsor. There were organizations in the Jewish community who would serve as sponsors. It didn't have to be an individual sponsor." The Hebrew Immigrant Aid Society (HIAS) assisted DPs. They had offices in Munich. Requirements satisfied, permission granted, once again Red Sea waters parted for Chaim.

Before leaving Europe, he wanted to visit his Swiss family one last time, for perhaps a long while. Fortunately, this time Xavier de Gaulle succeeded in helping secure the requisite paperwork. Chaim wore Onkel's coat to protect against the winter months and dropping temperatures. Their brief time together concluded and emotional goodbyes said, he returned to Germany.

First, he reported to Hamburg and later to Bremerhaven. As luck would have it, in Hamburg for three days before arriving at the dock, he met a twenty-one-year-old Hungarian Jewish woman who had lost her whole family too. She would prove a vital contact during the ten-day passage from Germany to the U.S.

Chaim's ship weighed anchor and left port. The USAT *General C. H. Muir* had already made several voyages to repatriate U.S. troops returning from the concluded war in Europe. His trip started at the end of 1949 with thousands on board, but no soldiers. "On a refugee ticket, they had all kinds of manual jobs I didn't want to do. They wanted us to go wash and scrub the floors outside the ship. Outside? It was freezing in November on the Atlantic! Outside or inside, I wouldn't scrub slick floors and risk injuring myself! They wanted me outside, sliding all over the place? They wanted me to paint in the rain. I said, 'No, I'm a violinist.' Was I free, or on a slave boat? I knew one thing. This was an American ship, and they were not going to throw me overboard."

At the outset, rolling waves took their toll in third class. "I was seasick." After two or three days the sea smoothed. "The northern route was very cold. They came and said, 'Mr. Arbajtman, now the sea is calm. You can play a concert.' I said, 'No, I don't have the steadiness in my legs, to be on the stage and play very demanding music.'"

Chaim had first refused the assigned outside duties, exposed to the elements, fearing it would jeopardize his playing fingers. Now he declined a command performance inside, feeling wobbly on his feet. As a result, he lost his food ration cards. "We had a booklet for so many days. You tore one card off for each meal, breakfast, lunch, and dinner. They took away the whole booklet because I wouldn't play. They punished me, so I couldn't eat."

His recently-made Hungarian friend had received assignment to the kitchen, and now learned of Chaim's situation. She made a plan to secretly supply him with sustenance below decks. "She brought me special first class food cooked for officers." Three feet away in the opposite bunk, a bearded Orthodox Hasidic Jew seemed perturbed by certain items and practices. "He used to spit into the air because the girl came to bring me food, not kosher, and I ate without a schmata or yarmulke (covering) on my head. She sat on my cot, waiting to take back dishes. She saved my life, but after this voyage we parted."

Interestingly, the USS *General Muir*, which brought soldiers back and refugees to America, later served in the Korean conflict. Eventually she went to private owners in San Juan, Puerto Rico, where Chaim would spend many future winters. He never saw the ship, but he did run into his helper from its kitchen. "When I was in Cleveland some years later I was invited to a party where we met one another by coincidence. She was married and had children."

Chaim docked in Boston, snow falling, on Friday, December 2, 1949, around 6:00 p.m. "I had a visa and waited in line. By eight o'clock, I was taken in a car with a woman and deposited at the train station." She may have worked for the HIAS. Corralled onto a secured train car by himself, no comparison to prior transfers by cattle car, he felt elated to have reached America. "The conductor locked me in, so I wouldn't get off anywhere. I didn't speak a word of English. They gave me a basket with some food. That was it. Unable to communicate, I was too nervous to be frightened, too frightened to be nervous. It was too much of everything. I didn't know where I was going. I wondered if I would ever see civilization again. Far away and all alone, America was so big. The train kept going for ten hours with no sign of humanity, just snow."

Arriving in Detroit, at 2:00 p.m. on Saturday, "There was an older lady wearing a written question worn on her chest, 'Are you Arbajtman?'" He moved towards her with raised hand. "For some reason, they sent me to Detroit. I had the green card, but you could not just go wherever you wanted. Everybody wanted to go to New York. They put you anywhere, but not New York. Once you were settled, you could later go wherever you wanted. This woman's agency was helping with placement and she took me by car to some Hungarian Jewish family who gave me a room."

"On Monday, I had to report in downtown Detroit to the Social Security services. I left early in the morning. Somebody directed me to the address. Well, it took me most of the day to find it. They measured my weight and height. I managed to get a Social Security number, but I couldn't find my way back, so I took street cars. I got on, I got off. They told me I was on the wrong car. It became dark."

Trying to return home alone, he found himself lost and deficient in language skill. "All I had was the address where I lived with this family. I approached a very tall policeman. Everybody was tall. I apologized in broken English, 'Me live...'" Recognizing the young man's struggle to speak correctly, "He put his arms around me and said, 'You speak very good.' He was probably a big Irishman and said, 'I will take you. Come with me.' He drove me about forty minutes. When we made it back, I was so happy to find my little hole in the wall. This could only happen in America." He marvelled at the contrast. Interactions with police in his native land never felt so friendly and helpful.

"On Tuesday, I was supposed to go to the Jewish Family Service. They said, 'We only assist immigrants with placement in the first four to six weeks. We help with English translation when needed. After that, we try to find them a subsistence job.' They found me employment in the automobile industry, twenty dollars a week I said, 'No, I won't work for a car company. This is not what I want. I have to study the violin.'" He quickly realized that they didn't support entry into professions such as medical, legal, or musical. "I went back home and became extremely sick with a high fever."

His host family members took note of these developments and kept in touch with the agency. Monitoring personnel there followed events with interest and concern. "If you were sick, Jews would be quick to try and make you well. For somebody hungry, they would do something. You never saw, anywhere in the U.S., homeless Jews. These Hebrew agencies served many poor people."

"After being there one week, Friday night we sat around their table for supper. They asked if I knew anybody in America." Chaim mentioned a cousin, Jack, in Chicago. They asked if their boarder knew precisely where the relative lived. "'Yes.' At that time I had the address because they used to send care packages. 'Do they know you are here?' 'No.' 'Why not?' 'After I graduate from school and have a job, then I want to go visit them.'" Hearing his answer, they became upset and expressed their displeasure quite loudly. Next, they picked up the phone and called soldier Jack Arbeit's father. He wanted to talk with his cousin. "Tomorrow there is a train at 8:00 a.m. from Detroit to Chicago. You get on that train," he said. "I will pay back the ticket cost when you come, if you're low on money."

"I went the next morning and the train arrived two o'clock in the afternoon. There were thousands of people at that hour in the Chicago station. I kept looking into all their faces. The Arbajtman family, they all looked alike, from the same mold. I had never seen him and we hadn't arranged a way to find each other. I guessed right, going over to a short man. He took me to the car, a big Oldsmobile. I knew nothing about cars, but was impressed to see such a big one. When he drove, I was wondering if he could see over the dash and out the windows." Chaim remained in a state of amazement at the size of America and her cities.

"We got to his house. He introduced me to his wife." Arbajtman men were "accommodating, and they tended to marry strong women. His wife said, 'Come with me.' She took me to the kitchen and showed me the refrigerator. Opening it up, 'Are you hungry?' 'No.'" Like his father said at the relative's shop in Warsaw, "If anybody offers you something, you say, 'Thank you, no.' But I was starving. She said, 'Whenever you are hungry, eat whatever you want.' They had two dry cleaning places. Two sons, one was already married on the west coast. I didn't see the other one. They invited me to stay, to eat for free, pay no rent, and work in either shop they owned for twenty five dollars a week."

Despite a second genuinely generous offer to help, the first when Joe Arbeit called his father from Germany after meeting a long-lost cousin violinist, Chaim declined once more. Our subject would visit his relatives in Chicago again a few years later, after establishing himself and launching a professional career in music. Just now, he had come too far to suddenly compromise and stumble before reaching his ultimate objective. "I arrived on Saturday. The following day, Sunday, I was back on the train to Detroit. I realized they expected me to stay for a few months, but I didn't have any time to waste. I had other ideas. They were probably displeased with me, but I couldn't help it."

One day at the end of December, an envelope with Swiss postage came in the mail. When Chaim opened it, a one hundred dollar note fell to the ground. After picking it up from the rainy pavement and pinching it between two fingers, he read the accompanying letter from his Geneva family. Knowing of a grave shortage of finances to eat adequately and regularly, they promised to send this same amount weekly. The very next correspondence, "I wrote my aunt, 'If you really love me, you must not send another penny. I am in this country now and I have to find a way to sustain myself. If you send me one hundred dollars a week, I will live like a king.' The end of 1949, with a hundred dollars a week, I could have bought the world."

The European "relatives" were familiar with and respected his insistence on finding a way ahead by himself. Their reply, "'You know how much we love you. If this is what you prefer, we will not send you money.' It became very bad, I didn't have any money. I struggled, but I needed that." Still, they could not totally refrain from tokens of affection, even shipping him some food by boat. Of course, he well knew their feelings for him, and gladly accepted special gifts at Christmas, Easter, and birthdays. Swiss chocolates tasted out of this world.

Everybody desired to help. But it sometimes seemed to Chaim that those with good intentions wanted to move him someplace else, in a direction that would take him where he didn't want to go. Returning to Detroit, the Hungarian couple remained willing to assist. "So, they asked me to come back to their home to talk. 'What did I want to do?' 'I want to play violin.' 'There is a famous string trio in Cleveland and they are coming to Detroit to play a recital.' One of them was a very famous violinist and they wanted to introduce me. I could play for this violinist and maybe he would help me."

"I spoke in German, 'I tell you what will happen. Yes, I can play for him. The violinist will like my playing, try to do everything possible for me, offer a scholarship to teach me, and maybe get a better violin.' That's exactly what happened and I said, 'No.' I still wanted to go to Curtis. I came to the U.S. for one reason, to study with Efrem Zimbalist."

Next, the Hungarian family disclosed they knew a rich family. "'You can stay with the rich family. They will take care of you.' I said,

'Thank you, no.'" Knowing what he actually required, Arbajtman again had to refuse uninformed help, even when most kindly offered.

Utterly clear to him, next he needed to write a letter to Zimbalist. But, saying what? How crucial the exact wording, but he didn't even speak English. He must seek a suitable translator and find how best to request the all-important audition. "Somebody wrote a letter. In Yiddish, I told what I wanted him to write. I asked him to address my letter to Zimbalist. I put the stamp on it and mailed it. I had no idea what was written because it was written in English, but I trusted the person. I accomplished what I came to do."

At this time, "The Detroit Symphony was on strike. Bernstein was asked to participate in a benefit for the Symphony. I asked the Jewish Committee if they would put me in touch with him. 'Tell him that I, Chaim Arbajtman, want to see him.' I was taken to Bernstein who was staying with a nice family. At his suggestion, I brought my violin. He offered to connect me with rich patrons who might be able to help. 'Mr. Bernstein, I don't need this kind of help. I don't want people to help me financially.' I needed a letter from him. 'I merely ask if you can give me a letter, but only if I deserve it.'" He looked and replied with a smile, "'You deserve it very much.'"

"Bernstein was already a big name, a genius, an extraordinary talent. He wrote such a beautiful, moving letter for me. His English was like a poet, describing my life very strongly in a few words. And it opened doors. The Committee gave me a typewritten copy." The extant letter reads, *I find Chaim Arbeitmann an extraordinary talent who deserves every possible encouragement and aid... He deserves the best. Respectfully yours, Leonard Bernstein.* This and Chaim's cover letter hit their mark.

"I got the audition with Zimbalist." His moment of opportunity had finally come. After so many years of dreaming daily, starting at age nine and always maintaining hope, he felt a nearly indescribable elation of triumph and validation. Passionate prelude concluded, he had finally come to his opening curtain; the long-awaited premiere before a world famous stage artist who, years previously, had entranced the heart of this boy in a Warsaw audience.

9
Curtis Institute of Music

"Two ladies returned me to sanity, Tante in Geneva, and Ingrid Bohlen in Philadelphia."

With Bernstein's introduction and the cover letter translated into English, contents not now recalled, an imposing door opened wide. Chaim paused before 1726 Locust Street on January 20, 1950. Checking to make sure his coat and tie looked professional, he felt like "the luckiest man in the world." Less than a couple of months after landing at Boston, he stood in Philadelphia before the Curtis Institute of Music. Here to audition, he climbed threshold steps without further delay.

Efrem Zimbalist, in his native Russia a student of Leopold Auer and acquainted with Rimsky Korsakov, came to Curtis in 1928. Three years later he headed the violin department, and later rose to director, a tenure longer than any in the Institute's history, from 1941 to 1968.

In an outer office, Chaim noticed the double take by a receptionist. Seeing his reaction to hers, she quickly explained what seemed the remarkable resemblance to their director as a younger man. When the supposed twin was ushered into his office, Zimbalist exuded a professional and all business air. If he glimpsed anything of himself in Arbajtman's face, he gave no indication.

The audition began with Mozart's Violin Concerto No.5. Despite inevitable nervousness, it went smoothly, over almost before it started. Unlike a more typical scenario with some period of waiting, he received immediate acceptance into the world-renowned musician's studio. After hearing, "You'll begin next week," Chaim blinked twice to reassure himself of a bona fide waking state. "I felt I was on top of the world, but I am not the type to shout my joy. I was serious. All through the war years, I was thinking, 'If I survive, if I make it, I have to go study with Zimbalist.'"

Of course, formalities and procedures applied before starting classes mid-term on February 1. A chest x-ray showed a spot on his left lung. Doctors speculated about tuberculosis. Arbajtman pocketed a bunch of dispensed TB pills. His intuition, that camp exposures or infections had left lungs scarred from battles fought and won, proved correct when chest films in later years came back showing no active process. Some might call this surprising, since he had started smoking cigarettes, then switched to and stuck with cigars in the latter half of the 1950s. Maybe strong defenses explained his nearly perfect radiograph.

"Zimbalist was a non-stop smoker. He used to come into his studio with big cigars, but they were the least expensive ones. During the day, nickel cigars, and I understood he smoked expensive brands only in the evening. I couldn't see him because the windows were not open and the door was closed. You couldn't complain or cough. After you left, you coughed," his former student commented in jest.

Efrem Zimbalist had no peer or competition for bowing technique. "My teacher had the best bow arm in the world. He could play an entire étude, down or up, in a single bow."

During the next four-and-a-half years, Chaim would study at Curtis, alternating lessons with Zimbalist and his assistant teacher. Known as a pedagogue, the director "spoke very good German with me." Unlike his first emotion-filled encounter in Warsaw as an audience member with a performer, now student and teacher related on an intellectual plane.

"I was very happy to be part of Curtis. I realized right away that I was going to learn so much from other students. It was a great environment."

Other important lessons in these early days at school boiled down to economics and language skills. A Jewish voice student from the Bronx, Saralee Liss (later Avery), spoke Yiddish and treated him at restaurants. "She was a singer and had a gorgeous, beautiful voice. At five o'clock we would go out in a group of six. I was happy to join them. I would tell her in Yiddish and she would order in English."

A classmate from Mexico, José Kahan, spoke English and Yiddish. He befriended Arbajtman and helped him with translation work. This included homework and exam materials. Chaim memorized answers, and would retain for more than sixty-five years the workbook with prompts by Kahan that enabled him to pass an early exam with high marks!

Chaim initially spoke little English. To every statement and query, his accented response sounded closer to German, "'Tank you.' I wanted to speak better and decided to go to University of

Pennsylvania for night classes." One evening, the group of all ages learned only a couple of words. "'It will take ten years!'" He took just two classes of formal language study, then promptly quit. He found their curriculum not just excruciatingly slow paced, but also of little practical utility. "I studied with the radio. I got a book, learned the alphabet, and started reading."

His roommate, Anthony "Tony" di Bonaventura, found any verbal faux pas amusing. "He used to go crazy laughing, completely hysterical with some of the words I would come up with. Speaking of Beethoven's 'Turd' Symphony, Tony said nothing. I asked, 'Why don't you correct me?' 'Oh, you are terrific, keep it up, you speak great.' He had fun at my expense." Tony and Chaim roomed together for three years. Di Bonaventura, a talented pianist, studied under the well-known Madame Izabella Vengerova, who also taught Sergei Prokofiev and Leonard Bernstein.

"After maybe a couple of weeks at Curtis, my first girlfriend that I met was a black girl. And she became very famous." Chaim met this exceptional female pianist, Natalie Henderson, when she studied at the Philadelphia Conservatory. She came from Ohio, studying first at Oberlin and later at Juilliard.

"I was trying to save up some money to invite Natalie to dinner. There was a nice, inexpensive restaurant in the neighborhood. We planned to meet for dinner at seven o'clock. I came about ten minutes to seven. There were three rooms, and they seated me in one that was empty. I sat until eight o'clock. Natalie didn't appear, so I went home. Later I called to see what happened. Natalie had come two minutes after I did and they gave her a different room. She stayed until after eight and went home. She was there at the same time I was! They didn't believe that the white and black would have dinner together, so they segregated us. Those were different times."

"This killed me. I couldn't understand, I just couldn't. As a kid, at primary school in Poland, seeing African kids in pictures or paintings, always I would ask questions. 'People exist, looking like this, black?'" Just the innocent curiosity of a European youngster, but after coming to America, "I found out the problem here. I started grieving over the situation, that whites didn't like the blacks. I was absolutely shocked."

Though others seemed to shun Natalie, "I took her to a student recital. The General Manager of Curtis Institute reacted, 'Last night you came with a negro girl.' I said, 'Yes.' He said, 'It's not good for you to bring a negro girl to Curtis again. You may not be able to become a citizen.' This was wrong, but I didn't know about racism in 1950."

Chaim and Natalie had grown close to one another. He found her skin particularly attractive, like when he encountered the tank crewman who liberated him in Germany. "She was twenty-two. We used to go with her friends, mixed black and white, but never spoke about color. I was totally blind to it. If she was black, green, orange, it was the same to me. In my mind, she was gorgeous and talented." Mutually tight budgets crimped their dating and the frequency diminished over time. "I stopped seeing Natalie regularly."

Two years later, the American State Department "picked up Natalie, and they were sending her all over the world. A terrific speaker, she was very bright and played beautifully." She changed her name to a more exotic Natalie Hinderas, signing as the first black television correspondent and personality at NBC. "Her name was around all the time, on Broadway and the big screen." Eventually, she performed under Eugene Ormandy's baton in 1971, the first black artist to play with a nationally ranked orchestra. "On their Walk of Fame at the Academy of Music, they have Eugene Ormandy, Rudolf Serkin, and Natalie Hinderas. She kept good company," he remarked with a twinkle in his eye. After her marriage to someone else, Chaim remained friends and socialized with both Natalie and her husband.

"When I started Curtis, there was a Jewish Family Service to help the sick and poor in Philadelphia. An anonymous man in Detroit deposited a sum with the center to help me. I received a small amount on a regular basis that lasted my years at school."

At the service center, Chaim had a weekly appointment for financial support and general counselling. "The first few months at Curtis, the money amounted to fourteen dollars a week (they raised it after six months to nineteen dollars a week). Even in those days — for sheet music, to rehair the bow, buy strings, to eat — fourteen dollars wasn't enough for everything. Sometimes you skipped a couple of meals during the day and had a bigger meal at night."

"I would get my check, going to the center, every Friday at 2:00 p.m. A social worker would grill me in German for three hours, and I got dizzy." Sessions ended at five o'clock when she went home and Arbajtman was unhappily forced to dodge cars while crossing streets during rush hour traffic. "I was a fighter."

"This counselor was about forty-five years old. I learned that the husband left her. She was divorced with two little babies. She herself was miserable and somehow thought she could help me. She started telling me that I must find a job to make some money. 'We will deduct from your fourteen dollars.' This made me very unhappy. She tried to tell me how to live and didn't want to keep giving me the full weekly amount. Nearly nothing, still fourteen dollars was fourteen dollars."

More motivated by a pressing need for adequate cash flow than any social worker's canned advice, he landed a couple of odd jobs. "I was bussing the dirty dishes in a cheap diner. There were customers that I knew who sat down, never paid a tip, never even acknowledged me."

"Horrible, they gave me a dollar a day and I could eat for one dollar," no real gain. "I smelled the butter, the grease under my nails and on my shirt. Nothing got rid of the odor. It stuck in your mind. I asked the owner, 'If I don't eat any diner food on the job for three days, can I order one expensive item off the menu?' He said, 'Yes.'"

Time away from music studies and chapped hands from so much dishwashing impeded progress. He returned to the Jewish Center on Friday at 2:00 p.m., telling the social worker, "'I'm making six dollars a week at the diner, so you can deduct six dollars. You don't understand one important thing. I have problems, and I know that fact much better than anyone. Among my problems, the biggest is that you think you can help and teach me. No one here is equipped for my kind of problem. The only thing to make things better would be to give me my check without any more counseling.'"

This last comment went over badly. "She lost control, got up from her chair, and yelled at me. I said, 'I am the client. I can scream. You make a note, but shouldn't scream. I need to see someone else.'" Thereafter, in the woman's place, he had weekly guidance appointments with the center's director.

Chaim proposed to him a potentially exciting way to obtain financial reward with his violin that would be much more appealing than cleaning diner tables. "'There is a competition on a good radio station. Winning first prize, the award is three concerts. They pay cash, and I know I can win. I am going to compete and intend to win first prize.' I was secure about trying my best." On leaving, he saw doubt on the faces of staff.

"I was sincere, but told myself an obvious truth: On a given day you could be great and not win. Even Bernstein once told me he auditioned in a competition for piano and lost. He auditioned in composing and lost. He auditioned as conductor and lost. And then he became the great genius, Leonard Bernstein." Arbajtman steeled himself.

"In under three weeks, I went for the audition, competed, and received first prize." Despite appearing overly confident or self-deceived to staff members, back at the Jewish Family Center he felt vindicated. Chaim explained himself to them, "I believed I could win the first prize, or I wouldn't have proposed this. The problem was you believed less in me, and I was not going to agree. The way I thought, 'I can do it.'"

Back at Curtis with a little more cash in his pocket, "I never complained. I never asked them for anything. Then Zimbalist's secretary calls me in and said, 'From now on, every month you will receive twenty-five dollars.' 'Why should I get twenty-five dollars I never asked for?' So, I went to Zimbalist. Though I needed it desperately, I said, 'Mrs. Lytle told me I was going to get twenty-five dollars. I never asked for it and would prefer not to accept.' Zimbalist raised his voice for emphasis. 'You will accept it or I will dismiss you from school.' So, I accepted."

Instruction by Curtis instructors proved solid. For composition, Arbajtman had Professor Andre Constant Vauclain. The final exam consisted of composing eight bars with the teacher watching. Chaim felt unfettered by conscience. Hardly a matter to alter his artistry on violin or impact future employment options, he proceeded to modify Hatikva. As it is said, "Talent borrows, genius steals." Fortunately, the national anthem of newborn Israel didn't ring any familiar bells, and he received an A+.

In contrast to his easy time in the composition course, "There were certain passages that I couldn't perfect. It bothered me and kept me up at night." He felt more determined. "One evening, I took out the violin and it came by itself, without trying. It was the easiest thing and I realized how wrong my thinking had been. I didn't use my brain in the right way, but you learned better for the next time."

"When I got into Curtis, technically I played right, but something was very wrong. I didn't play the violin, I was crying in my music. Not realizing it, I expressed a painful past through the violin." Professors gave him their critiques. "I was made aware by some of my teachers that you cannot do this. You cannot play concerts and fill them with pain."

Still far from graduation, and with no steady playing job yet, he reached out to a local branch of his family. Three of his father's male cousins had immigrated to the U.S. "Finally finding their number, when I was at Curtis, I contacted one in Philadelphia. I used to go to Friday night dinner with them." As recorded in ancient Hebrew, "Do not despise these small beginnings," the young man had "nuzzled" with members of his own fold; nonetheless, only music would continue to fill voids left by lost parents and siblings.

Student concerts occurred weekly. Mrs. Ingrid Bohlen, Swedish and tall in her mid-sixties, had a custom of attending. At the conclusion of Chaim's concert about five months from the start of his studies, she approached him wearing an elegant dress. In her British-accented English she asked whether her pronunciation of his name sounded correct. "'Mr. Arbajtman, listening to your music, I feel I know you. Would you consider coming to my house to dine?'" Not yet catching every word in English, he understood her generous and timely offer. "Not having enough money, many days missing meals, I would have had dinner with a maintenance worker."

Chaim replied simply, "'I would love to,'" then continued to listen and gleaned that she felt fondness for the intelligence and talent of Jewish people. Mrs. Bohlen also disclosed that her deceased husband had harbored anti-Semitic views. Francis Bohlen, law professor at the University of Pennsylvania, had lived with her at their imposing mansion in the suburbs, complete with chauffeur. Professor Bohlen's first cousin, Krupp von Bohlen, owned companies that manufactured everything from coffee makers to bullets.

Industries of the same famous German family manufactured Hitler's armaments. Krupp Works, twelve years before World War II, took out "government insurance" in case of a conflict with America. The U.S. respected this agreement and did not destroy family factories in Hanover. "That's exactly what happened. I was in Hanover after World War II ended. The only thing that stood in Hanover, Krupp factories."

Chaim visited Ingrid Bohlen regularly at her apartment near Rittenhouse Square, usually finding two filet mignons for him to cook, and drinks for them to share. Viewed in retrospect, being very modest, she claimed to come from peasant stock. "She was like a queen. Her son John was a big, distinguished lawyer."

As Arbajtman later described, "She loved me dearly, despite my starting discussions with 'You are wrong.' After I finished my objections, she looked up with this aristocratic air about her, 'My dear heart, how silly of me. Of course, you are right.' Her words made me feel good. Truthfully, she was polite and smart, realizing there was no reason to argue with someone so strong-willed. To realize this truth took me twenty years."

A younger female came into Chaim's life about this time. "I had a girlfriend from Canada who went to Curtis, Diane MacDonald. I was crazy about her. She rented a room and lived with this family in the suburbs. The streetcar and buses didn't run that far, so I would walk her home late at night. I remember it was May or June, and before she went in, we would sit on the steps outside her house. We talked all night long, until the sun came up, then I would leave. Though we had talked the whole time, going home, I didn't remember a single word."

"This was a special quality of life. We were young and in love. Already light, when parting I said, 'Good morning.' Summers she went home to Newfoundland. She wrote me every day, except Sunday. Every day I would get a letter. I would read the letter several times. I was so happy."

Meadowmount Institute of Music in upstate New York provided an escape from the heat in the summer of 1950. "At Curtis Institute, age twenty-two, twenty-three, I had no regular lessons through the summer. I asked my teacher if I could attend camp to study with Galamian. He said, 'Absolutely.' So that summer I studied with this world-famous teacher."

"Galamian came in for my first lesson. Sitting down with his violin, he spoke in a thick Russian accent. The first thing he said to me, 'There are three types of vibrato.' Demonstrating, 'There is slow vibrato, also medium and fast vibrato.' He also changed my bow arm technique to his way. Never before in my life did I have discomfort with my right arm. After one week or ten days, I had severe pain."

"I went for another lesson with Mr. Galamian. I said, 'Professor, I must be doing something wrong, because I have pain when I play.' He said, 'You should work through it.' I didn't buy that. I was doing something wrong and this was why I had pain." After leaving Meadowmount and resuming his own way of playing, "My pain stopped. To this day, it hasn't returned. If you have discomfort, you are doing something wrong."

Finally, the long summer of 1950 came to an end. Diane MacDonald came back and Arbajtman made plans to see her. "I saved up change to take her to Chinatown. First thing she said as we sat down, 'My mother doesn't want me to marry a Jew.' I said, 'Couldn't you have waited 'til after the dinner?' And that was the end. So, three weeks later she called me, she wanted to start again. I said, 'You didn't want to marry a Jew.'" Chaim always tried not to repeat the same mistake.

In August, at Curtis, Arbajtman got to know cellist Ron Leonard and his future wife, violinist Norma Auzin. He also first ran into clarinet student Don Montanaro in September of the same year. Don and his future wife, harpist Margarita Csonka, both became long-term close confidants. With them, Chaim formed personal and professional relationships that would last decades.

Roommate di Bonaventura began dating Franklin Delano Roosevelt's granddaughter, Sara Delano Roosevelt, during Chaim's second year in school. The couple invited him on an outing for four. Tony and Sara paired him with her good friend Diana. "Saturday night they wanted me to join them. She was bringing me a blind date, a good friend of hers, who also went to Bryn Mawr. She was Harry Hopkins' daughter." Hopkins played pivotal roles in Roosevelt's WPA and Lend-Lease programs, serving as envoy to Churchill and Stalin. "I couldn't speak English, and here I was dating Harry Hopkins' daughter! It was incredible. This is America. There is no other country like this that has ever existed. I love this country almost as much as I love my life."

"After nine months in this country, I became more comfortable with English. The students were nice. They tried to help, all morning asking, 'How are you?'" If his responses came across as persistently glum, it had nothing to do with them. "I had to lighten the load of mistrust I was carrying. It took a few years. I don't remember exactly what or how, but I changed. To that point, humanity had shown me some of the worst things in life. At a young age, the liars and killers had tried to take everything from me. Then, I met wonderful people. Because I could trust them, a burden was taken off my chest."

Perhaps the greatest impact on Chaim of all the faculty came from French oboist Marcel Tabuteau, who conducted the chamber orchestra. Having tried growing a little beard at age seventeen, Tabuteau had claimed to be twenty-four, and auditioned for New York's Metropolitan Opera under Arturo Toscanini. The conductor asked him, "'Where are you from?' 'I am from Belgique,' because Italians tended to dislike the French. Everybody loved Belgium, they were no threat to anyone." Tabuteau roomed with the great harpist Carlos Salzedo, also from France. Toscanini, short and skinny, intimidated the musicians. He gave Salzedo and Tabuteau all kinds of grief. They confronted Toscanini about his seemingly unfair treatment, "'We are among the best in this orchestra, and yet you often pick on us. Why?'" He responded, "'With you two, there is hope.'" Bemusedly, Arbajtman could imagine from these two a final request of the conductor, that he keep picking on them.

Tabuteau had disciplined himself as a student with remarkable exercises. For example, he practiced breathing at different distances from a candle. "He would make a diminuendo with the candle light, not to blow it out, to control and make crescendo. This is very difficult. If you try doing this, it's almost impossible. He mastered it."

Spurred by Maestro Toscanini's high expectations, the oboist attained an exceptional quality of musicianship, which he subsequently both modeled and demanded of his own students. Marcel Tabuteau understood every instrument and "could teach an elephant to play." He maintained discipline in the class, especially during rehearsals.

Michael Tree served as concertmaster for a particular program in the Curtis student orchestra, with Chaim sitting next to him. Tabuteau had his pupils rehearse Schubert's Fifth Symphony twice a week for six months. Sometimes he directed focus on just two measures the entire rehearsal. "'If you understand these two measures, you understand a lot, but you don't understand yet.'"

Michael Tree described his string colleague and new friend Arbajtman as "getting his feet wet in the language." Tree used to tell him stories. One time at rehearsal, he whispered a joke and made Chaim laugh. Those days, once started, he could not stop laughing, ending in tears. "I was shaking, laughing," says Arbajtman.

The professor immediately halted the slow movement and angrily pointed, "'Stop, get up!'" "Never looking at you, but through you," Arbajtman and the student behind him, John Pintavalle, found themselves equally uncertain who had caused Tabuteau's displeasure. Neither moved. Tabuteau demanded, "'Get up, I say get up.'" Both stood. "'No, not you,'" he snapped. Both sat. "The whole thing broke us up like comedy hour, everybody was hysterical." Their teacher, now even more incensed, moved forward and shouted, "'Get up!'" He grabbed Chaim's collar and directed him from the building to an outside street. This effectively blocked further participation in class rehearsals.

Though Michael Tree had instigated the trouble, he and Arbajtman traded compliments, "It was one of those times you get stuck with somebody" and "I'm lucky I got stuck." They celebrated their friendship at midnight on 46th Street and Market with a thirty cent, humongous five-foot hoagie that took an hour to consume and wash down with beer. Chaim added, "We used to go to the concerts. On one occasion, we arrived a little late and only front seats were available. We sat together, started laughing and couldn't control ourselves. We were thrown out because we made noise. We had fun in life!"

Five or six weeks later, Tabuteau encountered his expelled pupil on the street after a Friday afternoon concert. The orchestra instructor approached Arbajtman. In a strong French accent he said, "You are very talented. Come back to rehearsals tomorrow." Chaim promptly did so. His temporary absence from rehearsals went unnoticed.

Moving from practice to performance after a few months, he showed pleasure when they played well. "He turned around to the audience, his body language meant 'Pretty good, huh?'"

Contrariwise, he scolded them during concerts for any single bad measure. Indisputably, Tabuteau "was a character."

"An organist, singers, they all would come to listen. When Tabuteau was conducting, we couldn't get a seat; everyone came." He promised his students, "'Right now you don't, but if you are lucky, maybe thirty years from now you will finally understand what I am saying.' This was his 'gift' to us that would arrive much later." The most intellectual of the professors, Arbajtman studied with him four-and-a-half years at Curtis.

Outside school, Tabuteau played first oboe in the Philadelphia Orchestra. He influenced every oboist in the country. "He said to all of us, 'If a time comes in your musical life when you are satisfied with your playing, that is the end of you.'"

A small gang of perhaps seven Curtis students chummed around together. They stood out as particularly dedicated and strong. In this group, Michael Tree and Arnold Steinhardt prominently took part. "We had a lot of fun, tried to work together and took it seriously. And we played well and were proud to play."

"We played for big names before anybody knew who they were. We played for Ben Gurion. We played for Golda Meir before she became *the* Golda Meir."

Heading into his first fall in the U.S., Arbajtman remained cash poor, depending on weekly visits to the Jewish family service center. "To give you an idea, if it came to be cold and you needed a scarf, you went to the community special desk. For people like me, they would not give you money," rather, a voucher. "They would know, let's say, Macy's had a sale on hats. It was two dollars and sixty-six cents for a hat. So, they gave me a two dollar and sixty-six cent voucher and I went to Macy's. Among the bunch of hats there, I found one that fit me, but it was two dollars and sixty-two cents. So, I said to the clerk, 'keep the four cents.' 'No, we cannot do that.' You had to start over and get another voucher for two dollars and sixty-two cents. So, I returned, taking another day."

"I went back to Macy's, but the hat was gone. And the hat price went up to two dollars and sixty-four cents, but I had the two more pennies to give them. 'No, we cannot do that.' I am telling you what really happened. A few pennies difference, but it had to be exact. I went the whole winter without a hat, every day running back and forth to check."

Several of Chaim's group excelled at eating capacity and gravitated towards $1.50 dinners. With such exceptional appetites that could bankrupt a restaurant, they found themselves barred from some "all you can eat" buffets. Operating on tight budgets, they might walk to Chinatown for savings on bus fare.

Chaim expanded his social circle to include some individuals who had little knowledge of other ethnic groups, even leaning towards outright prejudice. "Lloyd Oostenbrug, a wonderfully talented singer from Iowa, was tall and blond. The reason we became friends was that we spoke German together. As a singer, he had to take foreign languages. He told me, 'I never saw a Jew before I came to Curtis.' We became very good friends." Coming from the environment of rank intolerance undeniably pervasive in those days, this midwesterner would go on to discard a number of preconceived negative images. In Arbajtman's view, "You had to go through this garbage," baseless bias passed from one generation to the next, "but that was part of living free."

Chaim's new acquaintance would gain more understanding from their exchanges, the former object of intolerance beyond belief ardently advocated tolerance. Previously confined to a series of concentration camps without creature comforts, he loved to freely expand his chest and draw in the air of a city that birthed the American constitution and spawned liberty.

Sharing with his new student singer friend, he said, "You don't even know what a real anti-Semite is. I know what that is. I was in seven Nazi detention facilities. They put millions in gas chambers. This is the definition of an anti-Semite. You are not putting me anywhere and you wouldn't want to do this to me. You are a friend of Jews." Aiming to raise consciousness on this subject, Arbajtman employed gallows humor and satire to raise eyebrows and open eyes. Also, he tried to open doors for his friend Lloyd (actual birth name Lothar). Chaim introduced him to Samuel Rudofker. "Sam was crazy about opera. He was such a fan that he got his own opera house. Not the house, he got the company. It lasted for some years. Because of Sam, Lloyd was singing in Sam's opera."

"Sam was such a fantastic human being; fabulous. He helped so many people. Lloyd had a wife and little baby girl. One day we went out to lunch. A few hours later, Sam called. He wanted me to ride a few blocks with him in the new car he bought for Lloyd's wife. Sam was so happy to give it."

"Through another friend at Curtis, I met a Polish Jew who had immigrated. His name was Joe. Humongous and tall, he couldn't read or write. In the black neighborhood where he lived and had his butcher shop, the most important people came to see Joe, including the mayor, governor, and judges. He was a mastermind in helping people. Joe the enforcer never killed, but he may have ordered somebody."

"I used to go occasionally to Joe's for dinner. 'Spend summer with us. You can move into my house.' Curtis was closed, so I spent the summer with him, his wife, and two daughters. I had steak every day. I stayed there July and August, in '51 and '52."

"He befriended the chief of police of Philadelphia. He used to have dinner parties with important people every Friday night. We ate well and he always wanted you to listen to his never ending stories."

Later, "Joe invited me to a movie in the middle of the day. We sat only ten minutes before he fell asleep. A short two minutes later, he awakened and asked, 'You saw the beginning?' I said, 'Yes, but I didn't understand it.' He said, 'Still, do you have an idea of how it will end?' 'Maybe.' 'Good, let's go.'" The natural question was why did Joe buy theater tickets and leave after just a brief nap? "It was August, ninety-five degrees. He took out a gun in the middle of the street. I didn't know I was going to a movie with a loaded gun! The only white man in the neighborhood, he carried around a loaded gun that could have killed me."

"One day while staying with Joe for the summer, he said, 'Today is Shabas, I am going to deliver some gefilte fish, some challah.' There were eighteen or twenty Jews in prison, and Joe was interested in visiting them. Horrible words, I wouldn't repeat what they used to call him. He said, 'They don't deserve it, but they are Jews. They should have gefilte fish and challah on Shabas. He asked, 'Wanna come with me?' 'Yes.' So, he took me into the Eastern State Penitentiary." This facility had housed Al Capone and Willie Sutton previously.

"Jewish prisoners liked the things Joe brought when he visited." Going with "Joe, all the doors opened freely to get in, a cinch. For a prisoner to get out you had to use five different keys; a long process. I met a short, quiet fellow in his cell. He must have been fifty-five. The guard locks us in and I started to feel a little squeamish. This was not a good situation. He said to my strong and tall friend, 'Get me out of here.'"

The prisoner started to verbally abuse Joe. "He said, 'You promised to get me out of this shit house.' He said, 'You think it's so easy for an asshole like you to get out?' Before, Joe talked like a diplomat. Now he talked angrily. Joe was six foot five. The other was a little shrimp, five foot two, and he started screaming. Joe looks at him, 'You son of a bitch! If you don't shut up, this fist goes right through your brain!' Then I thought, 'I am living with Joe. What could he do to my brain?'"

"Finally, we left. I asked, 'What did this guy do to be here?' 'He killed five people.' I said, 'What do you mean, he killed five people?' He took out insurance on them, then killed them one by one. He was smart enough to collect insurance. After nine months, the government found out and took away his passport. They were afraid he would leave the country and they couldn't catch him.' So, he was there for life." Did the brief return to prison unsettle Chaim? "No, most of the people seemed normal. It was very deceiving."

"Joe wanted my attention all the time. He told me at night what he did the whole day. I didn't want to listen to all this, and finally left for good."

Back at school in the fall, each Wednesday Mary Louise Curtis Bok served tea and coffee for students around 4:00 p.m. In an open room off the main entrance, she hosted the traditional event, both elegant and well attended, as the school's patron. She founded the school in 1924 as the Curtis Institute of Music, to honor her father. A successful businessman, Cyrus Curtis owned the Curtis Publishing Company that printed the *Ladies Home Journal* and *Saturday Evening Post*. His daughter had a love for the school and its students, but left day-to-day management to department heads. Director Zimbalist would see her on official business a mere handful of occasions each year.

Arbajtman spoke further of his teacher. "Around 1910, he was the first western violinist to go to Japan, and they loved him. He was a powerhouse in Japan because he was the first one to make an international career of sorts, welcomed by the kings and queens. Heifetz and Zimbalist became the closest of friends. In 1920, Heifetz would go to Europe and play recitals. He would take Zimbalist as his accompanist. He was just as good on the piano as on the violin. All of the greats could play piano very well and they were also composers. They were true musicians." David Oistrakh compared him to Heifetz, saying, "While Heifetz conquered by sheer brilliance, Zimbalist captivated people by appealing to profound mysteries of heart and soul."

After coming to the U.S., Zimbalist had first married the Romanian soprano, Alma Feinsohn Gluc. Both became American citizens and assimilated well into their new culture. "Nobody could understand or imagine the prejudice. At the height of their careers they converted to Christianity."

"He didn't teach Beethoven Concerto to anybody. Very few ever played the Brahms Concerto with him. It was strange, these two concertos you learned after you left. At the end of a lesson, he would ask me, 'What would you like to bring next week?' 'I would like to bring the Debussy Sonata.' 'Good.' Vladimir Sokoloff came to accompany this time. I played from beginning to end. I wasn't sure what to do with the sonata. Zimbalist told me, 'I never heard this piece before. It's not a bad piece.' This must have been '51."

After his first wife's death in 1938, Zimbalist became romantically linked to Mrs. Curtis Bok. He joked about the rumors, saying he didn't know how he would adjust to seeing her more than twice a year. They married in 1943. She left a twelve-million-dollar endowment for Curtis.

Another Curtis friend, nineteen-year-old viola student Al Brown, approached friend Chaim about learning Yiddish. "We became very close friends. I said, 'Why do you want to speak Yiddish?' 'I want to be one of the boys.' He had a fantastic ear and I taught him Yiddish. We went to real kosher delis with the Jews. He was as black as it comes, and we would drive them nuts with his good Yiddish accent. In the deli we picked up stuff from the counter. We sat at a big table with benches, across from two Jews. They just started to eat, and Al

Brown says to me, 'Chaim, give me a glass of such and such.' In the 1950s, you never saw a young black man with a young white guy. This was something strange, hearing a black man speaking very good Yiddish. They were very startled, left the food and took off fast!"

As part of the music degree qualifications, Arbajtman's school required one year of viola for violin students. "After being at Curtis for one-and-a-half years, I went for my first lesson on viola. The instructor gave me her whole spiel for half an hour, to explain the differences." Without further clues or any previous guidance, playing the instrument came naturally.

Arbajtman performed in the Curtis orchestra. He played viola so well that he attracted the attention of fellow students and an impressed Zimbalist. His mentor offered the possibility of a double major in violin and viola, but this held no appeal for the young string player. He unhesitatingly rejected the proposal. He preferred to maintain his focus on the instrument which first caught his attention in youth, on outings with his father to the barber shop. The violin kept him alive during the horrors of World War II. With undivided devotion and loyalty, he continued his violin studies. No other sound could compare.

Between lessons, Zimbalist frequented Day's Delicatessen, a block or so from school. Arbajtman noticed he would slip in around 4:00 p.m., a less busy hour than lunch or dinner, to avoid crowds. He frequently purchased items that included gefilte fish and matzah ball soup. The teacher, seated against the wall, seemed unhappy for the student to spot him while on break.

Late night jaunts proved memorable in school for Arbajtman, especially with Curtis piano student Joseph "José" Kahan Pintel. "I had a good friend from Mexico, like a brother to me, he spoke perfect Yiddish. At 11:30 p.m. we would talk and walk eighteen blocks each way for a thirty-cent hoagie so large you didn't eat again for days. Not the nicest of neighborhoods, nobody thought anything in those days. Today I wouldn't go there in the middle of a sunny day."

Some other evening in a Chinese restaurant, "Winter time, and you could eat a lot for little money. Dinner for the two of us was three dollars and seventy-five cents. My friend said, 'You pay. I'll pay you back.' 'Actually, I was going to say the same thing to you.'" Neither classmate had adequate cash to cover what they owed, barely enough for one to take a bus home. "We decided who was going to go get money in the winter and the snow. It was eight o'clock. We flipped a coin." José was the "unlucky one" tasked to go for funds to cover their bill.

"I stayed at the restaurant. It took an hour-and-a-half. The restaurant closed at ten o'clock. They wanted to close, but nobody said anything. Finally, José found some friend who bailed us out, to pay the money." After the pianist returned, they settled accounts and left the second-floor establishment. "When we went out, I found a five dollar bill on the street." Not quite the hero with two zlotys before Sabbath in Warsaw, he enthusiastically suggested, "José, let's take a taxi home." Hard times, but "Those were the most beautiful days."

Artistic expression and economic realities required mixing, of necessity, especially as enhanced by a dash of providence. Around spring of 1952, with other students, "I got a job to play at a Protestant church. Then I thought to myself, 'They must not know I'm Jewish; otherwise, they would have chosen another violinist.' So, I went back to the church. 'You must have made a mistake. It's Easter Sunday and I'm a Jew.' He started laughing and said, 'We want you.' I played, got paid, and was happy."

"Pinching coins," an Israeli pianist in Chaim's building needed one more penny for the bus fare of fifteen cents to avoid a walk of eighteen or twenty blocks. "He called me and I said, 'I have a penny and I'll give it to you, but first try what I do. When I need change, I look by the sewers. Usually you can find a penny, and sometimes a dime. If I don't hear from you, I'll know you found a penny.' He found his penny."

"I never heard the words a 'big sound' or a 'small sound,' until I came to the United States. All I heard was a beautiful sound and an ugly sound. I went to Curtis and they started talking about a small sound. I asked 'What does it mean, a small sound?' I wasn't competing with a trombone. To me, if I could hear you play, it was not a small sound."

Some adhered to a school of playing that was all about "scratching and scrubbing. Something was lost playing very fast, loud, not missing a note. The sound was so big, you could hear it five miles away at City Hall. Beauty and greatness in music were forgotten."

The second-floor apartment where Arbajtman stayed, at 408 22nd Street, had no air conditioning. The heat took a long time to dissipate. "It was 90% humidity, horrendous. Nobody could breathe. We sat outside on the steps to cool off after two o'clock in the morning." Sometimes he would seek relief at a movie house. "Not the safest neighborhood at three in the morning, but for thirty-five cents one could sit through three films and enjoy the cool atmosphere."

Scrambling for extra money, "I worked as a parking attendant for summer concerts. I directed cars to a big lot. Parking was actually free, but the way the operation started, some enterprising guy told drivers, 'Pay me.'" The operation grew and he couldn't manage everything by himself. "Then the big shot decided, 'I will hire small shots, give them five dollars a week.' I was hired to help. After a few nights, the big shot came around and took all the collected quarters from us guys. I thought, 'Wait a minute. How about two quarters for him, one quarter for me?' So, I made another inside pocket and set aside maybe six, nine dollars a night. This was a fortune. Still, he got two times as much money. I thought maybe I was the only clever one. Actually, other attendants made three times more than I did, putting it in several secret pockets. Parking was legally free, but I was afraid of this mafioso. He gave us a roll of tickets that didn't mean anything and, in the end, they threw away the tickets."

"When vacation came along, all the other students went home. Where did I go? Nowhere, and I don't say this for anyone to feel sorry for me. I hope for humanity, and all the people I care about, never to be alone. The tragedy was, since age thirteen, I grew up and lived much of my life alone. So, for me being alone was not a disaster. A time with no money, I had to clean tables at the cheap diner and park cars. But, what did all this have to do with violin?"

Chaim had begun to verbalize an unfolding revelation that he would eloquently express in decades to come; violin as salve to the emotions. There remained other areas of vital need. "You just played and felt well? No, life didn't work this way, because it wasn't only the heart. It was the mysterious brain."

As regards internal healing, "I knew I needed a psychiatrist." On the invitation of a friend, he went to that person's nearby apartment for presentations of mental health topics. "There were five psychiatrists who came, professors at the university. They would discuss cases. I was an interested observer," not participating with those seated around a table, and who actively engaged in conversation until four in the morning.

After a few months, like English lessons previously tried, Arbajtman concluded these joint sessions would not ever serve his personal needs. "They invited me whenever new psychiatrists came. I needed one, agreed, but never returned. If I had a problem, I had to fix it. I didn't want anybody else to touch my brain."

"After the war, for years I was killed every night in my nightmares. Somebody beat me, shot me, drowned me, killed me one way or another. I knew that going this way I would be totally destroyed. I needed help, but that meant I had to surrender. I was too proud to tell these things that I didn't want anybody to know, even a psychiatrist. One said, 'We need eight months for you to lie on the couch for treatment. You will understand yourself better.' I decided I could help myself. I would heal quicker and better than if someone else helped me."

"Nobody knew how I felt, or of the bad dreams. I recognized keeping things to myself was a lack of trust, but when you seek to understand an important problem, sometimes there is no end of searching, no quick answer. I never searched. I admitted to myself that I had a problem. Did I want to live the way I felt then? No. If not, what was I going to do? I had to change my thinking. It took a long time."

"How did I do it? I didn't know how or have a plan. There was no guarantee, but change came little by little. In turmoil, I improvised, using instinct rather than conscious intellect."

"When I went to school I had a smile. Everybody thought I was the happiest kid. I didn't want to burden even my close friends. They were my problems, not theirs. When I went home, it was a whole night of tears. I was liberated, but brought with me all kinds of remaining issues from the camp."

"Not out loud, I talked to myself. I had to solve the problem, reasoning within, mentally changing my way of believing. It was a very slow process. I had to self-analyze. After many weeks and months, I changed one thing: acceptance of what I was given in life. I repeatedly told myself to be calm," along with other encouragements. "It took just seconds to say all this, but it took years to do."

In classic formulations, humans have a tripartite nature with body, soul, and spirit. The soul may be further divided into mind, will, and emotions. Chaim's emotions had long suffered from the raw wounds of losing his entire family at a young age, and resultant hatred for their murderers. He had a deep-seated mistrust of others. His will always held steady, the point fixed by the parental pronouncement "You are a virtuoso," buttressed by the core declaration he would study violin under Zimbalist. Regarding the mind, since facing a firing squad at Budzyn, he had felt in some sense protectively numb or dead. Now, through what we might now call "self-talk" he knitted back together the rift between thoughts and feelings. Reminiscent of his father's tailoring of striped garments into perfect alignment, the son now brought together broken pieces of his own heart.

"During almost seven years, every night I was like a tortured, scared child. I got to a point I understood much more about life, much more about myself. Finally, I didn't dream of horrors. I slept like a baby."

Having overcome his own dark past, did he ever see the recovery of a Nazi, freed from evil thoughts and deeds, now truly possessed of moral scruples? "Personally, I never saw it, but I would say that it's possible. I will not say 'no,' just because I never had the privilege to see this. It doesn't mean it couldn't happen. If I said 'no,' I would have locked the door for good."

He still wanted to open communication with long lost family. To his father's sister in South America, "I found the address and I wrote them when I came here. I explained who I was. Would she have a picture of my family? So, she sent me a picture and letter." The note plainly stated their harsh economic limitations, unchanged after leaving Europe. Arbajtman didn't want to burden anyone and hadn't asked for money. "Since that letter in '53, I never bothered writing again." Chaim would, however, subsequently travel to Argentina and call on them in person.

Stymied in overtures to his own relatives, Arbajtman sought new local connections. A daughter of New York Police Commissioner Arthur Wallender caught his interest. "What happened, she was the close friend of my friend's girlfriend. My young British friend told me about her and asked, 'Would you like to go on a blind date?' He went with his girlfriend and I with her. She was an Amazon of a woman, young at twenty-one, at least six feet tall. We got on the subway and held onto the handle. When she said something, I looked up and my neck started to hurt" from the obtuse viewing angle. Exaggerating in jest, "I got a little nervous, knowing her father was in charge of police in the tough city of New York. I had to behave myself." She later visited Chaim.

Anthony di Bonaventura and Sara Delano Roosevelt had fallen deeply in love. Arbajtman learned of their now obvious courtship. "Sara used to call me 'Papa,' not Chaim. It came about after Tony and I went to see this movie. In the story about an Italian family, all the younger people called an older movie character Papa. Since that time my roommate called me Papa. Everybody called me Papa." Seeing his folks and dating Sara, Tony continued to commute to New York on weekends.

Between Arbajtman's third and fourth years at Curtis, he moved to new living arrangements at 2028 Chestnut Street. Tony and Sara had decided to get married. The groom sensitively explained that a Catholic wedding dictated a Catholic for best man. His long-time roommate gave reassurances that he understood.

Di Bonaventura came from immigrant stock, the "son of an Italian barber who came to the country, still shaving" customers in a rundown New York neighborhood. Anthony's parents invited Chaim to the pre-marriage dinner reception. "A Rolls Royce sat there. The street was blocked off, as the New York Times reported on their front page. They had tents for extra guests. Sara was incredible. She used to do lots of charity work for people in need, donating substantial sums. She changed her name to anonymously teach in a black school in Harlem. Her step-father's family, the Whitneys, never permitted any magazine coverage or photographs. They were a special breed of people, giving everything, but not wanting anything printed."

Another classmate, composition student Luigi Zaninelli, stood with the wedding party in June of 1953. Becoming what we now call a power couple, Anthony and Sara would later climb into the chauffeured limousine of Arthur Miller and Marilyn Monroe when they went out to dinner with them.

After marriage, Sara di Bonaventura sometimes invited Chaim for the weekend at her mother and stepfather's place outside of New York City. "This little Jew from the Warsaw Ghetto was invited to the Whitney estate." Sara's mother Betsey had divorced James Roosevelt and married John Hay Whitney. They lived in Manhasset on Long Island. The "Greentree" estate consisted of 900 acres, 125 staff members, a 110-room mansion, 40 bathrooms, an indoor tennis court with 250 seats, indoor and outdoor Olympic-sized pools, as well as a theater where Alfred Hitchcock privately prescreened his work.

"Jock" Whitney, romantically linked to Tallulah Bankhead, Joan Bennet, Paulette Goddard, and Joan Crawford, palled around with Fred Astaire, and hosted the party when Clark Gable and Carole Lombard met. Whitney's support helped ensure Eisenhower's presidential bid, and Ike tapped him as his ambassador to Great Britain. All this prompted Chaim to ask Tony, "Does even a President of the U.S. live here? No president could afford this."

Once, "The guy who owned the New York Herald Tribune was there with Whitney. They were talking about how he was going to sell the paper. 'Have you made arrangements?' 'No.' 'I would like to buy it. We'll give you two million dollars.'" Arbajtman smiled, "How incredible! I wouldn't know how to write two million dollars. I would have to ask, 'How many zeros?'"

"Protocol was followed on the grounds in a most aristocratic way. No pictures were allowed at the mansion where I spent many weekends. The first visit, I didn't know how to use the toilet. I'd never seen so many buttons. Tony said, 'Don't touch anything.' There was an ashtray in the bedroom. I used to smoke cigarettes in those days and there were ashtrays everywhere. You could smoke anywhere. I put down a little ash and went out of the room. I came back and the ash was gone. I had never seen anything like it. Everything had legs. I never saw anybody."

"The next morning, I had breakfast with Mrs. John Whitney. Such elegance, she wouldn't let me be at breakfast by myself. At that time, I hadn't changed my name from Chaim. She understood and she practiced. She made sure not to offend me in any way. It was unbelievable to be invited. I met so many important people and was always treated well."

"Mrs. Whitney was first married to President Roosevelt's son, James. She hailed from Boston. Her father was the most famous brain surgeon in those days, Dr. Harvey Cushing. Her sister Barbara married the president of ABC, William S. Paley. A famous man, I met him at one of these parties. They had in the main room twelve of the most unbelievable paintings." After Mr. Whitney's death, his widow sold one Renoir for seventy-eight million dollars.

"I am very fortunate to have met great human beings. And I mean that in every sense of the word. They taught me, not by saying 'Look, you made a mistake doing this.' The greatest way of teaching is by example. A pair of special people never told me that I was wrong. They showed me. There were two ladies who returned me to sanity, Tante in Geneva, and Ingrid Bohlen in Philadelphia."

Four-and-a-half years at Curtis passed quickly. His fourth year in school literally flew. Mid-year, Chaim felt inspired to pass along a token from his great fortune in life. "From my Swiss Tante I used to get beautiful boxes of chocolates filled with liquors. I got one around Christmas time, 1953. I gave this box to Mrs. Curtis Bok. I received a beautiful letter, thanking me." He put her letter among his keepsakes.

The year 1954 began, and his time at Curtis was drawing to a close. One of his last recitals took place on March 3, at 5:15 p.m. For the second half of the program, Beethoven's Piano Trio in E flat Major brought together José Kahan, Chaim Arbeitman, and Ronald Leonard.

Later, "Zimbalist called and wanted to talk. After I finished my last lesson," the two spoke. Always addressed formally, never Chaim, "'Mr. Arbajtman, can you tell me what plans you have?'" Chaim began considering an orchestra position, now that he had successfully come through the country's premier music institute. Celebration with his class drew near.

"The internationally famous singer, Anna Moffo, was a close friend of mine. She went to Curtis with me for four years." Anna invited Chaim to work with her on organizing student outings. "We were on some committees together. A close friend, she used to come to the apartment I shared with Tony di Bonaventura. She was also Italian. She would sit on a chair, nobody near her, the religious Catholic. She was gorgeous and had a golden voice."

"Anna Moffo and I played a joint graduation recital," Thursday afternoon, April 29, at 5:15 p.m. They provided their jointly printed program to family and guests. "Anna was a wonderful girl who went on to sing in all the big opera houses of the world. She became famous," adding wryly, "I became infamous."

Music had filled most of his waking consciousness since coming to America. Though he did not take up Zimbalist on his offer of a double major, the professor would later have some very positive things to say about Chaim's musicianship. Graduation from Curtis Institute of Music in 1954, a milestone and great triumph, marked the door that would open to a series of excellent career opportunities.

"I have such a love for this country. It's phenomenal. I had no money and couldn't speak a word of English, but I was welcomed and had the fortune of meeting many kind and wonderful people."

David Arben (born Chaim Arbajtman) and his family, only this image survived. Left to right: cousin Shlomo, brother Israel, David "Chaim," father Abraham, sister Zysla, and mother Chaya, seated in Warsaw's Ogród Krasińskich park, circa 1931.

Chaim and his family attended Nożyk Synagogue, the only Jewish house of prayer in Warsaw to survive World War II. Picture from 1909 (used with permission: Jewish Community of Warsaw).

Abraham behind his two sons: Israel, Chaim, and nephew Shlomo, right.

A scene at Janiszów labor camp where Chaim worked on building a dam, as portrayed on embroidery and fabric by eyewitness Esther Nisenthal Krinitz (used with permission: Arts & Remembrance).

At the last moment, "camp elder" Noah Stockman saved a teenaged Chaim from death by firing squad in Budzyn concentration camp, 1944

Flossenbürg concentration camp entrance, Appellplatz, and Chaim's barrack #19 on the right.

Flossenbürg concentration camp entry log #14088 with Chaim Arbeitman's birthdate recorded in error (as August 15, 1927).

Arbeitman's initial screening at Flossenbürg concentration camp occurred in this isolation barrack.

At Flossenbürg, Chaim worked on manufacturing Messerschmitt airplane wings in a nearby facility.

Chaim played his recently "acquired" violin at Schwandorf a week or so after liberation in April, 1945.

Chaim and Joe, the "shoe thief," with friends after liberation.

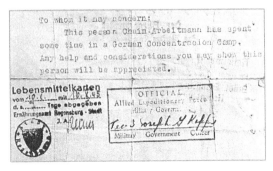

American Expeditionary Force credential for displaced ex-concentration camp detainee, Chaim Arbeitmann, issued in Regensburg, Germany, on August 16, 1945.

144

Montik, dem 10. V. 1948 13 a zejger in Lager Feldafing

Montik, dem 10. V. 1948 20 a zejger in Lager Landsberg

LEONARD BERNSTEIN

tret ojf far der Szeerit Hapleitah mit dem

Reprezentanc Orkester fun der Szeerit Hapleitah

un kinstler fun der Szeerit Hapleitah :

FOLKSZINGERIN H. DURMASZKIN ╱ TENOR M. GOLDSZTEIN

FIDLER CH. ARBEITMAN

PROGRAM

1. Ouverture fun der oper „Freischütz"   Carl Maria von Weber
2. Menuet un Farandol fun Suite L'Arlesienne . . . . . G. Bizet
   Reprezentanc Orkester unter lejtung fun Gast-Dirigent *Leonard Bernstein*
3. Sonate G-Moll . . . . Tartini *Ch. Arbeitman*
4. „Jeruszolaim" . . . . . Erec-Jisroel Lid
   Ch. Dormaszkin
5. „Kalanijot" . . . . Erec-Jisroel Lid
6. Arje fun der oper „Rigoletto" . G. Verdi
   M. Goldsztein
7. Arje fun der oper „Tosca" . . G. Puccini
8. „Rapsody in Blue" . . . . . G. Gershwin *Leonard Bernstein*

Der Gast-Dirigent akompanirt ale solistn

Leonard Bernstein in concert on May 10, 1948 with "Ch. Arbeitman,"
a member of the Ex-Concentration Camp Orchestra.

Beloved Swiss family at table in their Geneva apartment.
Left to right: Tante, daughter, and Onkel.

Chaim entertaining his "angel," Tante
in Sannemöser (near Gstaad).

Tante and Chaim stand
beside Lake Geneva.

Tante's daughter with Chaim at the wheel of Onkel's Peugeot, 1949.

Chaim immigrated to the U.S. wearing Onkel's gifted winter coat with secret pockets for hidden valuables, sewn and filled by Tante for his trip, November - December, 1949.

To whom it may concern:

I find Chaim Arbeitmann an extraordinary talent who deserves every possible encouragement and aid. It is my hope that he may be enabled one day to succeed as an artist and as a person, following his unbelievably difficult beginning. He deserves the best.

Respectfully yours,

Leonard Bernstein

Letter of recommendation for Chaim Arbeitman by Leonard Bernstein, January, 1950.

Mrs. Efrem Zimbalist
THE RAFTERS
NEW HARTFORD, CONN.

30 December 1953

Dear Marie —

We brought your wonderful chocolates with us, for we are spending the holidays here — I never tasted the equal in chocolate, of these you sent us. Bitro — We are all enjoying them greatly; and we send you warm thanks for your kind thought to give us such pleasure —

A Happy New Year to you!

Cordially yours
Mary Curtis Zimbalist

Thank you letter from Mrs. Efrem Zimbalist.

THE CURTIS INSTITUTE OF MUSIC

CURTIS HALL — THIRTIETH SEASON — 1953-54

RECITAL OF CHAMBER MUSIC BY
Students of Miss Tuttle

Wednesday Afternoon, March 3, 1954 at 5:15 o'clock

PROGRAM

I

Trio in E flat major, Op. 40........JOHANNES BRAHMS

Andante
Scherzo: Allegro
Adagio mesto
Allegro con brio

MARION ZARZECZNA, Piano
BARBARA SORLIEN, Violin
MARJORY BLACK, Horn

II

Trio in E flat major, Op. 1, No. 1
LUDWIG van BEETHOVEN

Allegro
Adagio cantabile
Scherzo: Allegro assai
Finale: Presto

JOSÉ KAHAN, Piano
CHAIM ARBEITMAN, Violin
RONALD LEONARD, Violoncello

STEINWAY PIANO

Curtis Institute of Music recital, March 3, 1954.

Curtis Institute of Music graduating class of 1954.
Chaim standing second row from the bottom, second from right.

Chaim in cap and gown with Ingrid Bohlen, on occasion
of his graduation from Curtis Institute of Music.

Only surviving European relatives.
Left to right: David, cousin Wolf Tuchmann, and wife Karola.

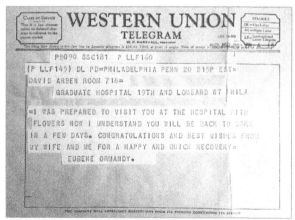

Telegram from a concerned Eugene Ormandy.

Arben's American solo debut with Cleveland Orchestra, March 23, 1958.

March 12, 1964, Centennial Celebration of Philadelphia Musical Academy, featuring Henryk Szeryng and Gary Graffman, with the Academie String Quartet (David Arben, Eugene Kash, Karen Tuttle, and Samuel Mayes). This photo sat prominently on a music stand next to Arben's grand piano in his Spruce Street apartment.

Henryk Szeryng and David Arben, 1977.

Arben performed the Mendelssohn Violin Concerto with the
Philadelphia Orchestra, William Smith conducting, December, 1979.

David embracing godson, great-grandson of Tante.

In Sarasota, Florida, David with Tante's second granddaughter, whom he affectionately called his Swiss "baby."

David returned to Warsaw in 1997 and recited Kaddish
in memory of his family at Nożyk Synagogue
(used with permission: Jewish Community of Warsaw).

Music in May, 2012, Santa Cruz, California, following the world premiere of Haim, by Polina Nazaykinskaya, a piece inspired by the life of David Arben. Left to right: Amy Yang, Carolyn Corbett, Jose Gonzalez Granero, Konstantin Soukhovetski, Polina Nazaykinskaya, David Arben, Rebecca Jackson, Ani Kalayjian, Alexandra Leem, and Dmitri Pogorelov (Photo: Scot Goodman).

Jack Terry and David Arben in 2013.

Philadelphia Orchestra friends for life, enjoying their decades-long tradition of dining in Philadelphia's Chinatown. Left to right: Larry Grika, Luis Biava, David Arben, Don Montanaro, and Jerome Wigler.

In Philadelphia, harpist Margarita Montanaro, David, and Sharon Kahan, daughter of his Curtis classmate.

*David with violin case and signature cigar beside the stairs to his
Philadelphia apartment building at 1517 Spruce Street.*

*In April 2017, friends gathered here to bid their final farewell
at Cape May, New Jersey.*

10
Detroit and Cleveland Orchestras

"Music is incredible, the most powerful thing in the world, more powerful than any bomb."

While yet at Curtis, Chaim met Mischa Mischakoff, concertmaster of the Detroit Symphony, who is widely considered one of the greatest concertmasters of the twentieth century. "You name the country, he had been concertmaster. He came on the same boat with Jascha Heifetz to the U.S. They were friends in Russia. I met him when he was invited to be a soloist with the chamber orchestra at Curtis."

"He came up to me during a break, 'What's your name?' 'Chaim.' 'You play very well.'" Initially startled by these words, Arbajtman listened intently to the offer that followed. "He said, 'If you want a job in the Detroit Symphony, here is my telephone. Call me. Come after you graduate.' 'I graduate in May.' 'The orchestra doesn't play in the summertime and I will be gone until September. Register with the union. I want you to be in my string quartet.' This was an honor, so I went to Detroit and thought I had the job."

When Mischakoff returned to town, "I called him. He said, 'Chaim, there is no opening.' My heart sank. I didn't have any money to eat, even live. I borrowed money and paid twenty-five dollars a month rent for one little room in a lousy neighborhood. It was a nightmare. I didn't know what would come next, but still I felt optimistic." He first rented at 661 Brainard in Detroit, later moving to 6603 Majestic.

"Mischakoff said, 'Our conductor isn't here, but will come in just a few days. I spoke to the conductor and he wants to hear you play. I will take you to his apartment.' He was a Frenchman, Paul Paray. The second week of the season I went to play for him. There was no opening, but the conductor had an idea."

"While I was there with Mischakoff, the conductor called the president of the orchestra board who was also president of one of the Ford company divisions and a major donor. Paray said with an accent, 'There is a very talented young man.'" He wanted to create another seat for Arbajtman. "The president was not going to overrule the conductor. So, I started playing the second week. I played about half of the season. I was last violin in the second violin section."

A wintry Monday evening in February of 1955, Mischa told Chaim to come to his home, a large place in the suburbs of Detroit. Violinist great, Jascha Heifetz also came on invitation that night, having just arrived in town for a Tuesday recital at the Masonic Auditorium. Fifty chairs, guests, photographers, reporters, and unexpected command performance for those assembled, all came as a complete surprise to their guest of honor. After dinner, Mischakoff motioned Arbajtman towards the home's library, there introducing him to Heifetz who had little to say by this point. At evening's end, already 1:30 a.m., someone needed to drive him with his pianist and a recording company executive to the downtown Sheraton Hotel. An anxious principal cellist volunteered his car. Chaim's friend Paul Olefsky who trained at Curtis with Piatigorsky, without any arm twisting, convinced Arbajtman to accompany him.

Increasingly uncomfortable silence reigned in the cabin, compounded by fear spreading from front seat to back, none willing to risk annoying a violin legend. Maybe twenty minutes into the ride, Paul gathered courage and blandly asked Heifetz whether he had seen Piatigorsky. "'Yes.'" After twenty more minutes of nearly unbearable stillness, Olefsky dared a follow-up question. "'Did you see him recently?' 'This morning, at the airport in D.C.'" That concluded the repartee, with icy conditions causing their vehicle to occasionally fishtail this way and that. Arbajtman and Olefsky felt incredibly relieved to safely drop off their intimidating passenger and two companions. Though 3:00 a.m., having survived a nerve-racking encounter, they searched until finding one bar open and ordered drinks to unwind.

On February 21, Abajtman played a recital at the Detroit Institute of Arts. Reviewer Dorian Hyshka at the *Detroit Free Press* called him "an accomplished technician with a tender, sweet tone… at his best in the Adagio movement of Bruch's Concerto in G Minor."

The Detroit Symphony Orchestra traveled to Chicago. Chaim stayed at Hilton Hotel on Michigan Avenue. "For people without much money it was very expensive." The time seemed propitious to again contact his father's cousin Jack. "I met them on my own terms, after I had a job." He called and the cousin's wife answered. "They met me at the hall. It was a Sunday afternoon concert. They asked, 'Where are you staying?' 'Hilton.' They didn't believe it and wanted to see."

"I took them up to my room. She saw two beds and asked, 'Who's sleeping in the other bed?' I joked with her, 'You can sleep in the other bed.' They thought I was hiding a woman there. You could not explain or convince them you were doing right. Finally I said, 'She is busy now.' They didn't ask any more. The wife of my cousin went to the bed to see if the mattress was good. It was so funny. These things were priceless."

"They lived exactly as they did before immigrating, fifty years ago. To me, it was beautiful because there was feeling, emotion, heart, caring. You could think it unimportant, but to me this was wonderful. There was nothing so beautiful as innocence. They had never stayed in a hotel, as far as I could tell. I remember she liked the room, 'a wonderful mattress.' Right away my stock went up," he laughed. "It took me five years to get approval, but I finally did. This was success, having a good bed."

"I did very well in Detroit, but for the symphony's next season, they wanted to rehire me with the same salary." Arbajtman made an appointment with the orchestra manager and named his figure. "I said, 'I need fifteen dollars a week more.' They said, 'No.' They offered me five dollars more. I said, 'No, fifteen.' 'Too high and impossible.'" Another of Chaim's tenets: if management fails to agree to a well-deserved figure, one must part ways. "By then I had decided to leave, and auditioned with Cleveland." They gave him the job, so he resigned from Detroit.

"After I became a citizen, I used to go to Europe. I always went on a ship. I had very little money. My salary for the year, when in Detroit, was $1,900. You could live, but barely. To fly to Europe in those days was $750. To take a boat was $400 round trip. Plane travel was an expensive luxury at that time. I chose the ship with a long ten-day passage because I saved on hotel expenses." And with an infectious smile, he added, "I didn't have to pay for food, so I ate everything."

By early 1955, after five years in the U.S., Arbajtman had attained naturalized citizenship. Years prior in Switzerland, his adoptive family could never treat him to lunch or dinner in nearby France.

How gratifying to have a passport and the freedom to cross borders at will! He had kept up with Tante, her husband, and daughter. "We were big writers, exchanging about two letters every week. The moment I got my passport I went back." The first overseas trip by ship, the SS *Flandres*, landed in June 1955. He preferred French lines because of the excellent cuisine. From port, he took a train directly to Paris where the daughter met him.

"From Le Havre to Paris, it took three hours by train, to see my Swiss relative." Tante's daughter "was a beautiful young girl. We spent a few fantastic days together. They continued on to Geneva, staying with her parents."

"They were happy to see me. I had the passport and wanted them to see it. Theirs was my home before I came to the United States. They were, in essence, my real family. We went to a place they had in the mountains. It was wonderful." They went together up to the Salève, off-limits to him in 1949.

Thinking back to when they first met him, "If you can think of the most ill-mannered person, I was worse than that. My 'war' in life began again after I was liberated. I was wild not only to myself, but to everybody around me."

His Swiss family couldn't believe how much he had changed. "I was a different human being. They said they never knew how one individual, not recognizable in any sense from before, could change so." Chaim thought his Swiss family should not feel so surprised. He couldn't have healed completely and durably without their unconditional love.

While staying in Switzerland, besides basking in the affection of his Geneva family, he considered an unanticipated option, should time allow before his new orchestra job. Germany had concluded six months of negotiations with Israel in September, 1952. The Federal Republic agreed to pay a reparations sum of three billion marks over fourteen years, starting in April 1953, to the Jewish State, on behalf of victims with no surviving family. Payments also started going to individuals who remained alive after torture in concentration camps. "If I would go back to Germany, I was entitled to a check, some kind of restitution." Authorities required the filing of legal papers to receive a small, but hugely symbolic payment by annual installment.

"In the late forties, while studying in Geneva, I had met friends. They were much older. A Polish Jew, a very famous lawyer and professor of law, his books are still studied in Warsaw. He managed to escape to Switzerland. I told him about the reparations. He gave me some advice. 'You need a lawyer. I have a friend who is an Israeli, with offices in Tel Aviv, London, and Frankfurt. You can talk to him by phone or go in person to Frankfurt.' I said to this brain, his name was Miecyslaw Warm, 'I cannot have Jews represent me against Germans.' Older by forty years, he looked at me and asked, 'Whom would you hire?' I said, 'I have to have a Nazi representing me. Germans will not think he lies.' He asked me, 'How are you going to find such a lawyer?' 'All I have to do is open the yellow pages under Attorneys. They're all Nazis.'" In fact, Arbajtman had preliminarily filled out initial paperwork pursuant to a compensation claim on October 17, 1949.

Leaving Geneva, he headed to Germany. He very much wanted to reunite with his beloved cousins and then could look for a local attorney. At Prager Strasse 8, "I stayed in Munich with Wolf and Karola. The law office, ideally, had to be close to where I stayed. I found a Nazi lawyer. The whole process took about two years." The violinist had hired a German lawyer who submitted the proper forms. Waiting had just begun.

"Whenever I went to Munich, I would go to his main office. I remember his huge room and a long bench. Up to ten people could sit there at a time. On the far end was a short German, a feather in his Bavarian hat. All of them sitting nearby were Germans. We all waited until the lawyer would scream a name. I was not going to respond like others when he came and called out like an animal. I didn't jump up right away, hearing 'ARBEITMAN' in his ugly growling voice. I stood up slowly and screamed back, 'ARBEITMAN IS NOT HERE. MR. ARBEITMAN IS.' To everybody else in the country I was Arbeitman. To him, I was Mr. Arbeitman." Germans transliterated the Polish spelling of Arbajtman to Arbeitman.

Before Chaim left Germany, late summer of 1955, Heinz Crucius invited him to play with his Resort Orchestra in Bad Wiessee. A reviewer wrote, "Mendelssohn's beloved only Violin Concerto was emotionally performed by Arbeitman from Philadelphia with effortless mastery to soaring effect. After the thrilling final movement of the charming and sparklingly boisterous Allegretto-Allegro vivace the amiable artist was showered with seemingly endless applause."

This same itinerary — summer in Europe, a stay in Switzerland and visit to Germany to see his cousins — became a travel ritual each year. Chaim took the French Lines' SS *Flandres*, their first new ocean liner after World War II which sailed the Atlantic 1952 to 1967, on more than one summer getaway to Europe. After a long and storied history, even serving as inspiration for the Love Boat television series, this ship would end up making a call in San Juan, Puerto Rico, each Saturday until ending her career in 1992. Coincidentally, the violinist from Philadelphia would soon establish a pattern of staying near his old ship's last harbor each of more than fifty winters.

The next position, already secured in Cleveland, lasted four years, from 1955 to 1959. "Everybody was nice and cordial. I started rehearsing on a Monday. I was sixth chair."

Brand new in the organization, for a period of months Arbajtman carefully considered his options to earn better pay, not wanting to precipitate some unnecessary crisis. Chaim knew the orchestra's management held the reins of power. "Speak fewer words, but meaningful words. If they won't give me more, then I will have to leave. It took a lot of thinking." No immediate action required or taken, he bided his time.

Later the same season, "Conductor George Szell, concertmaster Josef Gingold, and I met. I got nervous, not knowing why they wanted to meet." Szell and Gingold, believing he had a promising future, encouraged him to change his name. "They were right. Nobody knew how to say my name. At Curtis they butchered it, calling me 'Chain,' because they had never heard of Chaim."

After graduating and leaving Philadelphia, he missed seeing a particularly close confidant, Mrs. Bohlen. When the Cleveland Orchestra took time off, Arbajtman went to visit Bohlen and consulted her about dropping Arbeitman, his official patronym with Germanicized spelling since leaving Europe. Agreeing with Szell and Gingold, "Mrs. Bohlen also said I should change. 'Let me work on the family name.' She wanted to keep part of my name, spelled out the first letters A-r-b-e and added n, Arben. Shorter and easier, clever! My father's father was David, and I loved Grandpa David." David in place of Chaim, he changed his professional name to David Arben.

"We were paid about eighty dollars a week. They would renew our contracts on March 15." In the spring of 1956, Arben contacted Szell, whom he addressed not as Maestro, but rather as Dr. Szell, per Gingold's recommendation. David brought up his insufficient compensation. The conductor advised him to exercise patience. Undeterred, "March 1st I called on orchestra manager, Mr. Beverly Barksdale. 'I came here today to talk to you about my pay. I didn't come to bargain.'" David then continued with an approach that would serve as his trademark in future negotiations. "'I am not going to ask for the amount I truly deserve. But I will not accept less than a figure I am going to tell you.'" When Arben specified how much, Barksdale replied, "'That we cannot do.'"

David started to exit, confident that his musicianship deserved what he requested. The manager quickly stopped him. "We started negotiating." Indeed, Arben prevailed when Beverly verbally accepted his requested figure. Days passed. "On the afternoon of March 15, I called on Barksdale. He said, 'We need a few more days.'"

"About a week later we were on tour, and while overnight in Columbus, Ohio, Beverly Barksdale calls me into his hotel room. He said, 'You want twenty dollars more per week for the thirty week season. That's six hundred dollars. We want to give it to you, but we have to justify this and can give you ten dollars extra a week. For the remainder, would you consider playing a concerto with the Cleveland Orchestra?' I would have given them the six hundred for that," he recalled with a smile.

The balance of their season, he developed a fast and durable friendship with associate concertmaster, Anshel Brusilow. They both had attended Curtis Institute of Music and studied with Efrem Zimbalist. Former students in the trenches under a famous professor, they would remain comrades-in-arms for life. During breaks at Cleveland, they dominated the game of hi-low poker.

Nearly summer, Arben's thoughts settled again on Switzerland. "They were all happy that I did so well, managing to get into a top orchestra, but Tante was ailing." He returned to Europe in the summer of 1956 on a French ship, likely once again in the Flandres, departing from New York. "When I first got on the boat, a man on staff arranged that I would not dine by myself. There were others alone, so he put three women and two men around one table. Nobody knew anybody. We became friends. There was a young 30-year-old Arab. From Alexandria, he was an educated man. The three females included a very nice girl from Connecticut."

"The girls got off at Le Havre before the Arab guy." One of the ladies from Arben's table kept in touch by letter for a period after the voyage. "She lived in New York and I was in Cleveland. I met with her once or twice when the orchestra was on tour in New York."

The Arab from Alexandria and the Jew from Poland went ashore in France together. They traveled by train to Paris. To save money, they rented a room together. For two days they went out to eat and enjoyed the city sights.

The new hotel roommate proved "respectful, he knew I was a Jew. He spoke several languages and was working for the United Nations. He was an elegant, good looking man, and civilized. But that first night I kept one eye open and didn't sleep. He turned out to be a nice man and we kept in touch for a time."

In fall of 1956, the next season started. Initially a section first violinist, unbeknownst to Chaim who transitioned to David, behind the scenes Brusilow had personally recommended him to Szell for a solo performance. Less than twelve months after coming to Cleveland, management had approached Arben, broached the subject, and offered him a solo debut opportunity. Following these negotiations, for the first time in Cleveland Orchestra's history, they permitted section players to perform solos. Prospects appeared bright to David, veritably walking on air. Of course, he had already shared his good fortune with Swiss family members.

Early in the first month of 1957, Josef Gingold invited Arben to lunch. Per usual, "I called him 'Mr. Gingold.' He said, 'My name is Joe and, if you like, call me Josel,' a Jewish phrase." Gingold expressed his belief that David had talent that the world needed to hear. "'You should give more concerts in Cleveland.'" The young violinist appreciated the encouragement but asked, "'How can I do this with no money to rent an auditorium? I don't have the money to hire a pianist, to print the programs.'" He responded, "'I will do everything. All you have to do is play.'"

Gingold volunteered his help, procuring the concert hall and a pianist. "Before I arrived at the hall, he went to my room and left a package of food with a note in Yiddish, 'Eat in good health.' I still have the note some place."

"Gingold, in every way, I remember nothing but the best. He was an incredible man. He was a prince of a player, an excellent teacher, a big-hearted person."

The event took place January 28, 1957, at the Cleveland Music School Settlement. Not known to David, George Szell attended. After the recital, Gingold and Szell came backstage. At the sight of the maestro, "My heart started pounding. It's a good thing I didn't know he was in the audience." All the efforts helped advance his career and forged long friendships.

After the performance, *Cleveland News* critic Ethel Boros wrote about his American premiere of Bernard Reichel's Sonata as "quite absorbing, with real conviction, in fluid, graceful style... He plays with such facility that the violin seems to be a part of him." Handel's Sonata No. 6 in E Major, Brahms' G Major Sonata, and Bruch's Violin Concerto No. 1 rounded out the program. She quoted fellow orchestra members as calling David Arben a "violinist's violinist," "a real talent."

Arben always remained in close touch with his Swiss family. During the performing season, he kept up with regular letters and phone calls. Before the recently concluded recital, they shared his joy over the imminent performance opportunity. A source of concern, the health of his beloved Tante had entered into decline. Diabetes, a goiter and heart trouble added to her difficulties. "I found out these details years later. She had always attended to the needs of family and others, leaving herself to last."

Eventually, complications of her poorly controlled diabetes prompted hospitalization that January. Compromised circulation in a leg, quite severe and end-stage, dictated amputation. Before going to the operating room, she exacted a promise from her daughter. She knew of their Chaim's preparation for a recital within the week in Cleveland. "'If something happens to me in surgery, don't tell him until after his performance.' She tried so hard to do the right thing." She didn't want to break his concentration with any bad news about herself. On January 23, Tante died perioperatively, at age fifty-five, and an obedient daughter honored her wishes.

She called in seven days, after the important musical event. Tante's adopted son responded with violent emotion. "I was angry, really angry. I was deprived of something that meant so much to me. 'Why didn't you call me when she was sick? How could you keep it secret from me? I loved her like my own mother.' 'Chaim, she loved you like a son. She always tried her best to protect you and your talent. I wanted to call you, but she made me promise to wait. Please understand.'"

He found it unacceptable, never having the chance to drop everything and rush to her bedside. After all, Tante had ministered to him selflessly each night for thirteen long months. "She was like Mother Teresa. She gave to everybody, of any religion. I became more of a human being after knowing her." The sense of unfairness compounded his grief, which lasted a long time.

One example of the quality of Tante and her concern for him already cited, "She called on the chief rabbi in Geneva. 'I want to prepare kosher food for a young Jewish boy from Poland.' I lived a very rich life through the dignity of her whole family."

As soon as practical after Tante's death, he returned to his family in the Alps. Coincidentally, Cleveland Orchestra embarked on their first European tour in May 1957. During this trip Arben reunited with the Swiss daughter. They would resume playing together. Music always helped healing, in this instance to re-equilibrate the emotions of loss and profound sadness.

The Orchestra had boarded two planes. Their itinerary included England, France, Portugal, Spain, Belgium, Netherlands, Switzerland, Austria, Germany, and Poland. Arben contemplated a return to his native land, but the U.S. State Department dissuaded him from going, due to concerns that he might be detained. "'You are an American citizen, but the Polish government has the right to detain you,' because of the laws at that time. Once born in Poland, you were always a Pole, according to them. 'If they want to keep you, there is nothing the U.S. can do. So, we suggest you stay out of Poland.'"

After the first stop, Antwerp, their route took them to Brussels, Belgium. They then flew to Bremen, Germany, next to London, England. They arrived shortly after noon, had a brief rehearsal at 6:00 p.m., then the Royal Festival Hall concert at 8:00 p.m.

"Afterward, there was a dinner, then a beautiful reception in the ballroom." U.S. Ambassador Whitney — stepfather of wife to Curtis classmate, Anthony di Bonaventura, appointed by President Eisenhower in 1956 and serving from 1957 through 1961 at the same diplomatic post as his grandfather — hosted the musicians. "They gave a fantastic party for the whole orchestra."

"There was a man in uniform who announced your name upon entering. 'Mr. and Mrs. Ambassador, George Szell and his wife.' I was next in line. Mrs. Whitney saw me and said, 'Join us, Tony and Sara are here.' I sat at the Whitney table, the sole orchestra member in this private room and table for only eight people."

"The most important world magazines were snapping pictures. Nobody knew who I was. George Szell and his wife kept looking at me, David from the Warsaw Ghetto."

"Near midnight when the festivities ended, Tony and his wife invited me to see the residence of Mr. Whitney. We went out, finding two chauffeurs in uniform. One car was a stretch Cadillac like I never saw before, one a stretch Rolls Royce. Tony, my ex-roommate, asked 'Which one would you like?' I felt like I was dreaming. Little Chaim would never would have believed all this in a million years."

From London, the tour took the Cleveland Orchestra to Barcelona, Madrid, Lisbon, Porto, Bordeaux, Berlin, Stuttgart, and Basel. One very special experience stands out from this trip. With George Szell conducting, the Cleveland Orchestra performed in June at Basel, Switzerland. As part of their program Rudolf Serkin played Beethoven's Emperor Concerto. Next came Beethoven's Pastorale Symphony, which launched what Arben later would repeatedly describe as the transcendent moment of a lifetime. In this Swiss city, on that stage, under Szell's direction, the music lofted them to a realm beyond the material. "Everybody started to shake. It happened to everyone playing in that concert."

At first, David and others thought they were coming down with a flu when they started trembling. "The music took over and everybody was speechless at this inexplicable occurrence. It was something out of this world. Our conductor said he had a dream for thirty-nine years of how that symphony should sound. And this was the night it materialized. He waited thirty-nine years. Music is just incredible, the most powerful thing in the world, more powerful than any bomb."

Their visionary performance had brought about something ethereal. Strange involuntary shaking of body and emotions closely resembled the ecstasy experienced by religious mystics.

The orchestra moved on to Lugano and Geneva. "Onkel was so excited when we came to Geneva. He got dressed up with his derby hat and looked like the handsomest man on Madison Avenue. I introduced him to George Szell."

Next came four cities in Poland during June. "It wasn't the right time for me to return. Instead, I went to Amsterdam. Gingold brought back a book on violinists, and wrote a little inscription to me in Polish."

Having started smoking cigarettes around 1955, Arben switched to cigars that summer of 1957. David never inhaled and considered Cubans too strong, preferring a Dutch brand, *Agio*.

After diverting to the Netherlands, David waited for his colleagues. On their arrival, he rejoined them and resumed performances together. "After we finished our concert at 10:30 the principal bass player, a very close friend Larry Angell and I walked the streets of Amsterdam all night long. Darkness until the sun came out, we saw a different world."

The Cleveland Orchestra finished their European tour. Before returning to the U.S., in August 1957, Arben traveled to Bad Wiessee, approximately 55 kilometers south of Munich, to perform Brahms' Violin Concerto with the Resort Orchestra directed by Heinz Crucius. "He conducted in the wrong time signature. We stopped and started nine times. Everybody was up in arms. This rehearsal was a total disaster. During break he called me to his room and said, 'I am inviting you the next three years to be soloist. No matter what happens in performance, don't stop.'"

A reviewer at the concert, Walter Keilberth with *Münchener Merkur* commented, "The soloist was able to thoroughly enthuse through his bowing technique (which one will not soon find again), a gentleness of tone which nonetheless carries and rings in even the most pianissimo passage, and, of course, his mastery of all technical difficulties. Arben's determination to obtain the most musicality possible from the work caused him to make unusually strong personalized changes, which however never strayed from the essential musical line."

During summertime, concerts at Bad Wiessee took place outdoors on their open stage. "At a performance two weeks before mine, another soloist continued playing even after bird droppings landed on his fingerboard. Eventually, he stopped, wiped it off and returned to the beginning of that movement. Can you imagine?"

Colleagues had warmly embraced Arben on the European tour. Back in the U.S., orchestra members invited him for meals. Arben perceived Cleveland as nice in general, populated by good Midwestern people. He loved his time there, living at 1932 East 97th. For a period, he shared apartment #211 with Ron Leonard, the cellist whom he knew from Curtis.

Through correspondence by letter, increasingly neglected in our own time, David still kept up with his friends. In late fall, Sara di Bonaventura sent their announcement, dated November 25. "Dearest Papa-Chaim-David, we have a beautiful 9 lb. 2 oz. boy! Tony's concert was an enormous success, good reviews, except they didn't like Rachmaninoff." The parents chose to name their son Peter John.

In a groundbreaking 1957-58 season, George Szell had selected orchestra members to play concertos: David Arben, Ronald Leonard (later principal cellist of the Los Angeles Philharmonic), and Daniel Harold Majeske (concertmaster of the Cleveland Orchestra, 1969-93). Incredibly, after just two years David had attained this elite and exclusive fraternity.

Szell attended a rehearsal for Arben's scheduled solo. Afterward the Maestro made his way to David as he walked off stage, to deliver a pronouncement on his impeccable musical taste. With this said, the conductor left.

"My American solo debut was playing Mendelssohn Violin Concerto with the Cleveland Orchestra in 1958." After his Sunday, March 23 performance, Ethel Boros with *Cleveland News* called Arben's playing "the essence of fine feeling, with a clear, firm intonation that had a delightful, creamy texture on the low notes." This imparted to the slow movement "not only the expected lyricism but an unexpected, graceful serenity."

That same month, with contract negotiations looming again, David approached the conductor. "'Dr. Szell, what I'm paid is not sufficient.' 'Mr. Arben, wait a few more years.'" David mulled over such a dissatisfying reaction while living in his second Cleveland residence at 2065 Cornell Road, Apartment 15. Perhaps hearing of Arben's disenchantment, his old Detroit concertmaster Mischa Mischakoff wrote from summer residence in the Chautauqua Symphony Orchestra of job openings with the New Orleans Philharmonic.

David had much to consider about his next step professionally, but took opportunity to balance work and social life. "On a Sunday I was invited to a party in Cleveland, and there she was." Arben immediately recognized the woman who, while on board in 1949, provided him food from *General Muir's* officers' kitchen. "What an unbelievable coincidence!" He surely had his share of small world stories.

During the regular season, word came from Switzerland. Tante's daughter had decided to marry. She wanted her beloved Chaim as best man. With playing duties Arben could only offer, "'My soul will be at your wedding.'" She would have none other as witness. According to David's schedule, he could only depart for Europe on a Monday after the weekend performances. He would immediately grab a plane and arrive by air without further delay. Accordingly, she switched her wedding date to Tuesday, July 1, 1958. This hardly pleased members of her family who worked during the week, but she refused to reconsider.

On arrival back at the bride's residence, most everything seemed ready. She wanted Arben to play an excerpt from the first movement of Bach's E Major Violin Sonata, accompanied by Pierre Segond, organist at St. Pierre's Cathedral. David had brought his violin, but no music with piano part. A handful of hours before walking down the aisle, Tante's daughter quickly drove her Ford Anglia to a violin teacher's nearby home to procure the full score. Then she picked up Segond who didn't drive. When they arrived at a small village named Vesenaz where her wedding would take place, the organist realized he had forgotten his music as well! This required another round trip to town.

Just one other crucial task remained unassigned that morning. With a nearly completed checklist in her mind, the bride drove to an American singer friend Irma's place, now time to dress and finish readying herself. Arben had ridden along and, when he heard that two key guests had no transportation, promptly moved behind the Anglia's wheel to fetch them. Jean-Pierre Larderaz, godson of Tante's daughter, appreciated a lift. Later, the betrothed couple would choose him as godfather to their second child. A parish priest who came from Onion, France, would perform the wedding ceremony and didn't drive. David had confidently volunteered for this chauffeur's job in a loaned car that required a manual shifting of gears. Arben felt sure he could handle it, having just received his license in the States, even though to that point he had only driven cars with automatic transmission.

With the two passengers on board, David never got out of first gear, not yet experienced using a clutch pedal. They lurched and lugged along, particularly up hills, barely faster than walking. The country friar, relatively unfamiliar with cars, could only say, "'These English cars are no good. We don't have the quality and smoother cars that you have in America.'" Arriving at Vésenaz's Catholic Church with no time to spare, their story turned a wedding party's anxiety into mirth.

That same summer, David's thoughts returned to his former teacher Ignatz Weisenberg, who still lived in Switzerland. "If he had wanted to come to Cleveland, I could have helped him get a job in the orchestra. I suggested, 'I can arrange a meeting with my conductor.' He agreed to it." The meeting took place in Salzburg, and Szell offered Weisenberg a job, but he couldn't accept, because his wife's ill-health precluded moving to America.

Having left Switzerland and Austria, Arben crossed into Germany to see his cousin Wolf in Munich. This also afforded him an opportunity to go to the attorney's office nearby to check on progress of his request for reparations. He was told little. Leaving their building, a legal secretary followed David to the street. With empathy, she divulged, "'My father was anti-Nazi and they put him in Dachau. Your money should be coming in ten days, but the attorney you have is going to take a lot first. If you can, fire him. Ask for the lawyer to write a letter that he no longer represents you. Then you will get all the money.'"

Soon thereafter, Arben reappeared in the office and announced his decision to settle accounts. "I said, 'I have been very patient, but my patience has run out. I am not happy and I feel I should be happy. You no longer represent me. I will pay you whatever work you put in, just give me a letter stating you no longer…' and he started screaming. In the end, he gave his secretary the letter and I gave him the money."

"I read it downstairs. I didn't know what, but something wasn't right. I read it three times. I finally saw it, no signature! Without it, the letter didn't mean anything. I went back and banged on his table. 'How dare you do this! I paid, you took my money, and no signature. Sign it.' And he did." Did David remain indignant? "I did not. I was selfish. Lasting anger would destroy my health, my wellbeing, my balance. This was part of hate. I liked myself too much to hate."

David wanted to thank the secretary for her honesty. "I took her for lunch and gave something additional in consideration of her kindness."

Before leaving Munich and environs, in the fall of 1958 David performed Beethoven's Violin Concerto with Heinz Crucius and the Resort Orchestra. Crucius invited him again as a soloist, as in 1955 and 1957. Once again, Walter Keilberth wrote a review: "We already know him from last year, when we heard him perform the Brahms Violin Concerto. The (positive) impression that he left behind at that time has been reinforced: in David Arben one has an artist who is alien to all artistic showiness, who just wants to step behind the work and only be its servant. In his playing he avoids every move into the virtuosic, as well as into purely violinistic effects, only to express the tremendous conception of the work and thus shows himself best as a musician who has been deeply inspired by Beethoven. We thank him for that."

After returning from Europe, David's concert schedule kept him moving. On September 25, 1958, he appeared at Mexico City's famous Palacio de Bellas Artes. There is a quote in the program for this recital from a June, 1949 *Voix de Genève* article, reading: "He is destined to have a great resonance in the music world. We have a young artist who plays in a fine and distinguished manner." He performed Handel's Sonata No. 6 in E Major, the Mexico premiere of Herbert Elwell's Variations for Violin and Piano, Brahms' Sonata No. 3, and Mendelssohn's Violin Concerto.

"Salomon Kahan came to a concert which I played. The South American equivalent of *Time Magazine* is called *Tiempo*. It reached readers from Mexico to Argentina. He wrote an article about me and it was published with big photos. The funny thing was, on the same page where I had a large picture, Casals had a tiny photo. Can you imagine this?"

The new year got off to a quick start. On January 4, 1959, David, Daniel Majeske, Ernest Kardos, and James Barrett appeared as soloists in Vivaldi's Concerto for Four Violins with the Cleveland Orchestra at Severance Hall. On March 10, Arben performed Brahms' Double Concerto with cellist Rolf Storseth and the Akron Symphony, directed by Laszlo Krausz.

Anshel Brusilow left as associate concertmaster in Cleveland and, recruited by Eugene Ormandy, accepted the concertmaster position with the Philadelphia Orchestra. Brusilow arrived June 21, and eight days later he wrote a letter to David. Referencing Ormandy, Brusilow said, "He is a great conductor and knows how to make an orchestra sound." The letter reached Arben in care of the Tuchmann residence in Munich. Wolf and Karola had by then relocated to Schraudolph Strasse 15.

In the summer of 1959, David returned to Europe to visit family. For the first time, he decided to buy a car while there. He bought a Simca to drive around France and Germany. He could later ship the car back to America, eventually selling it there. This system proved economical. Happy with results, he later repeated this several times.

On August 29, Arben was very proud to drive Tante's daughter and her husband in the new Simca to visit one of her cousins, Liliane Gall, near Thonon, on the French coast of Lake Geneva. David had always liked Liliane. Many years before, she had told him that he should write a book on his amazing life story. The next day, Tante's first granddaughter was born. When Tante's daughter came back from clinic with the baby, Arben stood near. The new mother had no idea how to take care of the infant. David commented, "'My dear, I never saw you so disconnected!'" They had good laughs together trying their best to bathe, feed, and dress a newborn.

He later returned when Tante's daughter had her second daughter. During their childhood, he developed close relationships with both youngsters. With the younger, he "became and remained very close. I was there, three to five months each year, in their summer residence. They had a couple of vacation houses, one in France, the mountains, one in Switzerland." Later, the second daughter would leave Europe to visit Arben in the U.S. every year.

Violinist Henryk Szeryng taught a series of masterclasses in Nice during the late summer of 1959. Arben went to see and ended up doing some teaching. There he met Cécile, a French violinist. They spent time together, traveling around Europe in his small car, becoming very close. After some few weeks and at the end of class, David went to Germany. They kept in touch. Years later, they saw each other again in Paris.

"The first thing when I got my jobs in Detroit, Cleveland, and later Philadelphia, was I established my reputation as a musician you could depend on, prepared and on time. Get music from the orchestra library in advance, come forty-five minutes before a concert, practice everything quietly by yourself. Arrive early to every rehearsal and concert. Play well because everybody including management observes you, whether you are serious or not. I did not do this only for management. I liked to play well for me and for people in the audience."

"Cleveland was good to me, but my first home was Curtis. I came to America because of Zimbalist. I came to Philadelphia because of Zimbalist. I still had many wonderful friends there. My first audition for Philadelphia Orchestra, I didn't get the job. I made adjustments. A few months later, I tried again and made it. My first year in the Orchestra I was in the second violins."

Frank Brookhouser of *The Sunday Bulletin* gave Arben a hearty welcome to the Philadelphia Orchestra in an article dated October 11, 1959. The music writer termed this newest string player, "an alumnus of the Chopin Academy of Music in Warsaw, the Music Conservatory in Geneva, Curtis Institute of Music, Lysakow, Budzyn No. 1, No. 2, Wieliczka in Poland, Flossenbürg in Germany." Thus delineating a remarkable arc in Arben's life and experiences, the article continued with a quotation from David: "It is strange to think of it now,' Arben says, 'but even in the camps I still had great beliefs. My parents expected me to become another Heifetz and I thought I was something special. That may be one reason I am still alive.' David Arben was brought to this country on December 2, 1949. He landed in Boston and wanted only to come to Philadelphia. 'This was my first city. But I had to get orchestral experience before I could play with this great orchestra. Now I feel that I am home again. I came back home…'"

11
Philadelphia Orchestra, 1959–93

"A great and fabulous life, I consider myself to be very fortunate to have been able to create a life of harmony, joy, and wonderful friendships."

In the fall of 1959, David left Cleveland to play in the Philadelphia Orchestra. He wanted to move back to his old neighborhood where he spent four-and-a-half years at Curtis Institute of Music. The same inaugural season, Anshel Brusilow had already resigned from Cleveland and joined Philadelphia as the new concertmaster. In recognition of their arrival, both violinists received mention in Philadelphia Orchestra's sixtieth anniversary program. Their friendship would last far beyond their years together on stage.

Arben recounted a first impression. "When I joined the orchestra, I was lifted by the beauty of the sound. Oh, it was fantastic."

Maybe five weeks after being hired for the new job, just before going on stage at a Saturday night concert, Eugene Ormandy pulled David aside to comment on disappointment with his playing. "I was backstage. Ormandy said, 'You sit and look so bored when you play your violin in the orchestra. Are you so bored with your girlfriends?'" The violinist immediately responded, "'My girlfriends don't complain and I'm surprised you do.'" Arben didn't know yet that the famous conductor always tested new members. "If you were weak, he would give you a heart attack. If you were strong, he wouldn't bother you." He continued on stage, but deemed any further disrespectful comments utterly intolerable.

The next Monday morning, the orchestra's newest member, in his probationary year, headed to the maestro's office. "I knocked on Ormandy's door. I knew he was going to fire me on the spot, but I didn't care." Arben asked the secretary, Mary Krause, to see her boss. "Many years older than me, he was very smart from experience dealing with thousands of people. When I came in, he started eating. I must have had an upset expression."

Noting David's face, Ormandy said, "'Come in, what can I do for you, Mr. Arben?' 'First, you can never talk to me again like Saturday night.' He looked at me with a grin, 'And if I do…?'" Now in the lion's mouth, David thought quickly on his feet. "'Then you will force me to return to Poland.'" Ormandy burst out laughing. Then he switched to the violinist's native language, "'Varshava, Katovitze, Bosna,'" simply names of prominent cities back home. "'I just need a promise you will try to play your best. And, by the way, how's my Polish?'" Arben curtly responded, "'I didn't come here to talk Polish pronunciation with you and I cannot promise to try to play my best.' He said, 'Why?' 'I always play my best.' I slammed the door. Three days later I got a permanent contract. After testing me once, he realized I was strong."

"From that time on he was my best ally. During break at rehearsals, he used to eat a big sandwich. His secretary already had the sandwich waiting for him. He said, 'Mary, cut my sandwich in two and give half to Mr. Arben. Also, he needs a cup of coffee.'"

"I became like his adopted son. Ormandy was a caring person. If anybody were sick, he would be the first one to come and help." The maestro would sometimes pull David aside and ask, "'Do you need clothes?' 'I'm fine, thank you.' He wanted to give me from his wardrobe." Arben declined the hand-me-downs, impossibly small, since Ormandy was barely five feet tall.

Now established on his career track, a yearning to reach out to remaining family, even distant relations, overcame any prior reservations. His father's cousins had come to America years ago and taken up residence in Chicago, New York, and Philadelphia. Not wanting any of the relatives to consider him a potential burden, David circumspectly approached the local branch. Before 1959 ended, he received a return call from Louis Arbeit. On invitation, Arben used to go for Friday night dinners prepared by the cousin's wife, Gussie.

"When I got into Philadelphia Orchestra, Mrs. Bohlen became sick. In her mid-seventies, she could move around some, but was mostly bedridden. A few blocks from the hall, my pleasure was going to her apartment every Saturday. Her staff would have bought food and wine. I cooked and served Mrs. Bohlen filet mignon and baked potato with salad. Just once she forgot all preparations before I came. She looked me straight in the eye and said, 'If you have a good drink, you can never have a bad dinner, even when there is no dinner.' She always had a bottle of Southern Comfort and her favorite drink was scotch whiskey. I put some in ice cream and gave it to her. Every time I met her, which was each week for years, it seemed like meeting the most interesting human being for the first time."

Ormandy showed concern for David's social life. He even tried to set up Arben. He told the concertmaster, Anshel Brusilow, "'I don't want him to know I'm arranging this. Come to my office after the Friday concert. I will introduce you to a Swedish girl. Take her and David Arben out for a drink.'"

"Before the concert Brusilow said to me, 'It is no secret, Ormandy wants you to meet a girl. Wait for me after the concert.' I waited and he introduced me to Inglid asking, 'How about we all have a drink?' I went along, and acted as if I didn't know."

"We sat down at one of the hotel bars. Anshel suddenly said, 'I have to go. I have an appointment.' He left me with Inglid, the twenty-seven-year-old Swede, nice, tall and blonde. We talked for half an hour. Late in the day I explained, 'This was all unexpected and I have to go to a dinner.'" They left the bar together and parted ways.

Consumed with curiosity, the conductor telephoned Brusilow for a report the following day. "Saturday morning came a ring. It was the concertmaster. He had gotten a call from Ormandy, 'Why didn't David take Inglid's phone number?'" The truth of it all was that Arben preferred not to mix personal life with work life. He simply wanted freedom to play his violin. "All I wanted was to go on stage and play my best. Always prepared, I simply did my job, always."

As for what to tell Ormandy, David gave a suggestion to the concertmaster, "'Simply say I forgot to get her phone number.' My luck was that a few weeks later, Inglid got a job in the Swedish Embassy in Washington. I felt relieved," though just temporarily.

"We went to play in Washington a few times a year. On one visit, Anshel shared what Ormandy told him. 'Tonight Inglid is coming to the concert. Make sure David Arben comes back to my room.' After the concert, I had Anshel come with me. Ormandy saw us beside Inglid and said, 'Hello. Mr. Arben, are you going to marry her?' After that I made sure that the Brusilow stayed with me. She drove us to Georgetown to eat, then took both of us home. That was the end and I never saw her again."

On a trip to New York's Carnegie Hall, Anshel drove Ormandy to the concert. During this same trip to Manhattan, David experienced a deliriously happy reunion. By way of background, "There was one Yiddish newspaper, *Forverts* or *The Forward*. This man,

Mr. Schmulowitz, said, 'I'd like to come to Philly and write about you.' We made an appointment. A very nice man of about sixty, he was at my place for a couple of hours." Arben's interviewer took copious notes. This encounter impressed the man, and he left aglow.

On July 12, 1960, "He wrote a big article with my picture and where I worked." Of the members from the old "gang of eleven" that coalesced for mutual support in the chaos after the war, 90% were in Brooklyn. "They read this article. So, one of them wrote a postcard, 'David Arben, Philadelphia Orchestra, Philadelphia.' No exact address, but it reached me."

"I also got a call from the one who stole a red violin for me in Germany." New York served as the stage for Arben to reunite with his long-lost friends. "The orchestra was going to Carnegie Hall in a week, so we agreed to meet at the backstage entrance at 4:30 p.m. before our performance. I chose this because a music shop with big windows stood directly across the street." David could conceal himself behind a storefront pane and observe their arrival before meeting.

The day came. "I could see what was going on, but they couldn't see me." He paused and watched from the other side of the avenue. He wanted to see how they appeared, to detect any hint of unsettling body language. After their separation so long ago, departing early one morning in Germany without explanation to his comrades, how might they receive him? Taking several moments to survey the scene from a distance, David opened the door.

"When I crossed the street, they all ran towards me. The two girls and three guys were there. Big hugs, I had so much emotion. This was unbelievable. And they were all doing well. Joe, who stole the violin, married one of the ladies. The other woman married another guy from the group and had kids of their own. We had a great day, then made plans for me to come see them for another big reunion on a Sunday."

"I went to one of their houses. I saw stacks of many recordings, operas, symphonies." They had voted David in as their president during adolescence because they thought he had something special. They still felt that way, and exhibited pride in the life he made for himself on U.S. soil. They, too, had done well in their new country.

Later that summer, David crossed the Atlantic again. Although the Philadelphia Orchestra continued to play during the summer season, Arben skipped this separate schedule and vacationed most every year in Europe. "I had my suitcase packed and took the first flight to Europe." He added with a grin, "I didn't waste time." He wanted, if possible, to see his Swiss family and join in their activities. "They went on vacations and I went with them wherever they went, including to the Alps, where snow storms could hit in July."

Once overseas, on excursions, Arben took every opportunity to enjoy the outdoors. "In Paris, I walked all day until three in the morning. On a separate visit to Amsterdam, I started at midnight. I walked the whole night and loved it. It was more peaceful at night."

"Nearby German countryside was very beautiful. Touring seaside towns, I used to sit in outdoor cafes and read a copy of *Herald Tribune's* European edition. One day beside the beach a German man, about forty, saw me reading the paper in English. He came up and talked to me. He was with his family at a resort. Finding out I played violin with Philadelphia Orchestra, he signed the cross. Born in Berlin, his parents used to take him as a child to hear the Philharmonic. He was exposed early and loved good music."

"This wealthy man invited me to stay in his home at Düsseldorf and wanted to host a reception. When explaining I was staying in Amsterdam, he offered to make the three-hour trip to drive me. After a while, I told him I was Jewish. He said, 'And you talk to me?' Because he asked, I spoke about concentration camps and my experiences. He said, 'You are an amazing man. If I would be in your shoes, I would never speak to any German and wouldn't even come to Germany. You are talking to me and shaking hands with me. I don't understand it.' I said, 'You didn't create the massacre of the world. People are people.'" David decided to decline a side trip to Düsseldorf, and the two parted with mutual respect.

In August of 1960, Brusilow wrote to his friend, still in Europe, mentioning a new television show on NBC that he had just started hosting in June. Anshel expressed pleasant surprise at his program's rating of one hundred and fifty thousand viewers. He suggested they perform an excerpt from Bach's Double Violin Concerto on one fall episode, with pianist "Billy" Sokolow; then David would sit for the featured interview. Formerly he performed on radio in Bavaria, now he would add a television appearance.

Henryk Szeryng again taught masterclasses in Nice, which was one long day's drive from Munich, eight hours or more. The two had first became acquainted in Cleveland. "He invited me to join him for two weeks. Having students from all over Europe, he spoke every language they spoke." Their friendship grew, and the two violinists collaborated on instruction.

"It so happened we ended up in French Riviera at a party around midnight with all kinds of people. And Szeryng said to me, 'I still have not heard you play.' I told him to be happy about that. Not getting the joke, he insisted and I agreed to play Bach Double Concerto with him."

"There was a young Polish woman who heard us play through the Bach Double. She said, 'Dawiszek,' David in Polish. 'Why don't you come back to Poland where we need good violinists?' She was a very famous Polish violinist, already traveling around the world playing concerts."

Her name was Wanda Wilkomirska. "We met and became friends in the sixties. She was a soloist under Karajan at Berlin Philharmonic and with New York Philharmonic. When Szeryng gave his Carl Flesch masterclass in Nice, she was one of the best violinists that came."

"She played Bartok's Second Concerto beautifully and passionately. Szeryng kept stopping her. She said, 'But Maestro, I think maybe…' He said, 'I don't care what you think.' She was crying."

"We got together afterward and she played for me, asking in Polish, 'Do I sound Jewish?' It was cute. I said, 'Yes.' She whispered, 'Thank you. This is the biggest compliment.'" He added with a smile, "'Sometimes you play too Jewish and it's no good.'"

David assured her he would intervene with his intimidating Polish friend. "The next morning I spoke with him. 'I like the way she plays.' Everything changed from that moment on. When the course finished after two weeks I took both of them to the airport in my car. She didn't fly back to Warsaw, but flew to Paris to study privately with Szeryng."

"My second year, Mr. Ormandy put me in the first violins." Ormandy had a reserved podium manner and didn't try to conduct every note, according to one orchestra member. Under his direction, the Philadelphia Orchestra grew in prestige worldwide, and their recordings attained universal recognition for quality. "He had a terrific track record for selecting talented musicians." The extremely busy orchestra schedule reached well over one hundred concerts per year in Philadelphia, as well as performances on the road.

One trip took them to Youngstown, Ohio. The concertmaster shared with David, "Last night Ormandy told me, 'During the encore, I looked and saw my new principal violist, David Arben.'" The concertmaster, David's good friend, told the conductor "'He's not a violist.'" The maestro remained convinced, "'He's my principal viola.'"

In the choice of a violist, he had an inside edge. Eugene Ormandy and Efrem Zimbalist used to have dinner together in each others' homes. Arben later learned that his former Curtis professor had spoken well of him to Ormandy. "This was because I played the instrument in a concert at Curtis."

Then came the confusion caused by advice that conflicted with his own ideas. His friend Anshel called Arben around midnight. "He said, 'David, once you become the principal violist of the Philadelphia Orchestra, automatically you become a famous name.' Not just doubling the orchestra salary, the gain was even greater with teaching and other playing jobs. After five days of not sleeping or eating, the answer was 'No.'"

Advisors and friends "didn't understand. I could have taken the money, but the violin saved my life. It took me out from the grave. I made my decision in five minutes, but it took longer because so much advice kept coming from so many people. After five days it was final, 'No.'" Of note, Carlton Cooley remained principal violist for Philadelphia Orchestra until 1963.

"Ormandy was angry. So, for fourteen years I was sitting in the middle of the section. People behind me moved up, and people in front moved back, through all this time. I was frozen in that chair fourteen years."

Despite the seemingly punitive block to his advancement, Arben liked the conductor and respected his genius for signing great artists. "He trusted his musicians and let them play. He was smart and knew how to make the orchestra sound good."

David, himself, displayed many different types of smarts. "Normally, a person doesn't have to learn such a high level of survival and fighting skills as I had. In November, 1960 I was mugged in Philadelphia. There was a big snowstorm. I was bringing food to a sick friend. There were no cars, nothing in the street. I heard footsteps behind me, but I refused to give in to fear."

"Two guys out of a little alley knocked me to the snowy ground. One grabbed a leg, the other grabbed an arm. They beat me and took my watch. It was an orchestra payday and they took my money, leaving me on the ground. In this country, I was a free person. There had been danger of harm, but I refused to run from it."

"Police came quickly. We went to bars, but couldn't find them. I missed the concert that night. Ormandy got a message from police. My colleagues told me that during intermission he kept saying, 'I hope David is okay, I wonder what happened.' I couldn't play and was out for three days."

"Skills developed during wartime lasted throughout life. What happened remained part of you. In war, if you didn't adapt, you vanished. It was not because I was so smart or great, no. I adapted. For years close friends wanted to know about these things. This part of human life was totally foreign to them."

Arben thought moving to a safer and more convenient neighborhood would make sense. The same month of November, he signed a contract to rent the second-floor apartment at 1517 Spruce Street for $110 a month. David had switched addresses to one around the corner from Curtis, very convenient to work. It suited his purposes perfectly. "When I moved in, there was a Mr. Kelch who owned the building. He wanted to sell it to me. I should have borrowed the money and paid. With several apartments and garages in the back, I probably could have had it for seventy-five thousand dollars."

"A Mr. Saichek bought it." The new landlord agreed to favorable terms and they established a good relationship. "He was so proud he had somebody from the Philadelphia Orchestra living there. He was an old timer, going to Saturday night concerts since the days of Stokowski."

Later, it came as a shock to learn that the landlord and his wife had died in an auto accident. Several days afterward the son, a prominent attorney, sent notification of increased monthly rates.

"This was the beginning of June. I called. He came on the line, 'Is there a problem?' 'Yes, and that's why I want to see you.' 'I'm sure we can resolve it satisfactorily over the phone.'" David detected a tone of reticence to meet face to face. This told him to insist on an appointment. "'My current lease goes to next November, and even then the rent shouldn't automatically go up, so what's your rush? I want to come up to your office and talk to you.' The more I persisted, the more he became nervous. So, I finally won. We decided on the time."

At their meeting, Arben asserted the attorney's father had agreed to a fixed rent for the term of his lease. Now an astute son wanted to know, "'Where's the contract?'" David, recalling people's trust in his own father's handshake, returned, "'He gave me his word.'" This didn't impress a savvy property owner. "'The price of doing business is going up and a verbal contract is not binding.'" Arben calmly summed up, "'Mr. Saichek, I see the way we are going. You are going to force me to hire a lawyer. I know you're a good lawyer. So, I am going to ask you. I want to hire you...to represent me... against you.'" His quick thinking and deft words went beyond mere chutzpah and attained to what the authors term an "Arbenism." The rent remained the same for two-and-a-half decades.

David returned to Switzerland for the summer of 1961. He found Tante's daughter with two daughters of her own now. This first chance to meet the younger six-month-old, her cuteness and care needs absorbed Arben. "When the second granddaughter came along, as years went by we became very close, my 'baby.'" Her parents called her by the pet name, "Raton." David made it sound more Polish: "Ratounetchka." He found his time joyous while encircled by this family.

At year's end, the preliminary development of publicity for a planned European solo tour commenced. Bernstein's quote from his earlier letter of recommendation, "an extraordinary talent," carried weight. On December 17, 1961 Ormandy wrote and called Arben "an exceptionally fine talent."

Long-time friend to David and grandson of the tailor who in 1903 founded what grew into an industry giant, *After Six* clothing, Sam Rudofker took over in the 1950s. Under his leadership, it became "the biggest formal wear company in the whole world. Sam's wife, Peggy

King, was an entertainer for years." They frequently hosted and socialized with the violinist.

In July of 1962, Arben again went to Munich, visiting the Tuchmanns, who still lived on Schraudolph Strasse. "Cousin Wolf was my only living relative in Germany. Summers in Europe I saw my family." Nearing his destination, David paused for a stop inside the main train station. "I know right where to go. Oh, I love sauerkraut. I have meat wrapped in a roll which is just baked and warm. And the German mustard, it tastes entirely different than any other, sweet and delicious."

While in Munich, renowned concert agent Wilfrid Van Wyck, manager of Milstein, Menuhin, Zino Francescatti, Rubinstein, and Szeryng, wrote from London with thanks for publicity materials Arben had sent. "Client Henryk Szeryng had many fine things to say about you and your art." Van Wyck suggested David drop by before returning home to discuss details of a European tour in 1963.

Back in Philadelphia, temperatures turned cold, heading into winter. Every Saturday, David continued to visit and keep up with Ingrid Bohlen. She called him before a scheduled lunch, "'My dear heart, you have to forgive me, can we make it another time? My nephew, Charles Bohlen, is coming from Washington. Kennedy just appointed him to be ambassador to France.'" This occurred the latter part of 1962, though he officially assumed his post early the following year. He had a long diplomatic career, including a term as Ambassador to the U.S.S.R. in 1953 under Eisenhower.

A tall, distinguished lady, not wanting to put on airs, "She would tell me that her family had humble origins." When he shared about an upcoming visit to perform in her native Sweden, she wrote to her nieces that they might go to Arben's recitals. This plan would come to fruition the following May.

Meanwhile, he had a winter escape plan. "The first time I came to Puerto Rico was in 1962, and I returned every year. I would stay for two-and-a-half months. I came the fifteenth of December and I left the end of February." Returning to a defrosting Philadelphia, it always felt like coming home.

Back at his apartment, Arben set about planning for a five-week European tour. "I thought of pianist Alice Shapiro. I met her at Meadowmount the summer after my first year at Curtis. She was a terrific musician. I hadn't seen her, but still had her telephone number. After thirteen years of not talking, she agreed to go."

"We flew over for the first concert in Amsterdam." They played in Stockholm on May 20, 1963. Ingrid Bohlen had already called ahead to relatives. "Her niece, husband of the niece, and others came. 'Can we take you to dinner after the concert?' I said, 'Yes.' Alice also came. It was phenomenal."

"The niece asked if I could stay any longer. 'Yes, I am staying an extra day.' She wanted to invite me to the house for lunch." Her husband had served as ambassador to multiple key nations. After talking and eating, they took David on a tour of Stockholm, Parliament, and the House of Nobles. Arben learned that huge floor-to-ceiling paintings inside the latter building portrayed Mrs. Bohlen's parents. Reportedly, the King of Sweden never held a party without inviting them. Not a peasant at all, Ingrid came from aristocratic stock and high society. Her father owned part of Swedish American Line passenger and cargo shipping company.

Eight days later, Arben and Shapiro reached Berlin. Some ex-concentration camp musicians refused to play in Germany. David never felt this way. "My heart was full of anger over murdered family, and I went there with the feeling that I must do the best to settle things. I would have been satisfied just to play in Berlin, but also played in Amsterdam, Stockholm, Munich, Vienna, London, and Paris."

Afterward, he rated his performance in Berlin as "the best I ever played." He received rave reviews in five of the city's newspapers. One important paper, *Der Kurier*, signed off their terrific article, "Not quite without envy do we state that such a standard of violin playing is no longer attained in Germany. One is convinced of the high standard of instrumental culture, intensely vibrant tone, the dazzling precision of the left hand, the masterful double-stop playing. An infallible sense of form and style, the free lyrical spirit is the beginning and end of violin playing." The world-famous *Die Welt* had this to say: "Arben counts among the best of his profession; he gave himself fully to his playing." In another publication, "his roots... from Poland... Slavic... all part of the growth, the seed of great violinists." Arben commented, "They didn't mention it, but they knew my history.

They wrote, 'Warsaw born Polish American violinist.' I still have the review in German from 1963."

In another newspaper, there appeared a roundup of all the concerts from that week, epic musicians, and even the Berlin Philharmonic. The major weekend paper's headline read, "Violinist David Arben Belongs to the Best." "Such reviews I never got in my life." He savored sweet vindication in accomplishing his aim. "Center of the Nazis, Berlin was the best concert I remember ever playing. Something happened when I had to show that Hitler did not destroy the mind or growth of a people. Hitler didn't achieve what he wanted to achieve. He didn't kill me and I had my revenge."

Arben's performance reminded German concert manager Robert Kollitsch of Mischa Elman's Berlin debut, which he attended in 1904. Kollitsch offered him a contract. Arben expressed interest in the proposal that he give concerts "all over," but only on dates not in conflict with Philadelphia Orchestra.

Munich followed, then Vienna. Rave reviews continued. The *Münchner Merkur's* critic wrote, "Arben possesses that particularly big tone which nowadays has become rare... technical mastery... romantic poetry... expressive melodiousness." The *Wein Express* added, "David Arben is a violinist with outstanding technique, a strong tone, a remarkable amount of musicianship, and always a personal touch. The pieces made great demands, which Arben met with mastery in every respect."

Nearing the end of their tour, the American violinist and pianist appeared in Paris. Tante's daughter and her husband came to Salle Pleyel to hear the program of Brahms' G Major Sonata, and Swiss composer Bernard Reichel's Sonata. Of note, Reichel also composed music for David's Geneva family, including a piano trio and a cello suite for Tante's second granddaughter.

In London, Wilfrid Van Wyck wanted to place Arben under contract. "He arranged for me to play at Wigmore Hall. Ormandy was conducting London's Philharmonia Orchestra at Royal Festival Hall. The *London Times* wrote him an unenthusiastic review and mine, lower on the page, was good. Ormandy was upset, but we settled that."

"Van Wyck already had a tour lined up — eight weeks in Australia— but only if I quit the orchestra. I didn't want to give up what I considered security. I didn't want to live out of a suitcase. If I had the confidence then that I have now, I probably would have done it. At that time, it was a little too soon for me."

"Even if you played like God, if you weren't signed by a big agency, nobody would hire you. When you had management, you worked for them. They arranged concerts and told you where to play. When they needed you, even at the last moment, you had to go or they dropped you. You were under their spell. You had no control. For me, this was not a life. My life was more important."

"If my father would have been alive, he would have wanted me to be a famous soloist or give up the violin all together. There were several European managers that wanted to take me. They would only take me if I resigned from the Philadelphia Orchestra. After a taste of the soloist's life in 1963, knowing myself and what I wanted, I said, 'No.'"

Back in Philadelphia David contacted Ingrid Bohlen to tell her about the events in Stockholm. She seemed happy her family members had attended his concert and guided some sightseeing. "Ingrid was a good friend and good to a lot of young musicians. She had a way of teaching without saying, a method I observed over the years."

The balance of the year, Arben took satisfaction from having proven himself on tour. Local press covered his artistic accomplishments overseas.

In late March of 1964, David performed Mozart's Violin Concerto No. 5 with the Philadelphia Musical Academy's Faculty-Alumni Orchestra. *Philadelphia Inquirer* reviewer Samuel Singer described it as "one of the finest of the season. Arben's performance was worthy of any concert hall and orchestra. Arben played with such aplomb and technical and tonal security, everything was so right, that music, violin and player seemed one."

That summer, David's friend since their first meeting at Cleveland, Szeryng again directed and taught a series of masterclasses. This time in Baden-Baden, around 330 kilometers west of Munich, the program ran July through August. He inscribed a bound copy of the syllabus, "Dear Friend – David Arben, With many fond wishes, Henryk Szeryng."

In 1965, Onkel and Tante purchased a little house in the south of France, in a village called Coursegoules, one hour northwest of Nice. David visited several times there in the 1960s. "A good wife, good mother and wonderful grandmother, she went to church every Sunday morning at eight thirty. Sometimes I think she prayed for me." With a trademark Arben humor he added, "I am still here. Prayer can't be that bad."

In his Simca, he explored widely by road for weeks. In southern France, stops included St. Paul de Vence's "Festival de Musique," once with outdoor concerts given by violinist Ivry Gitlis. At a very remote place called St Barnabé, near the Col de Vence, beautiful summer nights in Provence left indelible marks on his memory.

Anshel Brusilow served as concertmaster of the Philadelphia Orchestra under Ormandy, 1959-66. "A magnificent violinist, I never met anyone with his nerves. One example on tour, minutes before the concert started, Mrs. Ormandy knocked on the door. 'Anshel, Eugene wants to see you.' He left the room and came back a minute later." His face said it all. Suddenly the program would change because a principal wind player just had a car accident. "Ormandy asked the concertmaster, 'Why don't you play Brahms' Concerto?' Brusilow hadn't played it in fifteen years."

Arben assumed Brusilow would need the music. "I asked, 'What are you going to do?' 'I will tell you in three minutes.' Three minutes later he said, 'Forget the score. I'll play by memory.' This was guts; nobody else that I knew would even dare do this. And he did the greatest job, not missing anything."

"A few weeks later, Francescatti was scheduled to play Tchaikovsky Violin Concerto. Ormandy called at ten o'clock at night and said to the concertmaster, 'Francescatti is sick and cannot play tomorrow.' Brusilow played the Tchaikovsky with less than twenty-four hours preparation. Francescatti's next scheduled stop, Pittsburg, heard about what Anshel did in Philadelphia and they invited him to come."

In 1966, Ormandy led the Orchestra on their first tour of South America. Besides other stops, they stayed in Buenos Aires the better part of a week. Their May 27 performance would take place at the continent's largest hall. Teatro Colon compared favorably to La Scala in Milan. A program for that evening listed Piston's Toccata for

Orchestra, Bartok's Concerto for Orchestra, and Brahms' Second Symphony. Arben had limited free time, but wanted to try looking up his father's older sister. She had married a man named Morel and immigrated to Argentina before World War II.

As the reader will recall, Lazaro Morel had come from Argentina. He and Ester, Arben's aunt, met in Warsaw. They fell in love, got married and lived in Poland for two or three years. They had a son. After deciding to go back to Argentina, they couldn't take the son because immigration would not permit it. He had an ocular problem. "So, Ester left the boy with us. He was raised like a brother. Shlomo was eight years older than I. My aunt and her husband had two daughters born in Buenos Aires."

"After checking into the hotel, I picked up a phone book. A large city like New York, their directory was big." Not having the address or recalling any particulars, Arben opened to a long list of Morels. "It was like Smith or Jones. They only had initials for the first name. After so many years, I barely remembered his name. I could have spent all night calling every L. Morel."

Not knowing Spanish, he randomly put his finger on a single entry and called. A woman's voice answered in Spanish. He asked if she spoke Yiddish. She replied in perfect Yiddish, "'Yoh,'" meaning yes. He then asked whether she knew a Polish woman, maiden name Arbajtman, who married a Morel. She responded, "'Yoh.' This was my aunt Ester, can you imagine?" He exclaimed, "'I'm your nephew.'" Explaining to his aunt that the Philadelphia Orchestra would stay just five days for a series of music performances, he jotted down her address and hopped in a taxi.

Before the evening performance, a driver took him to his aunt. They lived in an unpretentious dwelling with inner courtyard, where the group of about fifty welcomed him. "I was introduced to everyone. After ninety minutes I tried to get up, but all the arms were on my shoulders pushing me back down in the chair. The experience was funnier than anything you could imagine."

Arben visited their modest home each day the rest of his stay. "About eighty, she was born a few years before my father. The lady was short and tiny, but feisty with a strong voice." She added gesticulations to emphasize and make sure all heard her points. "The husband looked on, a nice quiet man, cleanly dressed." It seemed this group never stopped talking, laughing, and eating. They begged David not to go.

"I had written to her after immigrating to the U.S. In that letter I asked, 'Do you have any pictures of my family?' She sent the treasured images from long ago, the only ones I ever had."

"A reflection of prior times, my aunt's family lived exactly the way they lived in the old country, seemingly without financial reserves." After five days, David left them with what cash he had in hand. They never saw each other again.

Back on the U.S. east coast, "The orchestra in 1966 was on strike eight weeks (starting September 16, for fifty-eight days). So, we decided to play a benefit concert by and for the musicians. Leopold Stokowski conducted. The tickets were five dollars apiece. I suggested Carnegie Hall, but they didn't have three thousand dollars to rent it." David offered to help find a source of funding. He went to his old friend Sam Rudofker, who happily wrote the check.

Ultimately, they decided against what Arben had recommended and for which his friend provided funding. Carnegie Hall commanded a much higher facility fee and the committee voted for holding their event in Philadelphia on October 14. It turned out a great success.

Off-season, per Arben's usual, he gravitated to Geneva. Particularly attached to Tante's second granddaughter, "When I came, she was about five years old. After dinner she surprised me. She sat in front of the piano and played, my first time hearing her. Next year she surprised me again, playing cello." A thoroughly musical family, the younger granddaughter played cello in a trio with her sister playing violin and her mother playing piano."

Founder of Philadelphia Chamber Orchestra (1961), Anshel Brusilow said goodbye to his associates with resignation from Philadelphia Orchestra in 1966. David and Anshel would continue their friendship over the long haul. "He is one year younger than I, born August 14, one day after my birthday. He was a fantastic concertmaster." Brusilow continued to command recognition. In 1970 he went to The Dallas Symphony Orchestra as music director.

Customarily taking his summers in Europe, David played with the Philadelphia Orchestra in 1967 for a single month during their two-month residency at Saratoga Springs, New York. He then flew to Europe.

In Paris, per his tradition, David bought a Simca, this time with just four kilometers on the odometer. A short distance away on that pleasant warm day, someone rear-ended him on the Champs-Élysées. Reaching for his identification, Arben got out to exchange information. It was none other than the "Chief Justice (of France's Supreme Court)! He wanted to pay cash." Arben didn't know what the figure should be for damages, so he took a card with contact numbers and said he'd return to Paris and reconnect. When contacted later, the judge treated all matters very fairly. Arben found things usually turned out this way when one focused on more practical and concrete dimensions, rather than the less quantifiable apportioning of fault.

February 27, 1968, at Civic Center Museum, David was featured performing Beethoven's Violin Concerto with the Philadelphia Musical Academy Orchestra, Maurice Kaplow conducting. Sam Rudofker and Eugene Ormandy, the Honorary Chairman, appeared on a roster of the Board of Directors. In a review, the *Philadelphia Inquirer's* Samuel Singer called Arben "an old pro. He performed with complete aplomb, demonstrating a splendid finger technique that easily encompassed the rapid runs, the delicate figurations and the cadenza's difficult double stoppings, with ease of bowing to match. His tone was sturdy and steady, often with a soft glow. Intonation was accurate always."

In May of 1969, Joseph Castaldo sent private correspondence from the Philadelphia Musical Academy. He wanted to formalize in writing and planned to announce David Arben as their new Chairman of the String Department.

The season wonderfully warm, Arben boarded a plane for his annual getaway. He arranged to stop and stay in Brussels several days, and took a Belgian Airlines flight from New York. "Next to me was a young German lady. She must have been early thirties." Learning he played violin, she wondered if he ever visited Germany, and invited Arben to visit the home she shared with her physician husband. "They were living in Munich." He told her that after Brussels he planned to head that direction.

"Invited by the lady, she picked me up for a fantastic party." There he met her husband, who had questions about Arben's Polish roots. Informed of David's Jewish background, the doctor seemed surprised he would even come to a German's home and sit at the same table without anger. David joked, "'Are you hiding something from me? More seriously, I don't get angry at a nationality, you weren't responsible for the past. You are responsible for the future.'"

"This group in their mid-thirties were very intelligent and great music lovers." They initially interacted with David as violinist and member of Philadelphia Orchestra, leaving his history as a Jew from Poland for later. "Another doctor was from Berlin and brought his Vietnamese wife. He shared about going to the Berlin Philharmonic as a young boy with his mother."

At the end of the evening, several guests from various professions had questions. "'Mr. Arben, we want to understand how you feel. If what happened to you happened to us, we wouldn't come to Germany. You are more generous than any of us could ever be.' I said, 'When I think of Germany as a whole, I don't feel so comfortable, but being with you, I am comfortable. I'm very happy to be here with you.'"

In the broader social context, Arben did not suffer from blindness or amnesia. "I never forgot, and as human beings we must preserve certain memories. The memories of where I came from, where my family went, symbolic of so many precious freedoms robbed and lives stolen; I was not fond of forgiving the whole country."

"Most of my years, I didn't hate my enemies. I didn't even like to say that word 'hate.' I may have liked or disliked, but I did not have feelings of hate." Did he work hard to achieve this? "I never thought about it. I just didn't like the idea of hate, period. When you hate someone or something, it will destroy you. I like myself too much to hate."

Stateside, a press release issued by Joseph Castaldo early in the first quarter of 1970 announced a coming fall appointment of David Arben as head of strings at the Philadelphia Musical Academy, designating him a "talent scout" when the Philadelphia Orchestra would return to Europe on tour in the spring. Celebrating the school's founding in 1870, the Academie String Quartet with Arben as first violinist had their next scheduled appearance in the "Centennial" Concert Series on March 12.

Four days before this aforementioned concert, a *Philadelphia Inquirer* article explained how their event had its inception the prior summer at Saratoga Springs where Szeryng appeared as a soloist with the Philadelphia Orchestra. David had approached him with the idea. They also invited pianist Gary Graffman. Their Academy of Music program at Broad and Locust would include the Chausson Concerto for Violin, Piano, and String Quartet. In addition to Arben, other members of the Academie String Quartet included second violinist Eugene Kash, violist Karen Tuttle, and cellist Samuel Mayes. An occasion for special recognition, Henryk Szeryng received the Mayor's Proclamation.

Sometime in May, the Philadelphia Orchestra stopped in Florence on their European tour. Maestro Ormandy observed the recently appointed music director of the city's summer festival, Riccardo Muti, and kept him in mind on a short list of worthy candidates for his successor. Call it serendipity in Italy, David remarked, "We stayed at an incredible hotel, the Excelsior. Bernstein was my next-door neighbor, while on tour with the Israel Philharmonic."

"One evening I went out with friends, returning to the lobby at about eleven o'clock. At the same time, musicians from Israel returned after their concert and I saw Bernstein, who gave me a big hug. He introduced me to everybody." The prominent conductor also invited Arben to an exclusive after-performance party.

There Bernstein introduced David as a wonderful talent he'd known since he was a teenager. Everyone was curious who this mystery man was. "He was great to me. It was unbelievable." Many years later, David recounted receiving letters from Bernstein's secretary. She conveyed, "'Mr. Bernstein is so pleased that you have done so well.'"

Arben had occasion to accompany a friend in the orchestra who couldn't make up his mind while shopping at a shoe store in Italy. "He needed a pair of black shoes." He tried on pair after pair, making the shopkeeper climb stairs to fetch more boxes. "With all the boxes on the floor, he couldn't decide." Arben's friend asked the man, "'Are you open tomorrow?' 'Yes, I will be open whenever you want to come.'"

"The next day after breakfast we went to the store, but he could not make up his mind. I felt so badly for the old man." Tortured indecisiveness had started all over again. David took pity on them both. To break their impasse, he led by an example of decisive action. Having perhaps learned from Tante's treatment of the peddler at her door, "I bought shoes I didn't need." Arben, re-humanized by his Swiss aunt's selfless charity, replicated a part of her noble character. The friend fell in behind, drafting in his wake. "The moment I bought the shoes, he said he wanted the same pair. It only took five minutes."

No less than Tante, David always credited his parents for modeling moral practices. "In my childhood, you respected older people, even strangers. Today, there is a big difference."

During 1970, Arben lived at 1517 Spruce Street, a block from the Philadelphia Musical Academy, at 1617. Under Jani Szanto's direction, the Academy had absorbed the city's Conservatory of Music in 1962. "In anticipation of fall classes, Joseph Castaldo wanted me to go to Israel to pick four Israeli students for the coming term." On May 27, the Israeli consul in Philadelphia wrote with contact information for David to use in Israel.

"On June 12, I arrived and checked into a room at the Tel Aviv Hilton. A waiting letter instructed me to call the local number and meet with a man who eventually brought the students who played for me. I picked three guys and one girl."

With Arben standing at the hotel's check-out desk, a man hurriedly asked, "'Taxi?'" Before he could respond, this fellow picked up his suitcase and hustled to a parked cab. When David reached the curb he saw his unsolicited baggage handler standing beside an actual driver who asked the destination. Arben provided it, but balked at a suggested tip for the self-appointed middleman. David calmly stated he required no lessons on tipping from anyone; furthermore, he informed the colluding taxi man that he could decide to take him as a customer or not, but to expect no tip himself after the presumptuous coaching. "He drove me and I paid him what the meter said. He lost his tip, because I didn't like this pushiness. The first time in Tel Aviv and they were already after me," he said with a smile.

Before the close of 1970, Arben began playing a Stradivarius owned by the orchestra. He would play this violin for twenty-three years. "When I first got the Stradivarius, it took me about nine, ten months to learn how to play it. Strads each have their own unique personalities. You could not insist. You and the violin developed together. I would get up in the morning, open the case and say, 'Please be nice to me today.'" David smiled at his funny characterization.

During Easter time in 1971, Tante's younger granddaughter visited Philadelphia with her sister, mother, and father. During their stay, Chaim moved temporarily to a friend's place, making his Swiss family feel at home in his apartment. They all went to eat in Chinatown at 930 Race Street, one of David's favorite restaurants, Shiao Lan Kung. This younger granddaughter in future years would try not to miss an annual rendezvous, either in Pennsylvania or Puerto Rico.

On programmed spring tour with the Philadelphia Orchestra in Europe, the planned itinerary took them to New York, then on to Frankfurt. "In New York we had an hour and a half before getting aboard TWA." The group included violinist Luis Biava who brought along his wife Clara, both close friends of Arben. "I went all out, wanting to send a birthday telegram to Clara Biava." David went to the TWA counter. They recommended Western Union. He took three dollars worth of quarters to the pay phone.

"'Paging David Arben, paging David Arben.'" He collected the telegram from TWA's message desk, went to a duty free shop, bought some champagne, and headed to the plane. Once on board this 1971 flight, David approached two stewardesses. He explained about his friend's wife and a special birthday surprise. Out of sight, Arben produced the Western Union message. "'About an hour after take-off, please bring out the telegram, champagne with glasses, and sing happy birthday.'" Clara Biava continued talking about this cherished memory for years. Many others expressed the same appreciation for David's thoughtfulness and fun-loving spirit.

At a stop in Monte Carlo on this tour, "Movie star Grace Kelly gave a party for Philadelphia Orchestra in the ballroom of Hotel de Paris. Prince Rainier and Princess Grace shared their table with

Eugene Ormandy and his wife. The Princess originally hailed from Philadelphia, was charming and well-liked by Monaco's residents."

Arben went to the party and sat at a round table for eight. "It was a beautiful scene." Mayor Tate of Philadelphia (in office 1962-72) also attended. He had come with the orchestra for this stop on their tour. Photographers took his picture with David which later appeared as a magazine illustration.

Princess Grace invited Tate to sit in the royal box when Philadelphia Orchestra played. Arben later encountered Mayor James Hugh Joseph Tate, and received an interesting review of their concert.

"I saw him the next day. He spotted me on the beach and called, 'Dave, Dave.' I had never formally met the mayor, but he knew my name. Sam Rudofker used to talk to him about me, so he was familiar with who I was." Tate explained to his wife, "'This is David Arben.' They were in shorts on beach chairs."

"The Mayor told me he and his wife were sitting with both Prince Rainier and Princess Grace. Tate said, 'A few seconds after you started playing the Prince started snoring. The Princess was elbowing him, "Wake up!"' 'He kept falling asleep and this repeated the whole concert."

Not far from Monte Carlo, Tante's younger granddaughter sat with David in the garden. "She was eleven, and spoke to me fluently in English. She started the conversation, 'Brahms wrote three violin sonatas, which do you prefer?' I said, 'The G Major,' which is the first sonata. She said, 'So do I,' then sang in solfeggio the entire movement, all by memory."

An unusual musical engagement in July or August of 1971 took Arben to Germany and Yugoslavia. He first flew to Munich and visited his cousins. "Later, Henryk Szeryng was scheduled to play at a festival. He did some recordings for German TV and would then head to Yugoslavia. Some weeks before he said, 'Why don't you come to Dubrovnik and we can spend some time together?' I knew the hotel where Szeryng planned to stay, but couldn't get a room." The festival drew a large number of concert attendees who packed the local accommodations.

"On the plane from Munich to Dubrovnik, I ended up sitting next to a woman about forty years old who spoke English." On landing and getting off the plane, David had to surrender his passport. This caused him grave concern. "After clearing customs, the woman I met on the plane was ready to board a broken-down bus. I didn't know how far from the airport Dubrovnik was, and invited her to come with me by taxi wherever she needed to go. She accepted my offer."

"I found out it was a 50-plus-kilometer taxi ride. This Yugoslav woman asked me, 'Why don't we secure a room for you?' She instructed the driver in their language. We found a room for one night and I took it. I suggested I accompany her to her final destination and then have the driver bring me back to my place. She said, 'Thank you very much.'"

Arben took note as they approached a mansion behind massive walls. "You should have seen where she lived. It was a gated palace with big iron doors." She said goodnight. "Riding back to my hotel, the driver who spoke a little German said, 'Do you know who this woman is?' 'No.' 'Her father is Chief Justice of Yugoslavia and he makes all the laws.'"

"He continued to speak in basic German. Nervous to have her in his car, he thought I was important because I was with such a famous woman." Happily, this highly connected lady in shining armor came the next morning and took him to find another room.

"At 8:30 a.m., my phone rang. The lovely woman wanted to help. I paused to consider. Maybe I would be better off with less notoriety, knowing her father was such a powerful man in the country and I didn't have a passport." Keeping these musings to himself, he thanked his heroine for any help to find lengthier lodging.

At the small upstairs boarding house that she found, he announced "'I want a room to rent.' An elegant lady, seventy years old, spoke German and gave me a cup of tea. I had a suitcase, my violin and needed a room, but she gave me a cup of tea."

"So, we were talking and talking. She said to me after about fifteen minutes, 'Are you Jewish?' I said, 'Yes.' She said, 'Shalom. I am Jewish too.'" His eyelids began drooping after prolonged listening to her voice. David explained he needed to go take a rest before that evening's concert.

Acknowledging their kinship, he invited her to come hear him and Szeryng play. She explained only twenty-nine Jews remained in the area and, as much as she wanted to attend, they all found themselves under surveillance. Regretfully, she had to decline his kind invitation.

"I walked around Dubrovnik, which was so beautiful. I saw Jewish street names, the Judengasse (Jewish Ghetto). Not far away, they specialized in pork where I tasted the most delicious dish." Precious few Jews remained in town, but good Yugoslavs had tried to protect them. Serbs saved many Jews during Nazi occupation. Most of those who survived left for Israel.

"Szeryng had arrived and the government assigned a guide to him during his stay in the country. This individual monitored and helped him with whatever he needed. The three of us shared every meal together, breakfast, lunch, and dinner." Time came to say farewell and Arben departed for home.

During the Philadelphia Orchestra's domestic tours to cities such as Baltimore and Richmond, the orchestra typically stayed overnight. "My friend in Washington and I always went to the same very fine Chinese restaurant. One day we went and it was closed for ten full days because they had a private party. Kissinger and his whole entourage were going to China and the restaurant taught them how to eat with chopsticks." They learned appropriate Asian etiquette.

"After Nixon and Kissinger returned from China in 1972, Ormandy received a call. The woman from the White House asked, 'Mr. Ormandy?' 'Yes.' 'The President would like to speak with you.' 'Which president?' And she said, 'The President of the United States.' He thought it was a big joke. Nixon told Ormandy, 'I want you to go next year.' After a couple of minutes he said, 'Mr. Kissinger would like to speak with you.'" Henry Kissinger outlined the proposed cultural exchange and ultimately made necessary arrangements.

Among a host of other firsts, the Philadelphia Orchestra achieved a diplomatic coup later in 1973, when President Nixon assigned them a mission to tour the People's Republic of China. No other American orchestra had visited since Mao Zedong had finally prevailed over the Nationalists in October of 1949. The orchestra already had a schedule for the entire season in place. The only window of opportunity turned out to be a time slot in mid-September, after the residency in Saratoga Springs and before commencement of their regular season in Philadelphia.

For half a year, orchestra manager Boris Sokoloff repeatedly inquired about the best venues, dates, accommodations, food, and other important details. In coordination with Ormandy, he proposed different music programs. No Russian pieces; instead an American selection. And perhaps The Yellow River Concerto, a new Chinese composition, could utilize the talent of a young and upcoming local pianist, Yin Chengzong. But the Chinese did not respond. Just a couple of weeks before the planned departure date, they transmitted one single stipulation. "Don't play Don Juan." Eugene Ormandy, actually rehearsing that very piece, stopped immediately. With no coordination or further guidance, time came to pack up and leave for Asia. A favorable reception as the first American orchestra to arrive in mainland China since communists took over would help open opportunities for all important cultural exchanges to follow.

Shortly after arrival and with a definite sense of pressure, through the Chinese emissary, a Mr. Liu, the orchestra manager learned of a special request from Madame Mao. She insisted they play Beethoven's 6th Symphony, not the 5th. Ormandy had a dislike for the 6th, and hadn't conducted it in years. Still, Sokoloff said with more timely notification he would have prepared it. At this point, an absence of parts for musicians and inadequate time to rehearse made it impossible to comply. Behind the scenes, a mad search for music proved fruitless. Then the Chinese promised to fly in scores and 115 parts from Shanghai. After a conference with conductor, the manager and staff, based on their unanimous recommendation, Ormandy agreed to it for their third concert in Beijing on September 16, 1973. He said, "If that's what they want, that's what they shall have. I am in Rome and will do as the Romans. I will forget my own rules."

As to David's first impressions, "Nine months before our China tour, a cameraman took each member's picture. I thought they might be for visas. The first morning at our hotel, I went to the front desk and asked for a cab to the friendship store. Without telling him my name, he said 'Mr. Arben, we'll have a taxi within ten minutes.' For nine months, they had studied every musician's face and knew every man and woman in the orchestra."

"At the hotel, they had the most lavish spread of the best fruits. It looked like an open-air shop, but there was no one to take money. Nobody ate anything because we found out too late that it was all for us. When you walked outside the hotel, everybody acted polite and friendly."

On a Friday night, the Philadelphia Orchestra played their first concert in Beijing: Brahms' Symphony No. 1, Roy Hankins' Symphony No. 3, and Mozart's "Haffner" Symphony. The performance unfolded while a rainstorm doused the grand domed theater off Tiananmen Square, a building commonly called Egg or, more formally, the National Center for the Performing Arts.

At the second concert, Madam Mao sat next to Mrs. Ormandy. They spoke through a translator. Despite the last minute change, they performed Beethoven's 6th magnificently. Violinist Herold Klein commented, "They looked like they had just heard something completely strange." Their audience clapped politely as the orchestra rose to their feet and the Maestro bowed.

At a reception, the red carpet stretched what seemed like half a mile. "We shook hands with as many as we could, three hundred men and women connected with the arts, actors, actresses, instrumentalists. It was really touching to see them react so warmly, moving past us the whole time. None of the Chinese would likely have encountered anybody wearing a tie, so our ties really grabbed attention."

"Philadelphia Orchestra made history again with Ormandy. Mao Zedong could not come because he had to meet with the Prime Minister of France, Pompidou. Mrs. Mao came and, for the first time after the revolution, she wore a long black dress. I saved pictures. There had been one standard way of dressing, everyone the same. Mrs. Mao broke that tradition coming to our concert. That made news in the western papers."

For a retrospective in the digital *New York Times Asia Pacific* section, dated May 7, 2010, Xiyun Yang wrote an article about post-concert activities: "Musicians were riding buses back to the hotel when military vehicles sped past and screeched to a halt, cutting them off in the middle of the road. 'One guy got spooked, I remember,' said Anthony Orlando, a percussionist. 'He went screaming off the bus. I guess it was too much Big Brother for him.'" Arben added, "After only ten minutes at the hotel, we were told Mrs. Mao Zedong wanted us to return."

"It turned out that Madame Mao had just wanted a photograph with the musicians and to hand us little packets of flowers. We went back and she gave us a little present, then shook hands. Also, she made a speech about how in 1945, the Philadelphia Orchestra had played a benefit for Chinese refugees. Because of this she told us, 'You are our friends.'"

"Before we left, two guys from the State Department told us, 'Don't try anything on your own.'" One would think they hardly needed such a stern warning to refrain from going out at night in a country virtually unknown to them.

Curious and uninhibited, Arben climbed on public transportation at a large boulevard. "They had a humongous street, 50 kilometers one way and wide. So, I decided to try taking the bus, same number out and back again. There must have been about twenty-five people waiting for the bus. When it stopped, nobody moved. Men and women were waiting for me."

"When I got on board, they were sitting like sardines and everybody got up to offer a seat. There was no room, even for standing. A woman collected money, but I didn't know how much to give. And she wouldn't take my money. At that time, if anybody came from another country, they were a friend of China. The government invited us and they treated us like honored guests." Satisfied with his adventure, almost as suspenseful as childhood jaunts in Warsaw, he took a bus with the same number on the opposite side of the street. It returned him to his hotel without incident.

The next day he called someone he knew through friends with diplomatic connections in Geneva. "The hotel operator spoke perfect English. 'Let me speak with the Swiss Embassy.' The moment they gave me the Embassy someone said, 'Hello, do you speak English?' 'Yes, may I speak with the Ambassador?' 'He is not here at the moment.' 'My name is David Arben. I am here with the Philadelphia Orchestra and I was hoping to speak with the Ambassador.' 'Just a moment.' The Ambassador got on the phone and we had a chat. This was around 1:30 in the afternoon. He said, 'I have to go to the Swedish Embassy. King Gustav VI Adolf died and has a memorial, but my wife will come to your hotel at 4:00 p.m.'" The King had died September 15, 1973.

"I was outside the hotel and saw this big limousine pulling up, the Ambassador and wife. We had a wonderful chat and exchanged little presents."

No matter where he stayed, Arben habitually opened windows for fresh air, and Beijing proved no exception. "I would open one, go out for five minutes, then come back to find it closed. They meant well for me. The air inside the room was much better than the outside air. In Shanghai, it was even worse, horrendous."

"The country was just incredible. We went to see the Great Wall, which stretches 3,000 miles. We walked a couple of miles. All kinds of tourists were snapping shots. About five years later a friend of mine found, at a store, on the front page of a book, my picture! A Canadian author had written about walking on the Great Wall. There I was. You can't get rid of me," he laughed.

"The next day they showed us the Forbidden City in Beijing and hosted a party. Parties were always fantastic. I had two young men assigned to me, one walking on the left side and one on the right. One of them turned to me and spoke perfect English. He asked, 'Where are you from?' 'Philadelphia.' 'Were you born in Philadelphia?' 'I was born in Warsaw, Poland.' Incredible, this pair of Chinese spoke perfect Polish. 'Where did you learn to speak Polish?' 'In Warsaw.' 'Is that all you learned?' 'No, we studied at the conservatory. We are both violinists.'"

"I've been to China many times since my first time in 1973. I met the main conductor of Beijing Symphony, close with Mao Zedong's wife during their Cultural Revolution. At that time, I didn't know he was a Chinese Jew, but with a typical Chinese name. There were many Jews who intermarried because of persecutions. They used to call them the 'night Jews,' as during the Inquisition. In Spain, by day Catholics and by night they were Jews. To survive, they did whatever they had to do."

Also in 1973, David rose to assistant concertmaster of the Philadelphia Orchestra. His fellow orchestra members had become another family to him. They performed together, spent leisure time together, and traveled together. Besides swings around the U.S., they went to destinations in Latin America, Europe, Israel, Japan, and China. "You name the country, we were there."

Domestic concerts usually started at eight in the evening and, depending on the program, ended around 10:00 p.m. Afterward, musicians tended to stay up late. After leaving the hall, they went out to eat. Another popular pastime, cards, brought out competitive tendencies.

Arben says of one fellow orchestra member, "We didn't talk for many years after a poker game." Suspicious of a bluff, "He folded and wanted to see what I had. 'I don't want you to see how I play.' He started to grab the cards and missed. I was too quick, so he punched me. After nineteen years, he finally apologized. We shook hands, but we still didn't talk."

Subsequently, "This musician auditioned to be promoted. I was part of the jury and he told his best friends, 'I trust David Arben. He is an honest man and, whatever he says, I believe him.' This was the guy who punched me. I would never have held anything against him because he punched me. When he played, the past counted for nothing. He got the job, but I still didn't talk to him."

Arriving spring of 1974, Arben played in a fundraiser for the New Jersey Symphony on March 24 in Dr. and Mrs. Alan Young's Metuchen, New Jersey, home. A review by Mirko Tuma in *The News Tribune*, of nearby Woodbridge Township, gave details of this program that included Mozart's E-Flat Major Sonata, K. 481, Bartok's Rumanian Dances, Franck's Sonata, and Wieniawski's Concerto No. 2. Having heard a rehearsal of the Mozart Sonata, Tuma wrote, "I have never heard Mozart's violin work with greater insight and lyricism." This same critic penned in a separate article after the concert, "Arben's violin playing has dimensions one can neither learn nor acquire by practice. One must be born with it. His tone is uniquely warm, velvety and luscious. His technique, his art of the vibrato, his economic and fantastically precise bowing are only prerequisites for his higher musicianship. In the Mozart Adagio, Arben virtually captures the composer's heroic search for truth. The labyrinthine modulations climax in an enharmonic change that indeed bares the depth of the soul. This very analysis offered by Alfred Einstein – an analysis which used to escape me until I heard Arben's rendition yesterday – is what this sonata is all about. Arben can accent a feeling by playing a diminuendo while deepening the tone-color. This is sheer virtuosity and poetry as well." Mirko Tuma dedicated his book of poetry, *Crutches of Dusk* (1974): "For David Arben, who understands Mozart."

A downward drag on the heart strings, Ingrid Bohlen's condition continued to deteriorate in her Philadelphia apartment. An octogenarian, soon she would no longer be able to live independently. "For nine months she began preparing me. She was going to New England, an old age place. 'They treat you well there.' I didn't know why so far away, when she had children closer. She said, 'There comes a time in life when you must make room for the people you love.' The months passed, and finally she left."

"I tell you, hers was an unbelievable brain. The goodness of this lady helped me find sanity." From his parents, later Tante and family, and again with Mrs. Bohlen, he had received "smart," intelligent love. Ingrid never criticized, never told him "do" or "don't do," but was purely a guiding light. In the year 1974, her candle extinguished.

Arben learned from fabulous teachers and from personal experiences. In Vienna on tour with Ormandy in the mid 1970s, David arrived at the theater, and on attempting to enter, was blocked by a guard. The violinist pleaded, and when finally allowed access, he found things amiss in "his" dressing room. He notified someone of the loss. "I couldn't find my trunk. Time almost gone, I went out on stage — it was not my orchestra!"

"It was the Vienna Symphony. At first I wondered, 'Who are these strangers on stage?' I suddenly realized *I* was a stranger, and at the wrong hall." Instead of the Concert Hall (Konzerthaus), he needed to quickly find his way to the Great Concert Hall (also known as Wiener Musikverein). "So, I ran. Boy, did I run!"

Back to the U.S., he entered New York on September 15, 1975. Later in December, according to a newspaper article, Henryk Szeryng had come from Los Angeles to Philadelphia and saw Arben. The two friends drove to visit Dr. Samuel Applebaum (father of Michael Tree) at home in Maplewood. There, an impromptu performance by the pair came as a surprise when they joined in playing with some New York Philharmonic players who were also in attendance. The reporter wrote of "the most inspired and brilliant rendition of the Bach D Minor Double Violin Concerto I have ever heard." The two violinists would eventually perform the same piece at least three times together.

Time in Europe appealed to Arben, whether working or vacationing. First going to Munich and his cousins, then he headed to Switzerland, often staying in Vuache, where Tante's daughter and her husband had purchased an old 1840 farm house. Thirty kilometers from Geneva in the middle of open fields, Chaim liked fresh air from mountains nearby and nary a detectable noise. He slept with the windows wide open, blankets up to his nose.

Days, he would lie in the sun for hours. And he always made for his family two favorite dishes: garlic chicken and onion potatoes. Everyone enjoyed their time together, fun for adults and children. They played games, dined royally, hiked, and enjoyed music together.

Describing another residence on France's Atlantic coast near Nantes, "The family had a summer home in the western part of France by the sea. It was maybe two hours by train from Paris. I used to stay there every summer for a few weeks. I loved the family. I wanted everybody to be good, to be happy. Tante's daughter called me, 'Chaim Kissinger.'"

"Once in late summer with just five days off, I didn't waste any time. I went by myself, a few days in September. I flew into Geneva, rented a car and went up to the mountains. There was a little chalet, and I rented the corner room. It had a balcony and I could see the mountains from there. It was a sunny day, 72 degrees, hillsides full of snow. I had lunch in my bathing trunks."

Early in 1977, "It was a great honor when my friend Henryk Szeryng invited me to play the Bach Double Violin Concerto with the Philadelphia Orchestra." Szeryng was playing in New York and Arben had called him to express regret he couldn't attend. To an interviewer, David recounted the dialogue. "He is full of mischief, and he asked me then what I would be doing on July 21?" Arben looked at his schedule and found on that date he would have finished summer performances at Philadelphia and left for Europe. The friend lamented that there seemed no point in coming, if David weren't there.

"I didn't know what he meant. It turned out later that he had asked Fred Mann (President of Robin Hood Dell Concerts, summer home of Philadelphia Orchestra) that I play the Bach Double Concerto with him in the concert." Szeryng finally unveiled his desire for David to join him on stage. "Of course, I stayed for this."

"Before the concert, we had a rehearsal in his hotel room. He had a guest conductor there who spoke Spanish. During the run through, at a section when I was playing and he was not, he said something in Spanish to the conductor. I heard, but didn't understand." As Arben and the conductor left together, he commented with a Latin accent, "He said your sound is like pure honey."

Then David's Robin Hood Dell debut performance day arrived. "It was a crowd of fifteen thousand at the outdoor theater, so we each had a microphone to pick up the voices equally. We walked on stage and took a bow. As people were applauding, he grabbed my microphone and turned it towards himself. As we played, I had to awkwardly lean towards the moved microphone. Szeryng was one of the world's top violinists. It showed me that no matter how rich or famous, that didn't always build conviction you were the artist you wanted the world to know."

Both violinists attended an after-concert poolside party hosted by Sam and Peggy Rudofker. Later, the two violinists came together again. "Henryk and I had lunch and he said to me, 'You and I are going to record the Bach Double Concerto in London. It's going to be recorded on EMI records.' I said, 'You are giving me the greatest privilege.'"

Their recording plan remained on track for but a short while, just until the reading of reviews. Newspaper writer Monroe Levin observed, "David Arben's solo talents may have surprised many, but not his orchestra colleagues. Their applause went well beyond the merely courteous. A full-fledged solo engagement ought to follow this belated debut."

According to Michael Caruso of *Main Line Times*, "David Arben's tone was the more attractive because it was the more mellow. No one can deny Mr. Szeryng his brilliance, but it proved to be just a little rough now and then while Mr. Arben's sound was an ever gentle one that always sang." David summed it all up, "This review killed the Bach Double recording project. And yet we remained close friends."

Friendship based on mutual respect may be easier to mend, if fractured. Later, "We met in Paris where he had a nice apartment.

He called me at one o'clock in the morning. 'Would you come over to my place?' 'Sure.' He had newspaper, magazine reporters doing interviews. I observed him trying to control what was asked."

"A great, knowledgeable, very smart, intelligent musician, he absolutely had a certain gift. He spoke about twelve languages, each in the native accent. We used to meet his friends in Paris. They said, 'When he speaks French, he speaks like a great poet. The French people don't know how to speak French as Henryk speaks French.' I talked to him only in English. Originally from Warsaw, he resided in Mexico."

With the announcement in 1977 of a future audition for the associate concertmaster position, the office instructed interested people to enter their names. Arben took note and waited for six months. "I purposely did not put my name down, observing the reaction. Ormandy looked back during rehearsals and concerts, seemingly irritated and upset with me." David kept his intent to audition a secret, "the kind of secret you keep even from yourself."

In November of that year, Arben addressed the Board of Directors of the Philadelphia Orchestra Association, presenting a paper related to his violin, which was on loan. The treatise covered its particulars and provided a general history of its maker, Stradivari.

All along, David had secretly prepared. "Right before, I called the personnel manager, nine o'clock at night. I said, 'Mason, I would like to audition.' I came out one of the three finalists. We each were on trial for a few months before the appointment."

Heading back to Asia in September 1978, "I took this trip from New York. It was Pan American, Flight #1, a daily route around the world. After an overnight stay in Los Angeles, the next layover was Honolulu. There I stayed two incredible days."

That first evening, Arben read a newspaper article about the local orchestra. He recognized the name Robert LaMarchina, and made a call. David remembered that he had moved to Honolulu, but hadn't learned of his appointment to music director with the symphony. Arben found a phone number in the directory. His old friend responded excitedly, suggesting they go to dinner before concert time and a reception following.

The next evening, David's colleague announced, "'We have a surprise guest, violinist David Arben, in the audience. Tomorrow he goes to play the Bruch's Concerto with Hong Kong Philharmonic.'" Applause followed this gracious acknowledgment, all reported by a press member. The next morning, Arben departed on Pan American #1 at eight o'clock.

The reader will recall that on board ship in the summer of 1956, David shared a table with three ladies. Later, one moved to Honolulu. The woman later assumed duties in management of the Honolulu Symphony, and had read with interest a newspaper account of La Marchina's reported welcoming of guest David Arben. When contacted, the music director said that David had already left for Hong Kong, but suggested a way to put the long-lost acquaintances back in touch. Arben would soon return home via Hawaii after concerts in Asia. "She had been looking for me twenty years." Their meeting constituted the latest in a lifetime string of "coincidences."

According to Mandarin Hotel stationery our subject had checked in by September 4, 1978. The next day, Hong Kong's *South China Post* announced his "Concerto on a 1681 Stradivarius." Subsequently, Myra Andrews posted for the *Hong Kong Standard* her interview around Arben's early background. David was quoted, "The beautiful thing about violin was that it was my choice. I had to do it right or not at all." In her article, Andrews succinctly captured Arben's own summary of important events along the path of his career in music, an offer to study at the Paris Conservatory, then American citizenship in 1955, the Cleveland Orchestra tour of Europe in 1957, and by now, three trips to Asia. Myra Andrews announced his appearance performing Bruch's Violin Concerto No. 1 with the Hong Kong Philharmonic the next evening, at Baptist College's Academic Community Hall.

Finally, David returned to Philadelphia. All three finalists for associate concertmaster received a call to the conductor's office on a Friday afternoon, after a two o'clock concert. Ormandy announced Arben as his choice, and the other violinists stormed out angrily.

The Maestro insisted David stay. Just as when offered half a sandwich in his boss' office after first joining the Orchestra, Arben felt uncomfortable. "He wanted me to share about anybody critical of him. I said, 'You know everything. I haven't heard anything.' I wanted to play, not be friends. I liked to respect my boss and I hoped my boss respected me. All I wanted was to go on stage and play my best."

On October 8, David presented a treatise to Swarthmore College about the 1681 Stradivarius he used on loan, an identical paper to the one delivered before Philadelphia Orchestra's Board one year prior. "Most violinists don't know much about violins, but my fascination began in childhood when I fell in love with an enchanting sound emanating from the mysterious scroll."

Arben's violin had once belonged to a Rothschild. "Someone from world-famous insurers, Lloyd's of London, called me. He was coming to the U.S. and wanted to see my violin. He spent three hours looking at it under a nearby lamp in the apartment. It was such a piece of art."

Do instruments deteriorate when not played? "That's the rumor. When somebody doesn't play well, someone insensitive, it could be much worse for the violin than not being played at all. Each violin is unique. Beautiful sound motivates. A better instrument will drive you, instead of you driving it."

Much later, after retirement, Arben would say, "All the years I didn't have one, strangers asked 'Do you have a Stradivarius?' But once I had one, nobody asked. What happened, did my appearance change?" The master of humorous lines smiled at his own joke. After retirement, he would find out the Philadelphia Orchestra sold his loaned violin for ninety-five thousand dollars. "I found this out just months after it was sold. The value went up to maybe six million."

Many months since auditioning and final appointment to associate concertmaster, no formal recognition of David's success appeared. Going to the personnel manager's office he characteristically demonstrated forthright communication style. "'I auditioned and won. I have proven I can do the job. Why is it that my title remains assistant?' 'I suggest you communicate with Ormandy in writing.'" As recommended, David wrote a letter on December 7. "I didn't protest publicly. I sat there expectantly."

On July 5, 1979, the inaugural International Music Festival of Santorini invited Arben and Tante's daughter to Greece. Prior to the concert, "At a dinner party in Athens, I sat next to young pianist Athena Capodistria (student of Tante's daughter in Geneva), founder and organizer of the festival. Her father was Minister of Labor in

Greece. We were at the same table with a group of fifteen high society types."

David discussed his upcoming performance. Capodistria turned and commented, "'Santorini is an experience. When are you going?' 'Tomorrow.'" She eagerly offered to make any further arrangements. This struck Arben as unusually generous. "She picked me up at the airport and we had drinks in her unfinished house on a mountain, followed by dinner."

On the island, Capodistria made herself available to help. David inspected an already scheduled venue in the Greek Orthodox community, an open-air courtyard of the one and only Catholic monastery. He regretted having to tell a French priest in charge that playing outdoors just would not do. "My instrument cannot be exposed to the direct sunlight."

Athena immediately looked for alternate indoor facilities. She found a Greek Orthodox church where they agreed to make available the enclosed sanctuary for David's concert. "I met the Bishop and took a tour. The stage was nice with good acoustics.'"

"I invited both Catholic priest and Greek Orthodox Bishop to my recital. I made sure that they sat together." After the program, Arben heard that representatives of Orthodox and Catholic faiths had not sat together on Santorini in one hundred and ten years. He chuckled, "I made history and it took a Jew from Poland to bring them together."

Stateside, Ormandy had scheduled Arben to make his debut on a subscription concert with the Philadelphia Orchestra. Called to the manager's office to go over details, David maintained a focus on formal acknowledgment of his promotion. "'I will be very happy when given what consideration others receive in this same position which I won.' The personnel manager answered, 'We cannot promise...' 'It's one thing if you choose not to grant my request, but don't insult me saying you cannot. Insults I cannot accept.'" Arben walked out, and delayed signing any new contract.

"I was willing to sign, but what I wanted first was respect. I insisted on what I had earned. You had to fight for your territory." Starting with the Philadelphia Orchestra's program for the 1979-80 season, David Arben's name appeared as associate concertmaster and remained so each year until his retirement in 1993.

On December 21 and 22, 1979, Arben performed the Mendelssohn's Violin Concerto. Beforehand, Arben had expressed himself poignantly in a letter to Ormandy, "I am very grateful for the honors you have bestowed upon me in granting me the title of associate concertmaster and of giving me the opportunity to appear in a subscription concert as soloist... In arranging this appearance, you have made possible an achievement that I shall always look back upon as the greatest of my life, and I shall always cherish the moment that this will take place."

After David's performance, James Felton wrote a review in *The Bulletin* from Philadelphia. "It was impressive. Arben's handling of Mendelssohn's Violin Concerto was relaxed, very natural and a delight... he played songfully and almost with self-effacement."

At the *Philadelphia Inquirer*, Daniel Webster opined, "David Arben had appeared for twenty years with the Philadelphia Orchestra, but until yesterday he had never been soloist with the Orchestra at the Academy of Music... Arben brought a gust of fresh air to this familiar work. He shaped a performance that avoided false heroics and overstatement, and focused instead on the musical shape of the solo line and its nuances... It was playing that reminded listeners that Mendelssohn wrote for intimate performance in which clarity and expression were valued above power and volume. With that understanding, Arben played with such sanity and lyricism that the music appeared almost new... In the transitional bars between the second and third movement there is a small theme that is repeated. Arben played the few notes with such sweet eloquence that it infused the whole following movement with an innocent glow."

One of David's classmates at Curtis, fellow violinist Ling Tung, now served as music director of the Hong Kong Philharmonic Society. As already indicated, in 1978 Arben had soloed with the Hong Kong Philharmonic Orchestra. Back and lodging again at The Mandarin in June of 1980, he received an invitation to a welcoming dinner that Philharmonic supporters gave for every visiting soloist. On June 27 and 28, he would perform Mendelssohn's Violin Concerto.

David's introduction to authentic Chinese culture and cuisine had come many years prior. Ling Tung invited him for meals cooked by Tung's mother in their residence. She knew both Madame Chiang

Kai-shek and Dr. P.P. Chiu, a major donor to the Hong Kong Philharmonic, and reputedly one of the richest men in China. "He was a physician who didn't actively practice medicine. Extremely wealthy, he knew important people all around the world. When conductor Karajan came to Hong Kong, he would stay in Chiu's mansion. He had palace-like private quarters for guests." A staff of more than twenty attended to everyone's needs.

Dr. Chiu enjoyed classical music, and Saturday mornings regularly scanned reviews of the previous night's performances. A review was especially positive and he went to hear Arben that evening. "It was nice that Dr. Chiu came backstage afterward to introduce himself and inform me of the closing night party he held for all visiting soloists. He also invited me to meet him Monday at twelve o'clock at the Hong Kong Club."

"A man at the door had my name. Another guy accompanied me to the table and asked me what I wanted to drink. 'A cocktail.' He explained, 'Dr. Chiu and his wife will be here shortly.' They brought with them three guests, a French woman, someone from the Far East, and a pianist. Chiu gave a present to each guest. He and his elegant wife spoke many languages. Later I found out that Hong Kong Club was very exclusive and membership was restricted to the top British subjects, but Dr. P. P. Chiu was a member. At the Club he took out the best. He had twenty-dollar cigars to give everyone, including me."

Later, "He wrote to me in Philadelphia. He wanted to give a dinner party for sixteen people. I still have this beautifully written letter. Underneath, all of the names of people invited to attend were printed. I was delighted to find two names that I knew. One was Ling Tung, whose mother graciously used to invite me every weekend to stay with them. I was very lucky in life to meet not just rich people, but to meet people with incredible character."

Over the years Arben himself shared freely, hosting parties of as many as sixty in his apartment. "I invited all kinds of people."

On later returns to Paris, Arben liked driving to Nice. There he could stay at a clean hotel, one-half block from the beach, for two dollars. He would pay sixty dollars to cover a whole month on longer stays. In local markets, he bought the best brie, a baguette, fruit and small bottle of wine, all for fifty cents. These he consumed seated with his folding chair at the beach, looking at sparkling reflections of sunlight on a gentle Mediterranean splashing golden sand. Best unrestricted view in the city, "I ate like royalty."

"I would drive 30 kilometers, somewhere between Nice and Monte Carlo, to have dinner. There was a restaurant called Chateau de Madrid. It wasn't a castle, but guarded by a man with white hat and uniform." Vaguely, it reminded him of the fancy hotel and bellhop his father took him to see in Warsaw. "I used to go by myself. You entered on the seventh floor and took an elevator down several floors to the sea. It was absolutely an experience."

"While on tour with Philadelphia Orchestra, six of us took a three-hour taxi ride to Chateau Madrid. We had the driver stay and return us to Nice. The old days, this was not the only place where we took a taxi to faraway places. I would go back tomorrow." Spectacular views of the water, seafood aromas and meat sauces left indelible memories.

"Monte Carlo was good. I went with friends to the casino." And he added with a twinkle in his eye, "For casino winnings, Monaco was good to me."

From France, he drove everywhere and saw everything. His longest personal drive went nonstop from Munich to Genoa, through "Germany, Austria, maybe a little touch of Italy."

As far as roadways and the towns of Europe, Ormandy himself knew them well. He came from Hungary. Born Jeno Blau, theories vary as to what inspired his name change. Ormand, a small town southwest of Budapest and halfway to Zagreb, may provide part of the answer. Those with certain surnames could not readily gain acceptance as conductors.

Ormandy and Zimbalist kept up a friendship. They both climbed the career ladder at times of great social and professional prejudice. "Each had a different story altogether. Completely different, but they were good friends."

Philadelphia Orchestra had made Riccardo Muti an offer in 1979 to replace Ormandy in 1980. Arben emphasized, "No matter who the conductor, my whole being was in the music."

On his own, the associate concertmaster had occasion to approach "Freddie" Mann about a donation to the Philadelphia Orchestra for a planned concert. This important man headed the city Cultural Affairs Council. In 1957, he had built Fredric Mann Auditorium in Tel Aviv, home to the Israel Philharmonic. The same individual traded home visits with the Shah of Iran and his wife, socializing with each other in Philadelphia and Tehran. Among Mann's close friends, even Rubinstein, Piatigorsky and Heifetz joined him in business.

Arben and Mann had dealt with each other for years. "I made an appointment to see him on orchestra business." When Arben entered the busy entrepreneur's office he found his barber making a "house call," behind the desk to give an on-site shave. The unintimidated and persistent violinist said he would wait to disclose the purpose of his visit. Whiskers cut and cream toweled clean, Mann bellowed, "I already know what you're here for and the answer is no. Everybody in town comes for money. Enough already." Without missing a beat, David countered "'I realize I made a mistake in coming. If I knew your feelings, I would not have come and won't come again. Because you don't know me well, you're making a bigger mistake, if you think I will leave without any money. Once I come, I don't leave empty handed.' I said it to him directly, and what I said I meant. He smiled and agreed to write me a check. Later, he invited me to a few dinners at his house."

"Know what you want and don't deviate. It's better to know what you want and not get it, than not know what you want and not get it. Once I was there in the office, I was not leaving without a donation. If I thought of the possibility of not getting what I came for, I would not have gone."

More "chance" encounters: Arben had his picture taken with Philadelphia Mayor William Green and his wife Pat, as published in the *Courier-Post* January 25, 1982. They all attended a celebrity ball, the Grand Old Lady of Locust Street's 125th anniversary celebration, in Bellevue Stratford Hotel.

On tour to Colombia in 1984, March 16, David performed at the Teatro Colón. He played in the Orquesta Sinfónica de Colombia's sixth concert that year. Under the direction of Luis Biava, music director of the National Symphony in Bogotá, Arben performed Mendelssohn's Violin Concerto. Apart from this collaboration in South America, their association spanned decades. Biava joined the Philadelphia Orchestra in 1968, attained principal second violin and conductor-in-residence. He openly expressed his gratitude to Arben for helping him prepare and ultimately win a coveted spot. David had gladly offered the mentorship which he personally did not receive before joining. Biava conducted his last two concerts with the Philadelphia Orchestra in 2004.

On June 22, David played with Orquesta Sinfónica de México at Teatro Morelos, a second concert at Municipio del Estado de México the 23rd, and yet a third concert at Teatro de la Ciudad de México the 24th. For all programs he performed Bruch's Violin Concerto No. 1. "I used to play in Mexico every year, both in recitals and solos with orchestras." These trips provided a chance to keep up with his friend José Kahan Pintel and his daughter Sharon.

The father of Arben's friend José, "Salomon Kahan was a very famous author and music critic in Mexico. Occasionally, I was at his house Friday night for dinner and Sabbath candle lighting. The most famous people came. They had a big house and were very hospitable. José and I were close and his daughter always remembered me."

Pursuing his own art, critics continued to lavish their praise on David. March 8, 1985, Tom Di Nardo, classical music writer with the *Philadelphia Daily News*, quoted the violin soloist. "I'm trying my best to embrace Mozart, and I hope he does not reject me." Di Nardo went on, "young students who zip through the notes should ponder these words of violinist David Arben, associate concertmaster of the Philadelphia Orchestra, a familiar sight on the Academy of Music stage for 26 seasons… None of Zimbalist's players sounded alike. He let you believe in your own sound. You couldn't have the emotional or the intellectual solely, there had to be balance. For musicians, playing is not a luxury, but a necessity. We have a need to play. You can't put a price on the hours, the pain, and the joy. Some days you get the notes, the exact sounds you want. The next morning you can't find them. It is a constant challenge to find that beauty… When Maestro Muti asked me which concerto I would like to play, I said the Mozart A Major. Mozart is constantly the most difficult music to play, and musicians play his music with much anticipation. It is so pure, the height of nobility. Nothing is more difficult than simplicity in a world that complicates everything. I was lucky to have good training in Mozart. There are so many ways of playing it correctly, but many more ways of playing it wrong. I tried to do the work justice, but Mozart kept winning. I mentioned to Muti that this was the pain of Mozart – no matter how well you played it, you didn't get everything. You could only try. He knew just what I meant. It was impressive how Muti saw and heard every reaction. On the spot he had the ability to analyze a complex problem, involving personalities as well as the notes, resolving it with a correct and fair solution. He was demanding, but he wanted everyone to be happy. If he believed he was right, he'd stick to his guns and never waver... Marcel Tabuteau once told me, 'If you are satisfied with your playing, you cannot grow.' And Zimbalist (who died two weeks prior to publication of Di Nardo's article) used to say, 'Don't think about the concert you just played. Think about the one you're going to play.'"

Concerning this March 1985 performance of Mozart's Concerto No. 5, *Philadelphia Inquirer* music critic Daniel Webster described, "Arben commands a sweet, silvery tone and a gentle attack, and he played the work without forcing or seeking any romantic show in such perfect writing." *Main Line Times* entertainment editor Michael Caruso wrote, "Associate concertmaster David Arben gave an incredibly Romantic reading to the Mozart. His tone was so meltingly beautiful and his phrasing so intimate and sweet that I found myself loving every sound I heard."

April 27, 1986, he collaborated again with Michael Tree of Guarneri Quartet. They performed Mozart's Sinfonia Concertante with the Philadelphia Chamber Orchestra. An inspirational venue on Rittenhouse Square, Church of the Holy Trinity hosted their Sunday evening event. Michael Caruso described Arben and Tree. "The two made a perfect pair, each complimenting the other efficaciously. On top of Tree's swarthy timbres, Arben placed violin tones of the purest character."

May 12 through June 6, 1986, Muti and The Philadelphia Orchestra embarked on their 50th Anniversary North American Tour. In a *Los Angeles Times* article dated May 25, 1986, when asked about the former conductor, David Arben recalled that, "Under Ormandy, there was a sense of gravity to everything we did, from rehearsing to recording. Everything we played sounded weighty, it never took off. We were actually drowning in the beauty of our sound."

Arben said more than once, "Ormandy trusted the musicians and allowed us to play. This was why it was so great. Because there was less turnover in the orchestra, it stayed intact and, like wine, blended better over time."

Some entire Sundays, Ormandy and the orchestra devoted to recordings. "We would begin at 10:00 a.m., take 45 minutes for lunch, one hour for dinner, then continue until 10:00 p.m. or later."

"The recordings in the old days, to me, were more true to how a violinist sounds. Today, the engineers want to hear every bit of resin, every scratch. This is not authentic to the real acoustic. When a violinist plays on stage, distance between the violin playing and audience smooths out a lot of the little noises a musician hears under their ear."

"When I was in the orchestra they used to record with different companies. Columbia Records was wonderful. Then came RCA Victor. I could hear more scratches. Then came EMI. I didn't like it at all. What they liked, I didn't like."

On December 19 and 20, 1986, David Arben performed Mozart's Adagio, K. 261, and Panufnik's Violin Concerto with the Philadelphia Orchestra. The choice of Panufnik deserves some explanation.

"Polish composer Andrzej Panufnik lived in London with his wife. He was an elegant man and wonderful conductor of the Vienna Philharmonic. In 1971, Yehudi Menuhin went to their apartment and said, 'I would like to commission a violin concerto that we will record on EMI with you conducting.'"

"I ended up being in Amsterdam with Philadelphia Orchestra when I finally met Panufnik." Afterward, they kept in touch. "I have some letters from him. He wrote, signed and sent me the book he wrote in Polish. Panufnik exposed and told the story of anti-Semitism."

"He was Catholic but in Warsaw conservatory students thought he must be Jewish. His two best friends were Jewish. The students asked 'Why do you associate with Jews?' He said, 'I admire their love and talent in music, their intellect, and their sense of humor. These elements are enough for me to want to be friends with them.'"

"The director of the Warsaw Conservatory thought that he was Jewish. Panufnik was sitting at a concert in Warsaw many years ago when Arthur Rubinstein came and played the recital. The director of the Conservatory told Panufnik he didn't like Rubinstein's Jewish sound. This was how big anti-Semitism was."

"Listening to Menuhin's recording of Panufnik's Concerto, it said something to me. I chose this as my next solo with Philadelphia Orchestra, getting a copy of the music from a British friend who had contact with the composer. It is wonderful music, full of imagination and colors."

Inquirer music critic Daniel Webster heartily agreed. "Arben's playing is refined and musical, and he sustained the mood of this work without a flaw. The solo instrument plays a soaring melodic line over orchestra support that characterizes musical economy. This was playing of a high order... The Panufnik work, being heard in its local premiere, too, continued the mood of Mozart in that it is an extended single vocal line for violin with string orchestra support. Arben's playing remained elegant, finely crafted and sensitively applied."

Arben wrote to Panufnik February 9, 1987. The composer had missed Philadelphia's premiere of his work. David sent separately to London a recording of the December performance, hand carried by Bernard Jacobson (professor, musicologist for Philadelphia Orchestra, and author of *A Polish Renaissance*). On March 11, Arben received a reply from England, expressing admiration for his performance. "The string sound…was out of this world for me! Thank you very, very much. I shall always treasure the tape."

Off hours from the orchestra, "Riccardo Muti used to invite me to lunch every month or so. Sunday I would meet him in front of his apartment. We would take a taxi to the Four Seasons Hotel. He had a table in the back where we sat for hours. He asked me intelligent questions about all kinds of things."

"Once I remember at lunchtime, he started, 'Mr. Arben, you must write a book.' 'Why, Maestro?' 'You have a story to tell that all human beings should read.'"

October, 1989 marked Arben's next five solo performances with the Philadelphia Orchestra. "Witold Rowicki was scheduled to conduct. I had already worked with him a few years prior, playing Bruch's Violin Concerto. This time I chose Szymanowski but he sent a telegram to the orchestra manager, recommending I pick a different concerto because this was his trademark piece with Wanda Wilkomirska and Warsaw Philharmonic. I said, 'No.' He died ten days before the scheduled performances."

Concerning these performances, on October 13 Daniel Webster wrote, "There are musical shepherds who take responsibility for repertoire lost, strayed, forgotten. David Arben proved one of those when he was soloist last night in Karol Szymanowski's Violin Concerto No. 1, a piece the Philadelphia Orchestra had not thought about in more than 60 years. He showed that his determination to reintroduce the piece was justified. Bringing the piece to realization was further complicated when the scheduled conductor, Witold Rowicki, suffered a fatal heart attack less than two weeks ago. He was replaced by Christoph Eschenbach, German-born music director of the Houston Symphony, who had about a week to learn the complex work... The piece is in one long color swatch, a series of scenes in which the violin soars high in its range while the orchestra isolates solo instruments and groups to frame and illuminate the solo line. Arben's playing was silvery and pure, his instrument clear and penetrating in that high flight. The orchestral textures and the elusive long logic of the solo line created a play of sound and mood that sets this piece apart from most of the repertoire. It leads eventually to a cadenza that ends with a memory of Beethoven — the timpani softly leading the violin back to the orchestral earth. The work and this performance of it set the concert outside any hint of routine."

In May of 1991, Arben traveled to a particularly gorgeous concert venue in Prague." I was on stage in my seat, warming up thirty minutes before the concert. A lovely woman quietly passed by, smiling at me. Later, she came back and smiled again. Just us, nobody else in the hall, the little tiny lady kept going back and forth."

Only later did someone disclose her identity, the U.S. Ambassador to Czechoslovakia, the Honorable Shirley Temple Black. "We shook hands. Afterward, she gave a nice reception and party for the orchestra."

The Philadelphia Orchestra traveled to Munich on May 29. "We arrived about 11:00 p.m. on a most beautiful street, Maximilianstrasse, and stayed at the gorgeous Four Seasons Hotel." Everybody marveled at its elegance. David told his colleagues of a nearby establishment that served absolutely delicious food, frequented by undying Nazi supporters. "I knew how to survive in these hostile environments, so I emphasized to my friends the importance of following my lead exactly and avoiding eye contact with anyone there. A short walk away, we reached stairs that led to the smoke-filled establishment."

"I used to go to these places by myself, to see where Hitler got his start. This was a single exception, when I went with musicians from the Orchestra. And I was on edge, only because I was with my friends."

David visited all surviving haunts of the Third Reich's chief architect, doing his personal kind of research. He wanted to know as much as possible about a ruthless leader's origins, sometimes encountering the unexpected. There were three thousand German women in Berlin married to three thousand German Jews taken to Dachau. After some months, the wives organized and started marching. "Hitler was not really brave." Cowering before a burgeoning opposition movement of females, Hitler released all surviving husbands, so a host of reunited couples managed to survive in the countryside. "This extremely unusual story fascinated me," so different from the countless tragic outcomes in the war.

"For years after the war I wanted to understand why. Certain things in life, you could live five hundred years and still you wouldn't understand." After such explorations of a cesspool-like cradle of evil, he instinctively sought fresher air and higher ground. Arben found this on a visit to Berchtesgaden. "It is one of the most gorgeous places in the world."

On European soil, he reminisced about his early musical connections. His father had arranged for him to audition and study with Szymon Goldberg. Abraham and son would arrive twenty minutes early for an afternoon lesson at two o'clock. "Their courtyard where he lived had corner apartments on both sides." He later came to perform with the Philadelphia Orchestra. Goldberg first played at the Saratoga Performing Arts Center in 1967 and started teaching at Curtis in 1980. "Backstage, I usually wouldn't approach him. But one night I said, 'Mr. Goldberg. When I was about eleven years old my father took me to your place to play for you. While we waited, we heard you practice the Bach No. 2 E Major Concerto.' He looked at me and said, 'I am still practicing.'"

"Szymon Goldberg, all the great violinists listen to his Mozart sonatas. He was the specialist. I listened to him when I was studying Mozart."

Leaving backstage, maestro Muti asked a question. "'Mr. Arben, I will be leaving the end of next year and I would like to you to pick a concerto to play.' He gave me the honor." With Muti on the podium, Arben performed Mozart's Violin Concerto No. 3 on February 6 and 7, 1992. Later the same year, Muti was named Conductor Laureate.

Riccardo Muti led the Philadelphia Orchestra on their first trip to Israel, the year of David Arben's "first" retirement in 1992, at age sixty-five. This splendid crowning of Arben's career, actually rescinded for a year, preceded the many "curtain calls" and "encores" that followed him into a new phase of life. The President of the Philadelphia Orchestra Association then asked David to stay on one additional year. Arben agreed.

In March of 1993, David played the last time as soloist for his orchestra family. He performed Mozart's Violin Concerto No. 7. This three-concert series took place on March 19, 20, and 23. About this final hurrah, Daniel Webster penned in the *Philadelphia Inquirer* on March 20, 1993, "Violinist David Arben has played in the Philadelphia Orchestra for 34 seasons, many of them as associate concertmaster, and has drawn the admiration of his colleagues for the refinement of his playing and the grace of his musicianship. He was soloist with the orchestra last night at the Academy, probably his last such appearance since he has said he will retire after this season."

From Daniel Webster again on September 22, 1993, "David Arben left the Philadelphia Orchestra at the end of the summer, but he won't be putting down his violin. An orchestra member since 1959 and associate concertmaster since 1979, Arben says 'Playing the violin is not a job; it's my life.' Orchestra audiences have valued this self-effacing violinist's solo appearances with the orchestra for the refinement of his playing. His colleagues admire his playing for its combination of meticulous detail and poetic lyricism. Orchestra audiences saw him in his usual place through the summer season. Only his colleagues saw him backstage when he opened the case and took out his violin. It was like a father greeting a child in the morning, and it is a ritual and gesture the other musicians will miss."

Arben himself reflected, "Over a period of forty-five years, everything that might happen has happened on concert travels. A travel case left behind at San Francisco airport was still waiting for me three weeks later when I returned from the tour in Japan. A mystery to me, wherever I went, I had remarkable experiences. See the tales you got out of me, a suitcase story?!" Arben grinned.

"I played solo with Philadelphia Orchestra twenty-seven times." Summing up a professional career, like memories of a lifetime of brilliant sunrises and crimson sunsets too numerous and breathtaking to adequately recount, David Arben elegantly and simply described the last thirty-nine years. "Life has been full. Post-graduation, Detroit for a year, Cleveland four years, Philadelphia Orchestra for thirty-four years. Before my retirement, I was active as a soloist in the United States, Europe, Asia, Mexico, and South America. I have been able to pass along this art by teaching at university and through masterclasses. A great and fabulous life, I consider myself to be very fortunate to have been able to create a life of harmony, joy, and wonderful friendships. The violin is the best thing that ever happened to me. It gave me life."

12
Return to Warsaw, 1997

"Spiritually, I feel them. I see them, but I cannot touch them."

For more than fifty years following World War II, David Arben never returned to his native Poland. In 1994, Steven Spielberg set up the Shoah Foundation. Urgently, he wanted to ensure accurate remembrance of the Holocaust through recording personal testimonies from those who endured its unimaginable horrors and remained alive. Three years after incorporating, the Foundation invited David to go on a one-week homecoming. Arben commented, "Though I wouldn't go out of my way to teach the world anything, they did a fantastic thing to educate the public." He agreed to this trip with one simple request.

David had learned that a small synagogue in Warsaw where his family used to attend Sabbath services still existed. He wanted to visit, call to remembrance, and play the violin. Finally, he would say Kaddish, a prayer usually recited daily in Hebrew for eleven months after the death of parents. Until now, he had not fulfilled that basic cornerstone of traditional Jewish life. David, as the oldest surviving son, would now say this ancient prayer and "complete things." The Shoah foundation agreed, provided him a car, driver, and guide. "Just three weeks from formal invitation to departure, leaving little time to process, I started feeling how important it would be. I was doing it for my family." The magnitude of the occasion had begun to hit him.

On this trip the Shoah Foundation was joined by Israel 50, a consortium of groups sponsoring cultural ties between Israel and the United States, which had already begun making advanced preparations for a celebration in 1998 of the smaller country's founding fifty years prior. David Arben had been selected as a representative of Holocaust survivors. Newspaper coverage by the *Philadelphia Inquirer* added to those planning to document it all. "They sent a writer and also someone from New York to film the whole thing."

"A Polish woman came to interview me in Warsaw. She spoke English very well. The interview was four-and-a-half hours with cameras recording everything. A good interviewer is part psychologist and draws you out with the right question. She was a wonderful lady but with her questions, I didn't open up completely. The questions were not deep enough for my heart to respond."

Adapted from his Shoah Foundation interview May 14, 1997: "Coming back fifty-six years later was difficult with memories of horrors in hell. Tomorrow morning I will be going to a synagogue to play Joseph Achron's Hebrew Melody and say Kaddish for my family. My family never lived to see any of the fruits of how they helped me. They instilled in me that you must strive for the best. So, after the war, there was no alternative thought. Without their dignity or support, my playing violin would not have come to fruition or ever happened. Violin was my life, and I end on that happy note until tomorrow. Tomorrow will be a note of reality, of painful loss."

Philadelphia Inquirer personnel had obtained permission to go to Arben's apartment two weeks before his departure. They took photos to help illustrate an anticipated newspaper story. "The article was one-and-a-half pages long. With my picture, it said I was born Chaim Arbeitman and changed my name to David Arben. I did it on purpose (to reach any reader solely familiar with his birth-name)." Daniel Webster, the *Inquirer* music critic, wrote of events as they unfolded in his article that came out May 15. "Arben, 69, flew to Warsaw on Sunday. Accompanied by five close friends from the orchestra, plus orchestra president Joseph H. Kluger, two camera crews and representatives of the Shoah Foundation and Israel 50, Arben took his violin to Nożyk Synagogue."

The date for the synagogue service corresponded to a space of time when the Philadelphia Orchestra would tour Europe. Opening in Warsaw and staying for a few days, their first visit to Poland, David invited four members of his former orchestra to go with him to Nożyk Synagogue. His guests included resident conductor Luis Biava who brought his wife Clara, clarinetist Donald Montanaro and harpist Margarita Csonka Montanaro, as well as violinist Larry Grika. Orchestra President Joseph Kluger and cellist Ohad Bar-David, point man for Israel 50, also attended. "I invited six, but eighteen or nineteen showed up and I was glad everybody came."

All gathered outside at Twarda #9, "the same synagogue where my father used to take me when I was five and six years old.

Miraculously, in Warsaw that was 95% destroyed, this was the only synagogue that survived." Originally underwritten by a prominent merchant Zalman Nożyk and his wife Ryfka for Orthodox Jewry, the building's neo-romanticist facade incorporated elements of Byzantine ornamentation. Designed by a Karol Kozlowski, also responsible for the Warsaw Philharmonic Orchestra Hall, another famous Warsaw architect Leandro Marconi may have directed construction. It opened in 1902. "All the famous cantors sang there."

When a Shoah Foundation representative noticed Arben and accompanying parties entering, she initially objected. "This is private, only you and movie cameras. No one else is permitted." Such would depart from the contractually agreed upon scope of their activity to be recorded. David explained, "Not just anybody, they're my family and part of me. If I cannot have them, we're finished. They'll come with me and I will go with them." Enough said, Shoah Foundation's agent stayed on a call to Los Angeles for forty-five minutes, ultimately hammering out the new contract.

"I chose to sign a new contract which allowed my musician friends to be included." Ultimately, more than Shoah cameras documented what followed. Crew from Polish and German television arrived on scene as well.

Daniel Webster, of the *Philadelphia Inquirer*, documented David's words before all those assembled in front of a platform raised at the synagogue's center, the bema: "'I am now at the Nożyk Synagogue in Warsaw, Poland. I would like to thank my dear friends of the Philadelphia Orchestra for being with me today to share the memory of my family.' He paused briefly, choking back feelings triggered by thinking and saying family. 'It was fifty-six years ago that our family was separated by the Nazis to never see each other again. It is on this soil that my entire family was murdered. Their only crime was being Jewish. It is here that I feel close to my family. Spiritually, I feel them. I see them, but I cannot touch them. I know that they are not resting in peace. I am dedicating the *Hebrew Melody* by Joseph Achron to the memory of my family.' The cuffs of his blue blazer quivered perceptibly, betraying the emotion surging through him as he picked up the violin. His first notes were hollow, but strength and color grew as he tucked more firmly under his chin the instrument that had saved his life."

"The melody, with its melisma and ornaments, begins in the middle strings and gradually moves upward. In his elegant, inflected hands, it began as a cry of pain in the lower strings and, in the highest reach of the E string, gradually arrived at a plea for peace."

"In the hush that followed, he laid his violin on the blue velvet covering and, before the tabernacle, began to walk to and fro. He put on his glasses, then took them off to wipe away tears. He kept pacing. No one moved. Then he walked to a lectern and read in Hebrew from the Kaddish, a prayer that praises God and is said in memory of the dead."

"Arben walked back to retrieve his violin and seemed to take strength from the familiar routine of putting the violin back in the case, loosening the bow, covering the instrument, closing the case and zipping its cloth cover. They moved him toward a waiting car and returned to their hotel. A few hours later, in his hotel room, Arben said he had just gone through the most moving experience of his life." (posted May 15, 1997, *Philadelphia Inquirer*)

Inner stirrings, triggered by familiar surroundings, brought a flood of recollections, both quite delightful and at the same time deep and dark. Selective suppression not possible, he felt an intimacy with his past not available elsewhere, but also inevitable aching from loss permeated all. He did not recoil, lest he lose lasting touch with his parents and siblings. "Heavy memories are everywhere I look. They cling to me. Of course, I don't want them to leave, because this is the only thing I have of my family — my memories."

Around four thirty in the afternoon, Arben interacted with the Orchestra President, Joseph Kluger. He shared about news coverage of the story, "David Arben returns to Warsaw." Also, the orchestra chief announced a concert that evening with the President of Poland Aleksander Kwaśniewski expected to come. Kluger requested that Arben attend and had reserved him a seat next to the country's top executive. David replied "Thank you, Joe, thank you very much. Today is a day for my family." Kluger urged again, "But you will sit with the President." The violinist said, "I am sitting with my family today, nobody can interrupt my family. My mind and my soul cry."

"The following day was a free day for everybody. My friends in the orchestra gave me a surprise party at one of the finest restaurants in old town Warsaw. It was fantastic.

"There were two books that I read, written by Polish Jews from Warsaw who survived. Both of them said that everything was destroyed. So, I didn't expect to see any part of it. The next day I met with the woman guide. I asked, 'Is anything left of the Warsaw Ghetto?' She said, 'Yes.'" The Nazis had invaded Poland in 1939. Three million, two hundred thousand resident Jews then constituted approximately one-fifth of the total world population. Forced confinement within the Warsaw Ghetto commenced thirteen months later. By 1945, 90% of Poland's Jewish population had perished.

"Later, I understood why someone who knew otherwise might state that the Ghetto didn't exist. The influx of visitors from everywhere, interested for a variety of reasons, could call the wrong kind of attention and spark even more anti-Semitism. But you cannot, and should not hide from the truth. We have to accept it, although many times very painful. Without acceptance, we will never know."

So, his guide took David to the Warsaw Ghetto. "I saw things like the Star of David with a gallows, the word 'Jude,' and phrases like 'Polish Jews, go to Palestine.' The guide approached an old man selling trinkets. 'Were you here during the Ghetto?' The man could hardly talk, but suddenly came alive. 'Jews were horrible.'"

"The guide started crying. Despite growing up here she said, 'I never knew this existed.' It had been so many years since I had lived here, but I was not surprised because of my past experiences. There was anti-Semitism both then and now. I learned there was a famous bishop in some region of Poland, preaching the worst anti-Semitic lectures every Sunday, but Pope John Paul stopped him."

"Next, she took me to an area I recognized as my neighborhood. My original apartment building had its courtyard and three entrances to the building. Here's another structure quite similar. We walked upstairs and inside they hooked up microphones where I gave testimony. This record belongs to the Shoah Foundation. I got a nice letter from Spielberg, thanking me. The experience was extremely difficult, but wonderful."

During this same time in Warsaw, Arben looked for the places connected to his childhood. At Kraszynski Ogrud Park, a site close to the Arbajtman apartment, David found where someone had snapped a photo of his family many years ago. "I found the exact spot, but didn't take a picture. It was the same nice park."

"I don't like to speak for any person or group, including Jewish people. Anybody has a right and should speak for themselves. But at that time, we were totally divided in society. If Jews had non-Jewish friends, it was very unusual. Even when we went to school, we didn't make friends with non-Jews for fear of stirring up anti-Semitism. But in those days, we couldn't avoid it. Today is a different story. It's a different life. Now I go everywhere, embracing different religions and philosophies."

For his sincere guide who tearfully confessed, "'I had no idea such prejudice against Jews remained,'" David had a simple comment. "'When you don't look for it, you don't find it.'" Arben admitted, when interviewed by the Shoah Foundation, that the average person living in Poland during World War II may not have known about the greatest crimes committed against humanity. "And today I think I understand better, but I still think the people of the world committed a big crime to let this happen. There were certainly powers who could have stopped the crimes, who could have helped, but didn't."

David came to the end of his one and only return to a land where he had spent the precious handful of years with his father Abraham, mother Chaya, brother Israel, and sister Zysla. A legacy for the parents and siblings he lost, Arben had an abiding wish, the fulfillment of which felt essential for a better future. "I hope humanity can find some kind of greater tolerance towards others."

13
Retirement Life

"I decided to live a lot."

The most recent twenty-plus years of life since retirement flew fastest. After leaving the Philadelphia Orchestra in 1993, David Arben settled into a routine of playing, teaching, traveling, visiting friends, and spending time with his few surviving relatives, as well as adopted and adoptive family members. He emphasized the enjoyment and quality of life.

Arben left when he could have played considerably longer, feeling it better to depart at the height of performance. "A problem with many players, no matter what age, they cannot face the truth. For example, they still think they are great, even when they are not. I always looked at myself in a mirror. Sometimes the truth is not beautiful. I say to many of my students, when you lie to yourself you commit a crime. If you have to lie to the whole world, lie, but never to yourself. Never fool yourself. Only truth will survive you."

Many individuals advancing in years do not notice or want to admit that their skills have started to decline. He never wanted to retire from Philadelphia Orchestra, but knew when to compose a letter. Careful and deliberate, he reflected fully before submitting it. "I could have kept it up, if I had continued practicing a lot, but I decided to live a lot."

Only blocks from Curtis, the Academy of Music, and later the Kimmel Center, Arben kept a practiced finger on the pulse of musical life. Students came to 1517 Spruce Street for lessons. The violinists he coached often secured positions with elite orchestras.

Besides students, Arben regularly socialized with orchestra colleagues, still family really. "Margarita Montanaro and her husband Don are very dear friends. For years, no matter the season, we have a tradition of having dinner in Chinatown. The Montanaros pick me up and we meet the Grikas and Biavas. Margarita organizes and we get together about every three weeks."

On March 14, 1994, David received a call from Tante's younger granddaughter, his "baby" in Switzerland. Her firstborn had just arrived. "She called me from the hospital three hours later. 'We had a boy and you are the godfather. Don't give me any rubbish that you're too old to travel.' Having been unable to attend her wedding, I was more than happy to accept."

Arben did visit the summer of 1994, and laid eyes on his five-month-old godson. A house move caused the parents to delay christening until September 1995. "I flew to Geneva where I became the godfather. This was an honor because normally, Jews are not part of a Catholic baptism.

This contrasted to events in June of 1953 when David's Curtis roommate Tony, owing to traditional guidelines, didn't feel free to choose Arben as best man in his Catholic wedding, and apologized. David had responded, "Choose anybody, I am fine with your decision."

Disregarding religious dictates and regarding him as one of their own, Tante's granddaughter included Arben in a sacred Catholic ritual. "I was official godfather. My godson is a nice boy and sometimes comes to visit me in Philadelphia. Since 1948, the family continues the tradition. All devoted to me, I am devoted to them."

How would Arben describe the relationship with Sam Rudofker? "He was a dear friend, a close brother, the absolute best. It was a great loss when he died at a young seventy-two in 1994." Their friendship endured forty years.

In Philadelphia for many years, "Felix Zandman was a good friend and great genius from Poland." He hid from Nazi occupation in 1943, spending seventeen months with four others concealed in the pit dugout under a country cottage of one virtuous Polish family. After immigrating to Philadelphia, he went on to found the company Vishay, with his patent on heat-resistant electronic components. Felix Zandman considered another invention, a crucial technology he gifted Israel for their defense, his greatest contribution in life.

The question keeps returning: from whence genius? "Do I think there is something greater from beyond? You know, there are many questions. Basically, humanity doesn't know. We don't know where we come from and we don't know where we are going."

Besides pondering the universe, unfettered in retirement by any fixed work schedule, Arben had the freedom to extend his annual holidays in Europe. Members of the Swiss family even came to see him during his winter stays in Puerto Rico.

Eventually Arben's Swiss "baby" came with her kids to visit him in Cape May, New Jersey. They spent several wonderful summer holidays there for his birthday. "Starting with her younger son around one year old, she wanted her children to get to know me. What an incredible fortune to meet the Swiss family. If there is an afterlife, I am convinced that my parents are responsible for sending the Swiss family to me."

"I kept up with all kinds of friends. Considering my concentration camp imprisonment, many didn't realize how powerful it was for me to be alive. How wonderful it is to be able to decide what I want to eat, to sit and be comfortable. Most take all of this for granted."

Even air quality he cherished. "A pleasant breeze at the beach, lovely plants, taking in a breath of clear air, it was marvelous. I appreciated it all."

In the summer of 1996, Arben attended the wedding of cousins Wolf and Karola Tuchmann's daughter in California. Seeing such a lovely bride, Arben reminisced about the initial encounter with her father. "When I first saw Wolf, he was already grown up, about thirteen years my senior. A wonderful person, everybody loved him. My father made the wedding dress for Karola. It was beautiful and she cherished it. Somehow the dress survived World War II, but before we met again, this treasure from my father was lost. Wolf regretted it so much, pain felt for me."

An enduring love, his cousin and wife lived out their final years in Germany. "He was a fantastic man, such a devoted husband. They had everything. She outlived her husband, into her early nineties. I used to stay up to two weeks each visit with her."

In January of 1998, Israel Philharmonic and Philadelphia Orchestra joined musical forces at CoreStates Center for a "Hear, O Israel" concert to inaugurate America's celebration of the fiftieth anniversary of Israel's founding. Some sixteen thousand attended this once-in-a-lifetime moment. The two orchestras played their respective national anthems. Next, Leonard Nimoy gave preliminary introductions. A sustained note by fifty ram horns, the traditional shofar, followed. On a giant screen, the audience viewed a segment, documenting the life of Associate Concertmaster Emeritus David Arben.

"History has pointed out that America is unique, like no other nation." As a naturalized citizen himself, David expressed amazement and took pride in the country's two-century history of absorbing immigrants seeking opportunity from all over the world. Depending on the decade, some had come to escape religious persecution, others desired better economic opportunity and notably, many who sought political asylum.

As described, the specific impetus to seek U.S. shores and background of immigrants had changed according to circumstances. In retirement, Arben kept up with one familiar transplant, Lithuanian Jascha Gurevitc, who managed the unique Ex-Concentration Camp Orchestra in post-war Germany. During World War II he had served with partisans outside of Vilna's Ghetto. Among other duties, he donned a German uniform as disguise, rode his motorcycle into the woods and killed a few German officers.

After immigrating to the U.S., Gurevitc and his wife lived in New York. They hosted David, whom they always knew as Chaim, for a first Passover Seder in America. "Everybody loved Jascha, including me. On weekends, I would go to their place in New York. He was so proud of what I achieved. He wouldn't have been as happy, if he had done this himself."

"Some years went by and Jascha saw that the New York Philharmonic had a special program. Leonard Bernstein was the Music Director. He said to his wife, 'I am going to write a letter to Bernstein's secretary, telling him that I would enjoy coming to the concert and that I don't have tickets.' Jascha's wife said, 'How could Bernstein possibly remember you?' He heard back from Bernstein's secretary with two tickets and a message. 'I remember you very fondly. Please come backstage after the concert. I would like to see you.' His wife couldn't believe it."

As previously detailed, coauthor Rebecca Jackson met David Arben at Festival of the Youth Symphony Orchestra of the Americas (FOSJA) in San Juan, Puerto Rico. During FOSJA's 1999 summer orchestral and chamber music festival, David served on faculty. His extraordinary musicianship and remarkable kindness made indelible impressions on her. Afterward she sent a thank you note. David's return letter arrived at her California home and friendship blossomed. His love of music and life itself very much inspired and carried to fruition the biographical work in our reader's hands.

In 2009 David made one last trip to Geneva, staying with his Swiss "baby" to surprise her mother (Tante's daughter). Though the thought would have never crossed her mind to ask him to make such a long trip for the occasion, she expressed delight that he came to wish her a happy 80th birthday. For this special occasion, they took Arben by high speed motorboat to the lakeside medieval castle Château de Coudrée.

That same year in August, Arben kept up his correspondence with coauthor Rebecca in August after her visit to Auschwitz. Their birth years separated by more than fifty summers, and birthplaces on different continents, she had sensed palpably powerful emotion at the site where his cattle car once stopped for 24 hours.

Another proof of a potent power to extend life's temporal and social boundaries, film maker Andres Faucher produced The Legacy in 2009. This film followed nine lives that were all saved by music.

Through Faucher, David also connected with someone the director had unexpectedly found immobilized by a flat tire in the streets of Los Angeles. He helped the man put on a spare, and during further conversation over lunch, Faucher and the grateful motorist, named Jack Garfein, learned of their mutual involvement in cinema. Faucher shared about filming a Polish violinist who had been detained at Flossenbürg concentration camp. Garfein said, "I was in Flossenbürg." Faucher added, "The violinist is David Arben." An astounded Jack Garfein exclaimed, "I know David Arben!"

Garfein, the seventy-nine-year-old survivor of eleven Nazi concentration camps, talked with Arben via borrowed cell phone, speaking perfect Yiddish. "He had immigrated as one of five Holocaust survivors to first reach America. Later, he played an instrumental role in the development of Actors Studio. He discovered Ben Gazarra, Steve McQueen, George Peppard, Bruce Dern, and Susan Strasberg. He also gave James Dean his first role in a stage production."

Arben tells the story of their first meeting. "From tire changing in Los Angeles with millions of people from all over the world, we met in New York. Can you imagine? In Brooklyn, we shared a lunch. It meant so much to meet this man. We were both in Flossenbürg at the

same time, same camp, same barrack. We chatted like two lost boys."
Did they know each other in the camp? "No, our barrack had six or
eight hundred kids. I was sixteen and he was thirteen. He was there
for a short time and then taken somewhere else. He lost his entire
family. Now I ask, 'From where does it come?' He was all alone when
liberated at fourteen years old, no family, nothing. How do you
become a known Broadway producer and film director with no
father, no mother, all alone? We both came full circle. From ashes
back to music and arts, where we started, it never finishes. This is
life."

Towards the end of 2009, David received a call, one very familiar
voice from the past. "I had not heard from Tony di Bonaventura for
about thirty-six years. The beginning of October last year, my phone
rang. It was Tony. I answered, 'I'm pleased you called.' 'David, I
don't know what to say. I am sorry I didn't call you for so many years.
If you don't want to talk to me, I understand.' He knew better." Arben
added with characteristic humor, "'It's okay, don't worry. But if you
call me thirty-five years from now, I may not answer the phone.' He
said, 'You cannot imagine how much it would mean to me if you
would come to my eightieth birthday in six weeks, in Boston.' Tony's
five children put on a most lavish Saturday night dinner for three
hundred people and Sunday brunch at the Chestnut Hill Country
Club. Tony invited his best man, Luigi Zaninelli. I had a phenomenal
time at this reunion."

In 2010, Heidi Waleson wrote in Curtis' *Overtones* magazine an
article titled, "David Arben Finds Beauty in the Violin." She quoted
him, summing up his feelings in the wake of near execution by firing
squad, but saved by his musicianship. The violin "became part of my
body. It was me." After reaching the U.S., he observed "people write
about freedom. They don't know like I do what freedom means. It's
like life itself."

In April 2011 Riccardo Muti and Chicago Symphony came to
perform in New York. "Years ago, I had prepared three women for
auditions and now they are in Chicago Symphony. They called,
inviting me to their concert. I asked for a ticket to the Sunday
matinee."

"They called me back after talking to the manager. All tickets were
sold. Knowing my former students, Muti asked them, 'Is David

coming? If he wants to come, we will arrange it. Tell him to come to my room half an hour before the concert.' When I arrived, we embraced. He helped me take off my coat and hung it up in his closet. I ended up sitting in a box with his wife. It was wonderful."

"Muti was music director of Philadelphia Orchestra for thirteen years. I greatly admire him. Without doubt, he is the greatest living conductor."

"After concerts, many people rushed to greet Muti backstage. He is the kind of person that even if a prime minister were talking to him and he would see me or another colleague, he would step aside and embrace us."

In the first half of 2011, eligible for a new German pension benefit to those who had been confined in ghettos, David applied. The amount, a pittance compared to what he had lost, meant far less than the principle.

"I have met people that went through similar experiences. Every one of us who survived has an unbelievable story, each unique. Even if we were in the same camp, depending on many factors — age, whether you entered with a sister or brother, your upbringing — our suffering and experience were not the same."

"If someone asks and is interested to know my story, I share." Can reading his history of miracles and successes provide others with inspirational lessons? Arben has his own questions, hearkening back to a first disheartening attempt to play for remuneration, in the Warsaw Ghetto. "Both parents watched me during initial violin lessons and took pride in my progress. But when food became desperately scarce, my mother sent me to a less poor neighborhood, to play for charity. I came home empty handed. Did my violin feed anybody in those dark days? If it had been possible, I can assure you, none of the family would have starved. Did my music save anyone from death, besides myself? No. I only wish that they could still be alive."

Recollections from 2011 of a meeting in Philadelphia serve to illustrate David's beneficence. Coauthor Rebecca shared, "I spent an entire afternoon and evening with Mr. David Arben, always an enriching time of listening, learning, and laughing. Just moments after I entered his Spruce Street apartment, Mr. Michael Tree called. What a coincidence!"

"Mr. Arben passed me the phone and Mr. Tree said, 'What a nice surprise! I was just calling David to invite him to dinner tomorrow after I finish teaching at Curtis. Would you be able to join us?'"

Rebecca continued, "The next evening I met Mr. Arben at the stoop of his apartment around 6:30 p.m. We walked. More accurately, we strolled, stopping every few yards so he could punctuate a part of his story. With only a few blocks to walk, we arrived at Mr. Tree's hotel rather early, so we took the extra time to walk to Curtis Institute of Music. As we passed this historic, ornate structure, he read my mind, remarking 'This building has changed very little since I first came so many years ago.' On our walk to Tree's hotel a woman stopped with her hands outstretched, asking to shake Mr. Arben's hand. She said his final recital touched her so much and she still remembers it vividly. Her husband, standing nearby, was the current piano tuner at Curtis."

"Moments after arriving back at the hotel lobby, Michael appeared. As the two men embraced, I couldn't help but smile, looking at the joyful look on Michael's face. Every time I visit David, he tells me Michael has been a true friend for all these years since they attended Curtis together. A loyalty we can all hope to share with someone."

"We decided on returning to La Viola (on the west side of 16th Street). Mr. Arben and I had shared many a meal there, but it was to be Mr. Tree's first visit. Over pasta and wine, Tree spoke of getting to meet the great old violinists because his father interviewed them. He trembled with excitement, meeting Heifetz at age nine, and was dazzled by the company of Kreisler at age six or seven."

"A scrumptious dinner with these two revered musicians at La Viola concluded my weekend in Philadelphia. Mr. Tree hailed a cab to make sure I got to the Amtrak station at 30th and Market. He saw me off with a kiss on the cheek. After shutting my door, he knocked on the window of the driver to tell him my destination. As we drove away, my cab driver said with a thick accent, 'A very nice gentleman.' I said, 'Yes, and did you know he is a famous classical musician?' My cabbie replied, 'So nice. So humble. We need more people like that in Philadelphia.' I agreed with him and thought to myself, 'We need more people like Mr. Tree and Mr. Arben around the whole world.'"

The two musician friends chose two distinct career paths. Michael Tree played in the renowned and enduringly successful Guarneri Quartet. David gave many solo performances, domestically and abroad, but preferred the stable life of an orchestral musician.

A fellow student from the first year at Curtis, a Canadian voice major, Diane had known him as Chaim. After many years, she called the Philadelphia apartment where his phone number had not changed. "Somewhere in Newfoundland, she told me, 'Every 13th of August I think of you on your birthday.' She herself was eighty-four. Can you imagine?"

Why did he remain single? "If I had chosen to live a normal family life, I could not have achieved my goal. I lost six years of playing violin, from twelve to eighteen, being in the ghetto and concentration camps. During those formative years, six years is like six hundred years, which is when you make your greatest progress. To catch up, I had to work very hard. My focus was the violin, period."

"A couple of years ago, I said something to one of my students. She blew up at me, but eighteen months later she started doing what I pointed out earlier. If I had pushed the issue, she would have backed away, so I hadn't forced matters, I planted a seed. People may reject something initially, but in the back of their minds it's there. It may take three months or three years, but with something positive, it will develop."

Did his mental acumen come from emulating parental examples, his own technique of focused relaxation, or something else? "I analyzed who I was and how I should live." Congruent with his conclusions, he adopted new ways to express inner thoughts, choosing words that aligned with better paths. "I was not always right. Many times I admitted to myself a need for improvement, and constantly corrected things."

"I am comfortable in my skin. I have no tension and let my body breathe naturally. It can heal and repair itself, because there is no pressure. The most important thing in life is to have no stress. When you can relax your body, not trying to manipulate matters, it's the most wonderful thing. Leave well alone."

"Whatever you do, become emotionally involved. It's important. When it comes to friendship, I don't want it to be superficial. If I get sick, some of my friends become concerned and call every day.

Sometimes I tell them I am better than I am. I don't want them to worry and want my friends to be happy."

In Arben's parlance, living smart attracts luck; one leads to the other. Perhaps an inadequate explanation for those with an analytical bent, but small world connections seemed to follow David always. One example: for the 1997 newspaper article about his return to Warsaw described in the last chapter, he gave an accurate rendering of his original birth name to interviewers. He had done this on purpose, for easier recognition by old world acquaintances, should they by chance read this article. When the Dean of Philadelphia's University of the Arts saw it, he immediately thought of a friend in New York who would take interest.

The Dean, with whom Arben had previously worked, sent a copy of the article to his New York friend. Dr. Jack Terry noticed a familiar name, Chaim Arbeitman. Armed with a phone number, "Jack called me and we got together in Philadelphia, the first meeting after fifty-two years."

"He was with me three years in the camps, the last one being Flossenbürg. For hours, we talked about everything. We couldn't stop talking. I didn't know it at that time, only finding out later, that some of the young people looked up to me in the camps." Quite naturally, these reunions oft repeated. "Jack and I meet twice a month. We go to the best places and have fun. It's a fantastic feeling to have a closeness with someone. I am a fortunate man."

Pursuing answers, Arben asked his own questions. "Throughout history, Germans were the most educated people in Europe. No one can legitimately deny what they did. How could they have been so brutal to us, to other human beings? This is what education does for you? Then it's better to be a moron."

He accommodated differing views. "I do not insist that anyone believe me. You can believe me or not. During a disagreement, a friend said, 'David, prove it to me.' I smiled. 'Isn't it wonderful that I have come to realize I don't have to prove anything to anybody? The only person that I have to convince is myself. Fortunately, I did this many years ago.' Then we switched the subject to humanity in general, universal values, and equality. She compared her formulation to a math equation. I said, 'Yes, I can agree on arithmetic. But when it comes to humanity, sometimes two plus two does not equal four.' She persisted, 'No, two plus two always equals four.' I could not accept this because I have seen the worst side of humanity, as well as the best. It's not a formula."

"Nobody understands everything. Humanity was created in such a way we will not understand everything. And this is why we don't know how it started, and we don't know where we are going. This is good. Sometimes, not to know is healthy. There is a reason for it, but I am not going to spend time looking for the reason. Humanity needs some mystery. But before I die, for people I care about, I would like to have two days to say goodbye. That would be nice."

Nothing renders crystal clear, so much as a near-death experience, the inestimable value of continued existence. David held up a picture of Noah Stockman, again testifying he owed this man his survival at Budzyn Concentration Camp. "One man, one moment in time, if not for him, there was no doubt about my being killed. So many close calls with multiple guns aimed directly at you, try putting yourself in my place. When looking at him I see my life. I owe my life to this man."

When the German government began inviting individuals who suffered in concentration camps to return, wanting to honor the living and the dead, Arben and Terry started going back together for special ceremonies at Flossenbürg. Both spoke of their experiences to educate school students, trainees at both police and military academies.

"We stayed in Weiden, a nice little town with a charming square about 15 kilometers from Flossenbürg. Unlike Dachau and Auschwitz, not enough people spoke up about Flossenbürg, but it's better known now. More people are aware."

The site of Arben's final confinement during the war eventually attained status as a concentration camp memorial. "The German government invited me to go to this camp. The director of the concentration camp came after me and said, 'We are building a new building and going to dedicate it next year.' He asked if I would be part of it and play. I agreed and it was an incredible gathering."

The formal ceremonies each year came to include speeches by prominent figures that received national and international coverage throughout Europe. Dignitaries attended, including many Presidents, Secretaries of State, and Ambassadors.

"In 2007 the President of Ukraine, Viktor Yushchenko, was at the gathering. He made a big speech. His father, an inmate, had survived Flossenbürg. All the dignitaries from Europe came and made speeches. Jack Terry spoke very beautifully, and I finished the program with music in the camp's former canteen. It was broadcast on the radio and televised live all over Germany. It was a very emotional experience."

"It was like the United Nations. There was a woman who did translation simultaneously. They sent me the tapes which I reviewed. When I spoke, it was also said in German. I had two little speeches. I played Meditation (from Thaïs) for the non-Jewish population killed. Second, I played Hebrew Melody for the Jews who perished. When I spoke about Meditation, she translated accurately. Then I said, 'I am playing Hebrew Melody for my family. For many years I experienced agony.' The word 'agony' never appeared in the translation."

"I was introduced to President Yushchenko. I had never met anybody with such pure, spontaneous passion. German secret police and the Ukrainian Secret Service surrounded him, about thirty to forty people. When he saw me, he came over, held my head like this, kissed me on the forehead, kissed me on this cheek, then on the other cheek. Then he grabbed my hand and started to kiss my hand. I didn't know what to do. I turned his hand and kissed his hand. Never such emotion, as this man, it was unbelievable."

"Afterward I went outside among the crowd. With no gate, people from the small town could walk in, and there was a young woman, maybe late twenties, who came in with another lady looking for me. The blonde woman, about eight months pregnant, had seen me on TV. She tried to embrace me but we couldn't reach because her baby bump was in the way."

"With tears streaming, she cried, 'My grandfather was a guard in the camp. He was a bad man. I am so sick over what he did. I hope you can forgive. You played so beautifully, you made me cry.' I said, 'You are a wonderful person. You mustn't cry, you had nothing to do with it. You will have a beautiful child coming soon and you must live a wonderful life. I wish you all the best.' She felt so guilty."

"I returned to Flossenbürg in 2008 and spoke to German military personnel in uniform, twenty-eight to thirty-year olds who had already served in Afghanistan. They gave me a big picture of the unit and a pin for my lapel. The insignia somehow looked swastika-like. They meant well. I hung their picture on a wall in my home."

"When I spoke to the cadets, I mentioned the word hate. Anyone who hates does not like themselves, whether they know it or not. Hate is such an ugly word, it should be taken out of the dictionary. I don't even hate people I call enemies. I know what hate is capable of doing. It's a waste of life. Hate poisons and I don't want to be poisoned. If I don't like something, I can disagree but I like myself too much to hate."

"At Flossenbürg, it is interesting to think that terrible things took place on ground that became very peaceful years later. Birds are singing, but if the walls could speak or could write, there would be shock. In the concentration camps they didn't hate, they just killed. There was not enough time to hate. They just shot you and finished the job."

"On some visits, Jack and I met with young people, high school and college age from all over Europe, non-Jewish boys and girls. Once they had two Palestinians, two Arab Muslims, and two Israeli youngsters who met together. I shared with them, 'It was a war, but there's more to this story. The worst massacre was in Poland. I have data which shows, of 3.2 million Polish Jews, only 10% survived. More than one million Jewish kids were killed in gas chambers.' I asked the students to consider their own lives. 'Look what you have already achieved. You don't know what these more than a million murdered children might have done for humanity. We'll never know. I am from Poland, and my entire family was eradicated. In France 76% of Jews survived, in Germany 31% survived. But in Poland the figure was only 10%.'"

"To the Germans I wanted to speak about love. In place of love, I used the word tolerance. And I expanded on this. Being tolerant doesn't mean that you have to love something. There are many things that I don't like, but I keep an open mind." Arben wisely refrained from retaliatory emotions. Still sobering to consider, countless civilian members of society in occupied territories, both individuals and groups, that lacked courage, human sympathy, and moral rectitude, had aided and abetted expansion of the criminal Nazi empire before and during World War II.

What do these annual events accomplish and for what purpose? "You honor millions of people who died at the hands of Nazis and honor those who lived. Anniversaries bring to memory evil in those years. They remind Germany of what they did, so nobody can deny what they tried to hide. We must not forget this was part of history."

"Now they have an archive with my playing, and Jack Terry had something to do with it. If somebody comes from anywhere around the world, sees my name, and presses a button, he can listen to me play."

"Flossenbürg is special, as far as I am concerned, because this is the place where I was liberated. When I first went back, we all sat down together and started eating. I said, 'Oh, they have made great progress. Food is much better than it used to be.' Everybody broke out laughing. And this became a joke that spread to all the tables."

After laughter subsided, the memorial setting stimulated serious self-examination. "People ask, 'How can you believe in God? Look what he did to the many nations of people destroyed and killed, including six million Jews.' My answer to them is, "God cannot make the judgment, good for one and burying another. God didn't do any of this. God is too perfect. I'm proud I never blamed God. Humanity is the problem, not God."

"There were so many interventions that extended my existence, not just one time being in front of a grave with the firing squad. A split second away was death, but I was the only one that came out alive. What did 104 do differently than I, to deserve being shot dead or buried alive?! I don't understand."

"My opinion is that young children of survivors should not be troubled with details of their parents' difficult past. If teenagers come and ask questions, showing interest, I would tell them, but they should not be made to feel guilty."

"Life is my specialty. I am in love with life. You must admit, it's fantastic to be able to sit, to talk, to breathe, to stand up, to move. I cherish this kind of freedom because I know the opposite."

Arben relished both breathing fresh air and a good laugh. He recounted when the Philadelphia Orchestra stopped on tour in Vienna. The reader will recall Wolfgang Schneiderhan as a teacher who had treated David (then Chaim) prejudicially just after the War. "I fixed him good one time." Anshel Brusilow offered to share with

Arben a portion of more ample dressing room space. Brusilow, as concertmaster, had received special accommodations. As the guest soloist, Schneiderhan also had access.

When David went to put a trunk away in the backstage room, he ran into his old teacher. "He didn't recognize me. I was ready to change and asked him, 'Would you please leave now?' He politely said, 'Yes, yes, yes,' and quickly left. I threw out my Nazi teacher who gave me a bunch of grief. It felt so good to stand up for myself."

Knowing full well how Arben withstood continued persecution after detention in Nazi camps, coauthor Rebecca still had not yet attended any formal commemorative event in Germany. In 2011, she came by her own inspiration on how to remember Arben's parents and siblings who perished. Later she wrote, "I just returned from one of the most special trips, traveling through Israel with my parents and sister. All the stories could fill a book, but I write about a very moving part of my trip. Even before crossing the Atlantic, I knew I wanted to leave a note with the names of David Arben's family at the Western Wall. I wrote them on a small sheet of paper, folded it up and carried it in my jacket pocket, safely next to my passport. When we arrived at the Wall in the Old City of Jerusalem I felt nervous. I wasn't sure what the traditions were and hoped I wouldn't do anything incorrectly."

"Most obvious was the way the wall was organized — to the left were the men and to the right were the women. As I walked towards the wall, I noticed people walking backwards away from it. There were many women crowded against the wall. Most were standing, some with their faces in small books, bobbing as they prayed. A woman in front was seated in a chair leaning against the wall, quietly crying. I patiently waited to find a place to leave my note. As I reached forward to place my note on a protruding part of one of the stones I reached above and laid my palm flat on the cold surface. A wash of sadness came over me, as I thought of David and his precious family lost during the Holocaust — Abraham, Chaya, Israel, and Zysla."

Rebecca made plans for another heartfelt tribute to David Arben in 2012. He had generously come each year to Santa Cruz, California, as advisor to the Music in May chamber music festival. After pick-up at San Francisco airport and transport to our driveway, we welcomed him "home." He wryly responded, "It's a face only a mother could love."

The festival's fifth season would honor David Arben and include the world premiere of a commissioned chamber work inspired by his life, entitled Haim. Polina Nazaykinskaya composed the work for clarinet, string quartet, two pianos, and narrator. Performing artists included violinists Rebecca Jackson and Dmitri Pogorelov, violist Alexandra Leem, cellist Ani Kalayjian, clarinetist Jose Gonzalez Granero, pianists Konstantin Soukhovetski and Amy Yang, and narrator Carolyn Corbett.

The evening of the premiere piece came off, not without an incredible hitch — classic David Arben! After the intermission, the musicians for Haim waited for the cue to begin the second half. David came backstage with Enda (a festival board member who was to present the Mayor's proclamation declaring May 12 'David Arben Day' in Santa Cruz).

David, visibly shaken, came straight towards Rebecca and gripped her arm. "I didn't think I was going to make it — I thought the time was an hour earlier. Once I realized, it was already too late. I tried calling your cell phone..." As he spoke, Rebecca looked at the monitor showing the stage and saw Enda announcing the proclamation. She interrupted David and turned him around, literally pushing him on stage mid-story. Her heart sank — not only had he missed the first half, but she wondered as to *how* he had finally arrived at the concert.

After taking a bow with his signed proclamation, Mr. Arben came through the backstage door and as if the "pause" button had been released, continued his story. "I had no idea where the theater was, so I just walked down your home street in a panic..." Rebecca interrupted, "David, I'm so sorry. I want to hear all the rest, but we have to go on stage to perform your piece and I don't want to start until you've been seated." Enda escorted Mr. Arben to his seat. Polina came to comfort and said, "Rebecca, now we must go out and perform. He is here. Everything is okay." The show must go on! And away they went.

It wasn't until the reception following the concert that Rebecca heard the full story. There had been a major miscommunication. Both coauthors thought the other was in charge of driving Mr. Arben to the concert. After getting ready, Mr. Arben glanced at his watch and realized the concert had started fifteen minutes previously. Only knowing Rebecca's cell number, he called and left a message, but her phone unfortunately was turned off to avoid interruptions. Next, he left the house and walked down the middle of the street, flagging down every car that passed.

In Arben's own words, "I was walking in the street, hoping to find a taxi. I went to the end of the street twice. It was getting a little dark. I thought to myself, 'They don't know I'm here.'"

"Eventually, a car stopped. It was a young man with his girlfriend. He asked, 'Can we help you?' I said, 'I am being honored at a concert tonight and I am trying to find a ride there. I will pay you, if you could take me to the Caprilla (actually Cabrillo).' The person said, 'We just came back from the pharmacy. We cannot take you but what is your name?' They had me spell my name." They apologized that they could not help him. The young man said, "Good luck," and they left.

A brief time later, they returned. "This young man saw my name on the computer. He ran out with his girlfriend and found me again. 'We are going to take you.' I said, 'I don't know where to find Cabrini.'" The fellow reassured Arben that he found the event venue online. Making small talk he added, "'I'm a student. One of my teachers likes music.'" Just that day in class his Professor had mentioned the festival. David innocently asked, "'What is his name?' He said, 'David Kaun.' I said, 'David Kaun?! I had dinner with him last night!' This story! They didn't comprehend what was happening either."

Arriving at the Cabrillo College campus, Arben and his two companions searched a bit before finally finding the hall. He invited them to attend, all finding a seat at the end of intermission, moments before start of the second half. As previously described, David and Rebecca were reunited briefly backstage. At her continued urging, he returned to his seat, right behind David Kaun (cofounder of the festival). "It could have turned out horribly. But it turned out amazingly well. These wonderful two people decided to take me. Who will go out of their way to help a stranger these days?"

At the conclusion of an emotionally charged and moving tribute to David Arben, performers, composer, and David bowed. Each received a single yellow daffodil as David took time to embrace everyone on stage. Walking off together into the wings, he confided that he had not experienced such powerful emotions in a long time. Wiping away tears he said, "I thought I was a strong man." Wiping their own eyes, everyone huddled around him and chorused, "Mr. Arben, you are the strongest man we know!"

14
Epilogue

"The world is so beautiful, I don't want to leave it, every day is a gift."

Years previously, Mr. Arben had granted us permission to record our conversations. Later, it came as great encouragement to receive approval of the first drafts of chapters in our nascent biographical project.

Wanting to shift into a higher gear, coauthor John and his wife Annette arranged to join him for three weeks during the traditional winter stay in San Juan, Puerto Rico. Always a gentleman, he and his driver met us at the airport. "Wonderful friends, it's my joy and pleasure to be with you, every part of me is happy." Over the ensuing days, per routine, he walked to nearby parks to watch people passing, smoke, and look at ocean waves. A mind ever clear for responses to questions about his past, he displayed the same chutzpah, gallantry, and humor that had always endeared him to us.

During our stay on the island, David took note of an upcoming CNN special to mark seventy years since the Holocaust ended. He spent hours each day keeping up on news. We had rented an apartment in the same building at his insistence, wanting us to live in a safe neighborhood. Since we had no cable service in our unit, David invited us up to his place. There we would watch the special which included a tour of Auschwitz and interviews with survivors.

Before the program started, he offered us snacks with something to drink, iced beverages of course. Viewing the coverage, we remained mostly silent. Interestingly, when the special broadcast concluded, he had little positive to say. "All sanitized, it makes me so angry. It's not legal to show on television the things that actually happened. They showed a picnic with barbed wire."

Today a question remains as to what people exactly knew at the time. "I will tell you they didn't fully know then. And you don't know even now. I am glad you don't know because I care about you. You cannot know unless you were part of it."

"It made me sick to see the lies they showed. This was nothing, some women next to barbed wire. I wish it had been like that without any killings. I would be happy to have everybody alive." David said all this after watching a *60 Minutes* television special on the seventieth anniversary, concluding with comments by Spielberg. From David, "I wish I had not seen death so many times, when so young. Did you see any dead? Did you see anybody hanging, shot? No, because it's television. It's a lie what they portray on television." Arben expressed amazement at himself, "that I can speak about it and not lose my mind."

"I had a lot of pain. Many times, mental pain was worse than physical pain. Violin pushed me in the right direction. Whenever I didn't feel good, I picked it up to feel better. Violin was a 'friend' I could trust. I believe there are no stronger words than musical notes."

Arben didn't merely survive deep suffering, he thrived. "I didn't know why exactly. I had to credit the violin. People who didn't know music or violin would say, 'He cooked up the whole story that he played the violin and it saved his life.' They didn't know. And I will never try to correct them. No, let them believe what they want to believe. Most people never understand the truth of my story. By asking so many questions, you (the authors) are trying to understand and you understand much more than anybody else I know." Like the story of Moses who ran from Pharaoh and encountered an eternally flaming bush, readers who have persisted to this point must turn aside and contemplate the meaning of David's many brushes with fire that didn't consume him. "How did I survive? Of course, not the way that any human being would pick, it just so happened that I was in this massacre of life."

"You see, I lived in the part of the world that was full of deceit. You always pay the price for rampant lies. I am able to interpret Germany because I lived there four years after the War. I couldn't get out and enter Switzerland for a long time because I had no passport and no money. I won the most unbelievable battle in life for humanity. I am here with you. This is fantastic."

"How many people that went through hell really enjoy life now? It's precious when you are alive and well, able to enjoy all to the fullest of your capacity. I lived phenomenally well. I made it happen."

"Years ago, people complained that I didn't take a good picture. There's no such thing. Even if they only take the back of your head, that's a good picture. The only bad picture is no picture."

"Small names are very big to me. The voiceless have a very big voice. If I met the King of Yenemsvelt (Yiddish for "Nowheresville"), just joking, it wouldn't mean anything. I don't even care whether people think I am important or not. What's important is what I think of me and of others. My life story is life from death, not whom I met."

Concerning an accurate timeline and how best to convey what happened, Arben shared advice with the older coauthor. "It's better to ask and find out yourself, than to depend on someone's article. They may be wrong. I want you to be right." Hasn't his life's story been previously reported widely? "I'm glad you think so. If someone knows or doesn't know, it's less important. The important thing is how I feel about my life, my thoughts."

"People want to stay in their comfort zone, but you should learn from mistakes and move forward. I gave myself permission to make mistakes." He added with a smile, "which I continue to do without trying. I tell my students the important thing is not to make the same mistake twice. And don't regret things you cannot change. Regret accomplishes nothing, so why punish yourself? Drop it. Don't collect problems, think only of solutions. Think positively. It's very simple."

Did violin playing somehow serve as a fountain of youth? Arben grinned, "Look at me now. My violin made me an old man. No, but really, my violin was good to me. Music was good to me. It still is, always will be."

"I was 100% relaxed when I held the bow and violin. So, I could play for a long time without pain. I approached the violin and bow the most natural way. I played forty years in the orchestra. It was hard work, but I never had a problem."

"I have been a healthy human being for many years. I accomplished the things that I never thought would be possible for me. I am lucky. When your life is given back to you, you develop it. All the different parts grow like branches on a tree."

Arben turned his attention to the coming spring, measuring time since liberation. "This will be a special celebration for the seventieth anniversary in 2015." Inspired, coauthor John, his wife Annette, and younger daughter Elizabeth made plans to attend the event at Flossenbürg. "Seventy years is a long time. I was one of the young ones, liberated at seventeen. The organizers are doing everything possible to mark the occasion because so few of us are left. Soon there will be no life."

We had peppered him with questions and he kept feeding us with his answers. The three weeks in San Juan sped by, filled with meals together, beverages in open air cafes on the main boulevard, looking over white sand beaches, enjoying Arben's wit and wisdom. Sadly, our allotted time together over, we departed after promising to call regularly. We planned to see him in each of the coming months. We made our reservations to travel with him to Germany and attend the anniversary celebration, seven decades after liberation from Flossenbürg concentration camp.

In March of 2015, coauthor John and his wife Annette Jackson joined David Arben in Sarasota, Florida, where their daughter Rebecca played in the opera orchestra. David shared further information for this biography, attended performances, and all socialized. Later that same month John and Annette went to Philadelphia to see Mr. Arben. They spoke of and looked forward to an anticipated trip to Germany the following month.

As unexpected events unfolded, it looked less likely Mr. Arben would travel to Germany in April. John asked, "Would we have your blessing to still go?" "All my blessings, and I would be disappointed if you didn't go. I hope to be there with you." In the end, Rebecca remained with David in Philadelphia while the rest of her family flew to Flossenbürg.

In August, with Elizabeth Jackson at his side, David traveled to Santa Cruz, California. His three-week stay included beach visits, dining out, and hours of conversation and reflection.

Breaking with Arben's longstanding tradition, he dropped the idea of wintering on Puerto Rico island. In February of 2016, his Swiss "baby" took him from Philadelphia to Sarasota. While enjoying sun and sand, she reminisced about another getaway, his last trip to Europe. They had shared fabulous evenings in Paris. Then David traveled to spend a week at Tante's daughter's summer place near Nantes. There, she and her husband, with Tante's older granddaughter and her son, the younger granddaughter, her two sons and daughter, all gathered together. Gazing over the three generations, their beloved Chaim spoke, "Tante would have been so proud of her family!"

Later in 2016, he again attended Music in May. That same summer, although ninety years of life may receive more frequent note, Rebecca felt urgency to organize a surprise eighty-ninth birthday celebration. Constrained by her opera schedule in Santa Fe, careful planning allowed for a twenty-four-hour dash to the East Coast. She gathered with many of those closest to him to honor Mr. Arben in Philadelphia.

Yet further recognition came David's way in October, 2016. John and Annette flew back to Philadelphia. A special concert at the Philadelphia Ethical Society sponsored by Carol Lidz featured the world premiere of songs by Polina Nazaykinskaya set to poetry by another Holocaust survivor, Mirko Tuma. Also, violinists Rebecca Jackson and HyunJae Lim, violist Tiffany Richardson, cellist Danielle Cho, clarinetist Antonello Di Matteo, pianist Konstantin Soukhovetski, and narrator Matthew Saldivar performed Polina's Haim in Arben's honor at the same concert. Tante's younger granddaughter flew in as a special presence, bringing her daughter and Arben's godson.

Rebecca last saw David Arben in February of 2017. He brightened to hear how many were hoping for his return to a tenth annual season of Music in May. The idea of going appealed, perhaps with assistance by Yolanda Brown (his personal attendant of two years).

Rebecca received an utterly charming Yiddish lesson from David with Elsie at his side. The respected virtuoso also coached her one final time on an excerpt of Mozart. Before departing, recalling her father's urging, she asked for Mr. Arben's blessing. He responded, "You deserve the best." Informally imparted, but considering the source, she could not have asked for more.

Rebecca reflected on all she had learned from this great man, and dear teacher for half her life. In a flash of memory, she recalled carrying the names of Arbajtman family members to Jerusalem's Western Wall, many strolls with him on Philadelphia streets, his visits to Santa Cruz, and their first meeting in San Juan.

Arben himself had once reflected on the makings of a consummate performing artist. He believed that equally balanced mind and emotions produced the best sound. In the immediate post-war period, David's violin always cried, as his teachers told him. The cerebral side of his performance eventually un-froze and matured. The rawness in his soul needed to mend. Finally, the two came together seamlessly, something like the craft of his father and grandfather, master tailors.

Abraham Arbajtman showed deference and respect for his Orthodox father David. Son Chaim took note. At seeming variance with promised longevity for those obedient to the fourth commandment, Abraham's life came to a halt before his deserved allotment. Chaim continued respecting his ancestors long past the grave, copying his father and even taking his grandfather's name. Chaim Arbajtman, David Arben, has lived life abundantly, successfully.

"When life starts, at birth, the child cries. That's the most beautiful music a mother and father, or anyone can hear. It's not a cry, it's the music of the child. The old days, you had both parents. You had responsibility and took care of your father, your mother, the family. Taking care of everybody was good discipline, discipline for life." What a fountain of joy and wisdom our friend is! "I hope so."

"I cannot explain to you why I liked the violin at two-and-a-half, why I picked up two sticks to make believe I was playing the violin and 'la la la la.' I have no idea. The violin saved my life in the camps and later. To me, the violin became my family. My violin became my emotion, my heart, my being. When I grew up, if ever something unpleasant would happen, I would pick up the violin, play, and it would soothe me. The violin is the best thing that ever happened to me, it gave me life."

"Nothing can substitute life. The world is so beautiful, I don't want to leave it. Every day is a gift. We go back to where we started. It never finishes."

David Arben (1927–2017)

15
Postscript

David Arben died peacefully March 13, 2017. Memorial services took place on April 14 in the Grant Room at Union League of Philadelphia. Attendees flew to be there from three different continents.

Violinist Yumi Hwang-Williams opened with solo Bach. Jack Terry spoke of enduring friendship. A replay of contemporaneous television news coverage documented Arben's return to Warsaw in 1997. The same musicians who had performed a short five months previously, Rebecca Jackson, HyunJae Lim, Tiffany Richardson, Danielle Cho, Antonello Di Matteo, and Konstantin Soukhovetski (this time with narrator Gwendolyn Rooker) performed the piece Haim, the first time without Arben present.

David's Swiss "baby" talked about her family's bond with him, spanning four generations. Sharon Kahan, daughter of Arben's Curtis classmate, read remarks sent by Sam Rudofker's daughter, ending with the same quote from Shakespeare read at her father's funeral:

> *When he shall die,*
> *Take him and cut him out in little stars,*
> *And he will make the face of heaven so fine*
> *That all the world will be in love with night*
> *And pay no worship to the garish sun.*

Elizabeth Jackson spoke on behalf of the Jackson family and their love for a man with the most potent love of life. A slideshow of David's images featured the 1963 recording of him playing Debussy's La plus que lente.

Violinist Larry Grika delivered the eulogy from which come the following excerpts:

"David was a theme with variations. He was, at times, a light-hearted minuet, sometimes a hilarious scherzo or a driving presto or a long-winded Bruckner-like philosopher. And at times, his counterpoint would interrupt and punctuate the verbal melody with mild dissonant chords ... The most poignant words I ever heard, were expressed by David. It was after his solo debut with the Philadelphia Orchestra. The Rudofker family held a reception for David at their home. David thanked everyone and then, with tears flowing down his cheeks, in a barely audible voice, cried: 'I wish my Mother and my Father could be here having *nachas* (Yiddish for parental pride in their child's accomplishments) from a loving son.' ... I end with this thought from Victor Hugo: 'The supreme happiness of life is the conviction that we are loved.' David... YOU, ARE LOVED."

The ceremony closed with a performance of the Bach Double Violin Concerto by soloists Yumi Hwang-Williams, Luigi Mazzocchi, and string quartet accompaniment by Rebecca Jackson, Eliza Cho, Tiffany Richardson, and Danielle Cho.

The following day, close friends gathered at Cape May where David had returned frequently to stroll, enjoying the beautiful sea and sky. John Jackson and Sharon Kahan led the group numbering about twenty-five in a responsive reading. Ashes were spread over ocean waters by longest-time companion Jack Terry. After an hour, others crossed back over the sand, but Sharon and Arben's Swiss "baby" lingered. Two women at an empty beach said their last goodbyes without words. Embracing in their fondest of farewell hugs, they departed comforting one another, shoulder to shoulder.

David Arben's memory graced the communal meal that followed, spread over several tables at a local restaurant, the same convivial atmosphere as he had always relished with dearest friends. Harpist Margarita Montanaro spoke warmly to Rebecca and those assembled about going as a troupe to Music in May 2018, the eleventh season. A solo violin work entitled Hope by Polina Nazaykinskaya had been commissioned and scheduled for premiere in memory of David. Those at the table heartily seconded Margarita's proposal. Finally, time came for all to leave, hearts brimming over with imperishable afterthoughts.

Though Mr. Arben often made reference to "luck," we do not believe he would disavow the written expression of our conviction that his life, despite unimaginable loss and against incalculable odds, proved that miraculous successes do happen. Here we pause to reflect on Lincoln's turn of phrase in his Second Inaugural Address, "the better angels of our nature." Also, we recall the words in Hebrews 13:2, that some "have entertained angels without realizing it!" In the case of Abraham and Chaya's son, Israel and Zysla's brother, we always wondered this from beginning to end.

A documentary film asked David how he would define music and recorded his timeless answer. "I gave an explanation that music is life because I experienced life in music."

"Music is life.
Music is hope.
Music is peace.
I cannot ask for more."

Appendix
Timeline

An abridged list of David Arben's recitals, solos, recordings, and broadcasts compiled from personal papers, private conversations, and research.

1935

Poland
Warsaw. Chopin Academy. Student recital (Vivaldi Violin Concerto in A Minor).

1940

Poland
January: Warsaw. Solo debut scheduled (cancelled after start of World War II and destruction of Warsaw Philharmonic Hall in German air raid, 1939).

1945

Germany

May 27: Emming. St. Ottilien Archabbey displaced persons camp. DP orchestra (for U.S. military personnel one month after liberation, and at sanitaria and other DP camps).

November 14: Landsberg. Town Theater. Jewish Orchestra of Bavaria.

1946

Germany

January 27–29: Munich. First formal Congress of the Central Committee of Liberated Jews (David Ben-Gurion attending). St. Ottilien Orchestra.

March 17: Munich. Young Men's Hebrew Association Soldier's Center. St. Ottilien Orchestra (Purim Festival).

May 7: Nuremberg. Opera House. Ex-Concentration Camp Orchestra (for international judges at the Nuremberg Trial).

August 25: Landsberg. DP Camp (converted Wehrmacht Barracks). Solo with Ex-Concentration Camp Orchestra.

1947

Germany

Fall, Winter: Cities and towns in Germany. Concert tour. Recitals with Michael Taube.

September: Munich. Radio München. Studio recording. Solos with Bavarian Radio Symphony Orchestra.

1948

Germany

May 10: Feldafing and Landsberg. Solo with Ex-Concentration Camp Orchestra, Leonard Bernstein conducting.

1948 continued

September 11: Fürstenfeldbruck. Jahnhalle. Solo with South German Chamber Orchestra, Adolf Mennerich conducting.

Switzerland
September: Geneva. Solo competition in Concours International d'Exécution Musicale.

1949

Switzerland
June: Geneva. Conservatory of Music. Solo with Orchestre du conservatoire, winning the Prix de Vituosité.

1951

United States
May 7: Philadelphia, Pennsylvania. Curtis Institute of Music. Recital with Toshiya Eto, Jeanne Gillam, and Jules Eskin.

1952

United States
April 8: Philadelphia, Pennsylvania. Curtis Institute of Music. Recital with Vladimir Sokoloff.

1954

United States
March 3: Philadelphia, Pennsylvania. Curtis Institute of Music. Recital with José Kahan and Ronald Leonard.

March 26: Philadelphia, Pennsylvania. Free Library of Philadelphia. The Musical Fund Society of Philadelphia. Recital with José Kahan and Ronald Leonard.

April 29: Philadelphia, Pennsylvania. Curtis Institute of Music. Graduation recital with Anna Moffo.

1954 – 1955   Member of the Detroit Symphony Orchestra

1955

United States
February 21: Detroit, Michigan. Music Study Club of Detroit. Institute of Arts. Recital with Jeanne Diamond.

Germany
September: Bad Wiessee. Solo with Spa Orchestra, Heinz Crucius conducting.

1955 – 1959   Member of the Cleveland Orchestra

1957

United States
January 28: Cleveland, Ohio. Cleveland Music School Settlement. Recital with George Silfies.

Germany
August: Bad Wiessee. Solo with Resort Orchestra, Heinz Crucius conducting.

1958

United States
March 23: Cleveland, Ohio. Severance Hall. Solo debut with Cleveland Orchestra, Robert Shaw conducting.

Germany
Fall: Bad Wiessee. Solo with Resort Orchestra, Heinz Crucius conducting.

1958 continued

Mexico
September 25: Mexico City, D.F. Palacio de Bellas Artes, Sala Ponce. Recital with Juan Tercero.

1959

United States
January 4: Cleveland, Ohio. Severance Hall. Cleveland Orchestra. Vivaldi Concerto for Four Violins and Orchestra: David Arben, Daniel Majeske, Ernest Kardos, and James Barrett, Louis Lane conducting.

March 10: Akron, Ohio. Buchtel High School Auditorium. Solo with cellist Rolf Storseth and the Akron Symphony, Laszlo Krausz conducting.

Germany
September 4: Bad Wiessee. Solo with Spa Orchestra, Heinz Crucius conducting.

1959–1993   Member of the Philadelphia Orchestra

1960

United States
February 17: Philadelphia, Pennsylvania. Temple University, Mitten Hall Great Court. Solo with Temple University Symphony Orchestra, Anshel Brusilow conducting.

Fall: NBC television. On program with Anshel Brusilow.

1961

United States

March: Philadelphia, Pennsylvania. University of Philadelphia, Houston Hall. Contemporary Chamber Music Society. Recital with Donald Montanaro and Natalie Hinderas.

1962

United States

March 25: Philadelphia, Pennsylvania. Coffee Concert Committee. Drake Hotel. Recital with Anthony di Bonaventura, Murray Panitz, and Stringart Quartet: Veda Reynolds, Irwin Eisenberg, Alan Iglitzin, Charles Brennand.

1963

European Tour May 17 – June 15. Recitals with pianist Alice Shapiro.

May 17: Amsterdam, Concertgebouw.

May 20: Stockholm, Konserthuset.

May 28: Berlin, Konzertsaal des Städtischen Konservatorium.

June 4: Munich, Sophiensaal.

June 6: Vienna, Konzertdirektion F. Cieplik, Brahms-Saal (Musikverein).

June 10: Paris, Salle Pleyel.

June 11: Berlin, Konzertsaal des Städtischen Konservatorium.

June 15: London, Wigmore Hall.

1964

United States
March 22: Philadelphia, Pennsylvania. Philadelphia Museum of Art.
Solo with Philadelphia Musical Academy Faculty-Alumni
Orchestra, Maurice Kaplow conducting.

December 13: Philadelphia, Pennsylvania. Solo with Philadelphia
Chamber Orchestra, Anshel Brusilow conducting.

1965

United States
February 7: Wyncote, Pennsylvania. Jenkintown Music School,
Curtis Hall. Recital with Monroe Levin.

Germany
May 28: Dresden. Konzertsaal der Hochschule für Musik. Recital
with Lothar Broddack.

Mexico
July 25: Mexico City, D.F. Universidad Nacional de México, Teatro
Alameda. Solo with Orquesta Sinfónica de la Universidad, Matti
Holli conducting.

1966

South America
May: Philadelphia Orchestra's first tour of South America.

United States
September 16: Philadelphia, Pennsylvania. Philadelphia Orchestra
Benefit Concert for and by the musicians on strike, Leopold
Stokowski conducting.

1967

United States
January 29: Philadelphia, Pennsylvania. Civic Center Museum. Recital.

April 12: Philadelphia, Pennsylvania. Moore College of Art. Recital with Marion Zarzeczna.

Japan and United States West Coast
April 30 – June 12. Tour with Philadelphia Orchestra.

1968

United States
February 27: Philadelphia, Pennsylvania. Civic Center Museum. Solo with Philadelphia Musical Academy Orchestra, Maurice Kapilow conducting.

September 29: Wynnewood, Pennsylvania. Home of John Merriam. Recital of Academie String Quartet: David Arben, Eugene Kash, Karen Tuttle, and Samuel Mayes.

November 1: Philadelphia, Pennsylvania. Civic Center Museum. Recital with Academie String Quartet, Winifred Mayes assisting.

1969

United States
April 20: Philadelphia, Pennsylvania. Philadelphia Musical Academy. Recital with Academie String Quartet, John Krell, Leonard Mogill, Donald Montanaro, and Maureen Forrester.

1970

United States
March 12: Philadelphia, Pennsylvania. Academy of Music. Philadelphia Musical Academy Centennial Concert Series. Soloists Henryk Szeryng, Gary Graffman, and Academie String Quartet.

1971

Germany
June: Hamburg. Norddeutscher Rundfunk. Recordings with Academie String Quartet.

Yugoslavia
July, August: Dubrovnik. Dubrovnik Summer Festival. Concerts with Henryk Szeryng.

Mexico
September 4: Mexico City, D.F. Casa del Lago del Bosque de Chapultepec. Recital with José Kahan.

September 5: Mexico City, D.F. Ciudad Universitaria. Teatro Alameda. Solo with Orquesta Sinfónica de la Universidad, Icilio Bredo conducting.

September 9: Mexico City, D.F. Tlatelolco. Auditorio de la Cancillería. Recital with José Kahan.

1972

United States
April 9: Philadelphia, Pennsylvania. Academy of Music, Ballroom. Recital with Academie String Quartet: David Arben, Luis Biava, Sidney Curtiss, George Harpham.

1973

Greece
June 8: Athens. Athens Centre for the Creative Arts, Auditorium of the Hellenic American Union. Recital with John Papaioannou.

China
September: Philadelphia Orchestra tour of China.

1974

United States

March 24: Metuchen, New Jersey. Home of Dr. and Mrs. Alan Young. Fundraiser for New Jersey Symphony. Recital with Irving Gelber.

December 8: Llewellyn Park, New Jersey. Home of Adolf and Ingrid Dingfelder, friends of Dr. Samuel Applebaum. Impromptu performance with Henryk Szeryng, Adele Young, a few regional professionals, and members of the New York Philharmonic.

Greece

Summer: Athens. Hellenic Broadcasting Company. Studio recording. Radio broadcast.

July 5: Santorini. Greek Orthodox Church. Recital with Tante's daughter.

1975

Mexico

June 14: Mexico City, D.F. Universidad Nacional Autónoma de Mexico, Casa del Lago. Recital with José Kahan.

1976

United States

February 21: Bryn Mawr, Pennsylvania. Bryn Mawr College, Thomas Great Hall. Recital with George Harpham and Joséph Bloom.

1977

United States

Spring: Philadelphia, Pennsylvania. KYN TV 3. Arben appeared on CBS program Report From, hosted by Bob Bradley.

1977 continued

July 21: Philadelphia, Pennsylvania. Robin Hood Dell West. Solo with Henryk Szeryng and Philadelphia Orchestra, José Serebrier conducting.

1978

Greece
July: Athens. Recital.

British Hong Kong
September 4: Hong Kong, British Crown Colony. Hong Kong City Hall Theatre. Recital with John Koljonen and Kyung-Sook Lee.

September 9: Hong Kong, British Crown Colony. Hong Kong Baptist College, Academic Community Hall. Solo with Hong Kong Philharmonic Orchestra, Hans Gunter Mommer conducting.

1979

United States
December 21, 22: Philadelphia, Pennsylvania. Solo debut on subscription concert series with Philadelphia Orchestra, William Smith conducting.

1980

British Hong Kong
June 27, 28: Hong Kong, British Crown Colony. Solo with Hong Kong Symphony Orchestra, Kenneth Schermerhorn conducting.

1983

United States
November 20: Princeton, New Jersey. Princeton High School Auditorium. Solo with Igor Kipnis and Jan Rosenfeld, and Little Orchestra of Princeton, Portia Sonnenfeld conducting.

1983 continued

December 9: Haddonfield, New Jersey. Haddonfield Memorial High School Auditorium. Solo with Haddonfield Symphony Orchestra, Arthur Cohn conducting.

1984

Colombia
March 16: Bogotá, Colombia. Teatro Colón. Solo with Orquesta Sinfónica de Colombia, Luis Biava conducting.

Mexico
June 22: Mexico City, D.F. Solo with Orquesta Sinfónica de México at Teatro Morelos, Jean Claude Bernede conducting.

June 23: Mexico City, D.F. Universidad Autónoma del Estado de México. Municipio del Estado de México. Solo.

June 24: Mexico City, D.F. Teatro de la Ciudad de México. Solo.

1985

United States
February 3: Princeton, New Jersey. Princeton High School Auditorium. Solo with Chamber Symphony of Princeton, Portia Sonnenfeld conducting.

March 8, 9, 19: Philadelphia, Pennsylvania. Academy of Music. Solo with Philadelphia Orchestra, William Smith conducting.

1986

United States
April 27: Philadelphia, Pennsylvania. Rittenhouse Square. Church of the Holy Trinity. Solo with Michael Tree, and the Philadelphia Chamber Orchestra, Lawrence Leighton Smith conducting.

1986 continued

May 12 – June 6: Philadelphia Orchestra's 50th North American Anniversary Tour.

December 19, 20: Philadelphia, Pennsylvania. Academy of Music. Solo with Philadelphia Orchestra, Gilbert Levine conducting.

1989

United States

February 24, 25, 28: Philadelphia, Pennsylvania. Academy of Music. Solo with Philadelphia Orchestra, Witold Rowicki conducting.

October 12, 13, 14, 16, 17: Philadelphia, Pennsylvania. Solo with Philadelphia Orchestra, Christoph Eschenbach conducting.

1991

United States

February 3: Philadelphia, Pennsylvania. Academy of Music, Ballroom. Recital with James Fawcett, Lloyd Smith, and members of the Pasquale Quartet, John Hood, and Wolfgang Sawallisch.

1992

United States

February 6, 7: Philadelphia, Pennsylvania. Academy of Music. Solo with Philadelphia Orchestra, Riccardo Muti conducting.

1993

United States

March 19, 20, 23: Philadelphia, Pennsylvania. Academy of Music. Last solos with Philadelphia Orchestra, Zdenek Macal conducting (Mozart's Violin Concerto No. 7).

1997

Poland

May 15: Warsaw, Poland. Nożyk Synagogue. Recited Kaddish for his family and played Hebrew Melody by Joséph Achron.

2007

Germany

July 22: Flossenbürg, Germany. Flossenbürg Concentration Camp. Solo recital broadcast on radio and television (Meditation from Thaïs by Jules Massenet and Hebrew Melody by Joséph Achron).

Authors

Dr. John Jackson, a native of the state of Missouri, travels nationally and internationally as a wellness educator. He received his B.S. from UCLA, pursued graduate work in Israel, worked as an analytical chemist for a Silicon Valley biotech company, received his M.D. with distinction from George Washington University, and finished an internal medicine residency at UCLA. Board certified and a Fellow of the American College of Physicians, after more than twenty years in private practice, at the start of 2007 he shifted emphasis from disease management to natural healing and prevention. Avocations and abiding interests include jogging, family history, and Biblical archaeology. He currently resides with his wife of forty-four years in Santa Cruz, California.

Violinist Rebecca Jackson is the founder and artistic director of Music in May (MiM). MiM is an annual chamber music festival held in Santa Cruz, California. She performs regularly with San Francisco Ballet and Santa Fe Opera Orchestras. Believing strongly in the power of music to heal and unite, she has performed in many marginalized communities across the U.S., Ukraine, Romania, Dominican Republic, Haiti, India, Nepal, Costa Rica, and Lebanon. Combining her passion for music and service, she is a cofounder of Sound Impact. Ms. Jackson received her B.M. from The Juilliard School and a graduate degree from UC Santa Cruz.

Meeting Mr. Arben

Rebecca first met David Arben as an eighteen-year-old violin student in Puerto Rico, the summer of 1999, while attending Festival of the Youth Symphony Orchestra of the Americas (FOSJA). FOSJA was directed by Maestro Luis Biava and, as a faculty member, Mr. Arben coached violin sectionals. Hearing Arben perform the Schubert Cello Quintet made an indelible impression on Rebecca. Soon after, during her studies at Juilliard, she started making trips by train to visit Mr. Arben in Philadelphia. Unstinting with his time, he spent countless afternoons giving her invaluable lessons on violin and life. After moving back to California, during one of her subsequent return visits, she interviewed him for a master's thesis. The content from their question and answer session in 2007 was the nidus of this biography. In 2008, Arben attended Music in May (MiM) and was hosted by her parents; the entire Jackson family finally meeting Rebecca's mentor. He attended MiM and lodged with his adopted California family almost every season until his passing in 2017.

Dr. Jackson, who once lived and worked in Israel, had long felt an interest in historical events leading to the rebirth of that nation. To learn more and document our subject's life story, John used a small handheld Sony digital voice recorder to capture most all the transcriptions utilized in this work. Interviews took place face-to-face in California; during an extended stay with Mr. Arben at San Juan, Puerto Rico; his Philadelphia residence; Sarasota, Florida; as well as on recorded telephone conversations. An ideal pair of coauthors, the Judeophile father and his career violinist daughter collaborated to complete their first book. Thanksgiving 2014 marked the day that Dr. and Ms. Jackson began in earnest their serious undertaking of writing this biography, with every intention of handing Mr. Arben the final version. Though he never saw the completed book now in your hands, he read preliminary drafts. In his voicemail left on June 19, 2015, David's words gave strength that lasted after his passing and carried both coauthors to the finish line. He spoke warmly, "Thank you for depicting my life very beautifully and accurately." David's father had said, "One day the world will know my sons." The Jacksons hope to be a part of helping fulfill his prophecy.

Made in the USA
Monee, IL
12 November 2020